The Sunday Post

Pass It On

Household Tips From The 1950s

First published in Great Britain in 2017
by DC Thomson & Co., Ltd.
Meadowside,
Dundee,
Scotland
DD1 9QJ

www.dcthomsonshop.co.uk
To purchase this book.
Or Freephone 0800 318 846
Overseas customers call +44 1382 575580

Typeset by Steve Finan. Cover design by Laura Hall.
Cover model Nic Hutchison.

Printed in Great Britain by Clays Ltd, St Ives plc

ISBN 978-1-84535-660-6

Contents

Dedication

TO my delight, I found my own grandmother's name among the tips. Elizabeth Anderson. She was an incredibly hard-working woman, who cleaned city centre offices from 4am to 8am each morning, then 5pm to 8pm at night. A single mother of six, she did this until she was in her late seventies. She worked because she felt the need to be a worker, a grafter, a provider. She taught me, by example, that if you take on a job you do it to the best of your ability. Not to satisfy anyone else, but because you take a fierce personal pride in everything you do.

With all her cleaning knowledge I should perhaps have been surprised that she sent in an inventive kitchen tip. But, in truth, she knew everything and could do anything.

She died, in her 90s, in the late 1980s. But I can hear her talk as I read her words. Her tip is on page 81.

I am very, very proud of you, Granny A, and I hope you'd be proud of me. I dedicate this book to you, with respect, fond memories and my everlasting love and thanks.

But my Granny A. wasn't alone in sending in a tip. She was one among tens of thousands. Those people wrote this book. It is their genius that shines out from these pages. It is their achievements we celebrate by bringing their words back to life.

Out of respect for them I have left the full names and addresses of all contributors intact, just as they were given and printed when those resourceful and house-proud readers originally wrote in.

I hope that readers today will recognise and remember some of these incredible people, be they relatives, neighbours or friends. I hope you find a name that is special and dear to you. Think of them with pride. Shed a tear for them and for past times, if you will, but remember their qualities and their desire to make the best of themselves and what they had. They were very proud of themselves, so proud that they wrote to The Sunday Post.

Steve Finan, Sunday Post Production Editor.

Introduction

THE Sunday Post has always been the newspaper of choice for a certain type of working-class people in Scotland and the North of England. The best type of people. The paper stood, as it does to this day, for decency and respectability. And for decades, throughout the 1940s, '50s and '60s, The Sunday Post ran a Pass It On column – week in, week out. Housewives, and some men, would write in with clever, innovative and frankly brilliant tips for cooking, cleaning, mending, ironing, saving money and...well, just about everything you could think of that good and decent people did.

The paper gave a half guinea or a pair of towels for the week's best tip. Sometimes, for no reason that can be remembered, the fee even went up to a whole guinea for a week or two. However, the prize (half a guinea is 52.5p in today's money) was only part of the reward. In those house-proud times, the woman who had her "tip" printed was regarded as a housewife of distinction. A super-housewife who was resourceful and thrifty and kept her home spick and span.

These were the days when women would compete to do the best job when it was their turn to clean the close. There could be no saving the reputation of a slovenly wife who left the stairs clarty.

For those who reached the hallowed ground of a tip printed in The Sunday Post, a light shone for ever on their housewifely prowess. The cutting might be produced to impress friends and relatives. Others would tell their friends they lived next door to a woman who'd had a tip published, as it was a general sign of a good neighbourhood.

In the pages of this book, you can hear these women talk. If you close your eyes you can see them, rank after rank, year after year, an army of capable, hardworking, resourceful women.

They have their sleeves rolled up, their apron on, there is a pot simmering behind them and a just-scrubbed table by their hand. They are your mother, grandmother, aunt, the woman across the street who told you off for misbehaving. They are the backbone of society, the centre of their family unit, the one you turn to when trouble strikes. They are working-class heroes.

Perhaps it isn't the usefulness of the Pass It On tips we miss so much as the mentality and standards of behaviour that went with them.

There is nostalgia here in remembering the troubles that had to be faced and defeated. But there is another type of nostalgia, a different kind that recalls the values of those days.

As a cautionary note, it must be said that the tips passed on were never tested by The Sunday Post. There may well be physical dangers in some of them. Not all will work. Worse, there may even be the chance of spoiling your mince and tatties. They are re-printed here exactly as they appeared in the 1950s—I possess neither the expertise nor the bravery to change what these women and men said.

So tread very carefully. What was considered safe in those days might not be safe now.

As you read, you may also be struck by a certain consistency of tone. Many of the tip-givers included an extra sentence, or perhaps just a few words, which further recommended the cleverness or usefulness of their tip. I believe it is those few words that most allow us to "know" the person who wrote in. You can hear their tone, see the tilt of their head as they speak. Some, I am convinced, were just showing off that they owned a refrigerator or had a different apron they only used in the afternoon. The contributors are human, with all that means. I can't help but admire them. I remember what these people were like. And I smile when I recall them. In many instances, strange though it is to say of a book consisting of sensible household advice, it often makes me laugh out loud.

Salute them and think well of them.

PASS IT ON!

You'll Be Amazed At The Extra Light You Get

IF you allow your electric lamps and shades to become dusty, you lose from 25 to 30 per cent. of light. To get maximum efficiency, dust them weekly, and wash them monthly.—**Mrs Robertson, Aberdeen,** wins a pair of towels.

HANDY REPAIR.

When crepe-soled boots or shoes wear down at heels, repair by fixing large-size rubber protectors. Use oval nails, longer than usual. — **Mrs McNally, 49 High St., Musselburgh.**

TIME SAVING.

When preparing swede turnips, first cut into thick slices and peel afterwards. They're prepared in half the time.—**E. A. Aspinall, 18 Hartingdon Rd., Preston.**

STICKY JOB.

Glue from a tube is spread more evenly if you use a cork.—**Mrs M. Priestley, c/o 25 Ramsay Rd., Kirkcaldy.**

SHOE TREES.

Fill a pair of old stockings with sawdust. Sew up the tops. They make good shoe trees. The sawdust absorbs perspiration. — **Mrs F. W. Bell, 18 Westlands, Sunderland.**

FOR FLAVOUR.

When making Scotch broth, add one teaspoon made mustard and a teaspoon sugar a half-hour before serving.—**Mrs M. Colville, Kinloch Place, Campbeltown.**

DUST REMOVER.

A chamois leather, wrung out of warm water, will free velvet cushions from dust more effectively than a brush. Rub lightly with even strokes.—M'ss L. Miller, 65 Coast Rd., Heaton, Northumberland.

CHAIR BACKS.

A discarded table or sideboard runner can be made into lovely chair backs. Just cut in half and sew on fringed cord.—**Mrs E. Sorbie, 25 Camnethan St., Stonehouse.**

QUICK DRYING.

If your coat gets very wet, turn inside out, place on a hanger. Fill a rubber hot water bottle and suspend from hanger inside the coat.—**Mrs C. McIndoe, 25 Rolland St., Glasgow.**

SMOOTH GOING.

Tack a piece of waxed paper to one end of your ironing board. Run iron over the paper while ironing. It runs smoothly and gives glossy finish to garments. — Mrs D Hardie, 6 Backmarch Cres., Rosyth.

Send your hints to "Pass It On," "The Sunday Post," 144 Port Dundas Road, Glasgow, C.4. Every hint published will be paid for.

Thanks to...

"1950s Nic" (Nic Hutchison) for being the cover girl.

Craig Houston, Sylwia Jackowska and Gillian Grierson for the encouragement, vision and belief that transforming a collection of cuttings into a book could be done.

The artistry of Laura Hall , John Barrie and John Wilkie.

The nimble typing fingers of Mel Webb, Susan Martin, Lynn Clark, June Riddoch and Kaye Gallacher.

The photographic skills of Andrew Cawley and Jeremy Bayston.

The clever ideas of Rebecca Moncrieffe, Fiona Armstrong and Kirsty Matthews.

The loan of props from Carnoustie Theatre Club and Isobel Morton.

The proof-reading discipline of Dawn Donaghey and Andy Clark.

The doors-opening influence of Richard Prest, editor of The Sunday Post.

The archives knowledge of Barry Sullivan and David Powell.

The technical expertise and e-awareness of Raymond Barr, Fiona Brown, Ross Crae, Gillian Furmage and Chris Kelly.

The support of Maggie Anderson and Fraser T. Ogilvie.

The first-hand 1950s memories of Bill & Chris Nicoll.

The steady patience of Carole Finan, Rebecca Finan and Lewis Finan, who listened to moans and explanations of problems long after the responsibilities of familial duty should have run out.

Most of all, to Sunday Post readers for the ingenious ideas, expertise, experience and downright brilliance...especially Mrs Harriet Smith, of John Street, Ruabon, Wrexham, who is this book's champion tipster with a magnificent eight tips printed. Harriet, I salute you.

To Begin, A Look Forward

ON Sunday, January 1, 1950, the first Sunday Post of the decade carried a message for its readers. It was intended to address the problems of the coming year, but it also spoke for the mood of the time and gives an example of the attitudes going into a new period of history.

This is what it said:

As the New Year begins, many people are asking—is Britain finished? Will this year see her slide definitely out of a leading place among the nations? The answer is—no. 1950 can be one of the greatest years in British history. Those who tell us Britain is a back number forget the solid mass of people who stand behind us.

First, the British Commonwealth, where faith in us refuses to die. Our people in the far-flung Dominions pledge themselves to stay shoulder to shoulder with us. Do you know that in the past three years every man, woman, and child in Australia has gifted us £4.10s? That makes £36 million in three years. Canada, New Zealand, and the rest have told us their immense resources are ours to draw upon. There is newly-discovered wealth in the colonies. And people there don't forget it was Britain who gave the first encouraging grip of the hand when they sought a better life.

We have behind us, too, another 200 million people in the sterling area whose purse is largely in our charge. Their hopes of security rest on Britain's success. They will give every support they can to our efforts.

In Europe 270 million people are watching us. Yes, they're a bit critical. They don't mince words when they think we've gone off the rails. But they're looking to us for a lead in bringing back European recovery and prosperity. And their berets will fly in the air, as they did in 1945, when we win through. Even in the Pacific there can be no peace unless

Britain plays a major part. There can be no breaking the U.N.O. deadlock without British help.

Make no mistake about it. In every sphere we have the opportunity to prove our greatness—and the world wants us to do it. Not only that, world conditions in 1950 are ripe for a full-blooded British recovery. World food shortages are disappearing. There are surpluses of many raw materials. The riches are there to be won—if Britain pulls up her sleeves. And there's no doubt we have the ability. Our scientists lead the world in radar, television, jets, machinery, and ship design. Given the chance, our salesmen have the pioneering spirit —like the couple who peddled a mechanical shovel 4500 miles across Canada.

Greatest of all is the British spirit of determination to win through at all costs. For years, business and industrial chiefs have taken nothing but punches on the chin. Yet, like the harassed housewife, they still come up for more.

Then what's stopping us? Nothing, provided the people of Britain are free to use all these resources to the fullest extent. The £ is accepted by the rest of the world as the symbol of British strength, enterprise, and leadership.

Lately it's gone down. But it's within our power in 1950 to make it rise to prouder levels—just by everyone working harder, giving value for wages and cutting out waste. Perhaps we're sometimes too self-satisfied. We're apt to look down on our Continental neighbours, and fail to see they're making a better go of it than ourselves in some ways. Isn't it rather humbling to learn that most of our Continental neighbours are building new houses at their pre-war rate, while we don't do better than two-thirds of our 1938 rate? Many of them have got rid of rationing—we haven't. They're winning coal at 96 per cent. of the pre-war rate. We stick at 88 per cent. We were told they'd get in a mess If they got rid of super-planning. But they haven't. Aren't we just a bit too proud to learn from those we used to regard as "poor neighbours"? But we can still beat them all if we come off our high horse and get "mucked in". We've got it in us. The world knows it.

Our King said—"Now is the chance for us to show the great qualities—courage, perseverance, endurance, unselfishness, public spirit." Let's go to It this New Year. If we do, next New Year will tell a very different story.

THE SUNDAY POST, JANUARY 29, 1950

The Sunday Post

Morning Special

PRINTED AND PUBLISHED EVERY SUNDAY MORNING.

No. 2318. [REGISTERED AT THE GENERAL POST OFFICE AS A NEWSPAPER.] SUNDAY, JANUARY 29, 1950. RADIO—Page 15 PRICE TWOPENCE.

TO-DAY'S WEATHER: COLD & WINDY

JOBS FOR ALL PLEDGED BY CHURCHILL

Attacks Doctrine—"Work Or Starve"

MR CHURCHILL last night laid emphasis on his pledge of full employment.

The maintenance of full employment is the first aim and duty of a Conservative Government, he said.

A few months ago the Socialists hoped to win the election on the issue of unemployment. The Tories, they said, would like to have unemployment, which they could use as a spur to compel greater exertions from the wage-earners.

However, the truth has become so widely realised that it is difficult for the Socialists either to make good their claims to have cured unemployment since the war, or their unfair charge that the Conservatives are not as resolute as they are to do everything in human power to prevent it.

Mr Churchill said that so far we are only at the first stage of the evil journey into Socialism. But already enterprise, daring and initiative are crippled.

Regulations increasingly take the place of statute passed by Parliament. These are contained in 28 volumes, which can be purchased for £65. In these you may find that there are thousands of new crimes, unknown before the war, now punishable by fine or imprisonment.

The right is claimed, in full peace, by the Government to direct a man or women to any work or any place a Minister or the officials may choose.

These are the words which Mr Isaacs, the Minister of Labour, used in the House of Commons on December 3, 1947, when defending the Order giving him absolute power over the livelihood and employment of all men and women between the ages of 18 and 50 and 18 and 40 respectively—

"If any specific case is brought to our notice of a person claiming conscientious objection to a particular job, we will give it our consideration. But we are not prepared to recognise that any one has a right to conscientious objection to going to work, unless that person is prepared at the same time to say that he will not eat."

This is the shameful doctrine of "work or starve" which no Government in Britain has ever dared to utter in time of peace for more than 100 years. It is the greatest affront offered in modern times to the dignity of labour, which rests upon a man's right to choose or change his job.

The Socialists have not dared to use it on any large scale as yet. They are waiting for a renewal of their mandate.

Conservatives and National Liberals, on the other hand, are resolved to expunge this blot from our industrial life.

In the face of sinister issues like these, cutting right down to the roots of civilised society, it astounds me that liberal-minded men of any party can doubt where their duty lies.

Picture to yourselves upon this background the small group of Left Wing

(Continued on Back Page.)

Mr Bloom Does It In Style

BECAUSE of the bus strike, Mr Stanley Bloom set off from his home at 16 Paris Street, Grangemouth, to reach his work by train.

But when he arrived at the station, the train had gone.

He set out to walk to Falkirk, a distance of five miles. When he had gone some way along the road a voice called, "Hello, chum, do you want a lift?" It came—not from a motor car, lorry or motor cycle—but a tandem!

"Jump on the back seat," said the owner. Stanley did, and got to work!

44-year-old miner, Charles Lees, St Catherine, Maddiston, stakes a claim for the longest walk since the bus strike began.

He left his home at Maddiston at 8.30 a.m. on Friday, walked to Hetherstone Colliery, at Denny, 11 miles away. He uplifted his wages, then tramped the return journey. He got home at three o'clock in the afternoon.

A Cup tie scene at Brechin.

After All The Hullabaloo!

IT didn't happen after all!

Celtic supporters rolled up to Brechin in 68 buses and a special train—but there was room for them all and tickets to spare.

About two o'clock two men from the West were offering ground tickets at their correct price at the main entrance to Glebe Park. But not for long.

As the stream of Celtic supporters increased, tickets were being given away. Takers were few.

Some of the Celtic men handed over as many as seven at one time to men on duty at the entrance. One tore up a ticket and threw the pieces away.

One Celtic supporter said many hadn't turned up for the buses at the last minute.

Another said the tickets hadn't been distributed in Glasgow in time for some regular supporters to make arrangements for getting off.

The crowd looked comfortable in the ground. There was a slight tussle between some men but it wasn't serious.

After the game the crowd kept the restaurants busy.

BUS STRIKE IS OVER

The 500 drivers and conductresses at Falkirk, who struck work last Monday, decided last night to return to work. They will go back to-morrow morning.

Dundee bus workers decided last night to resume work to-day.

An inquiry will be held into the cause of the stoppage, which brought out 1400 men.

Five main Scottish depots—Dundee, Perth, Crieff, Falkirk and Stirling—were affected by the stoppage yesterday.

Hundreds of people who work in Dundee were stranded yesterday.

Folk walked from Longforgan, Invergowrie and Monifieth, thumbing lifts when they could.

Some Carnoustie workers were able to get on the Stonehaven and Arbroath operative buses.

Cup-tie fans were hit by the strike. Travellers for the Brechin-Celtic game went home. Some booked taxis.

Alexanders asked volunteers to take Dundee supporters to Edinburgh. Ten buses had been booked. Five drivers agreed. Other fans went by train.

Patients discharged from Dundee Royal Infirmary were taken by ambulance to country districts, where normally they would have gone by bus. Patients in the outlying districts attending D.R.I. for treatment also made use of the ambulances.

Yesterday was visiting day at Ashludie. The normal buses were off, but two double deckers were driven by inspectors.

One Dundee taxi firm reported runs to Longforgan and Inchture because people couldn't travel by bus.

Just prior to holding a midnight meeting, Forfar bus operators received word that the depots at Dundee and Falkirk had decided to return to work. In view of these decisions, Forfar bus men decided to carry on at work.

Montrose bus drivers and conductresses, at a brief meeting late last night, decided not to strike.

CAMEO CASE TO BE RE-HEARD

ANOTHER JURY DISAGREES

THE 13-day trial of the Cameo Cinema case at Liverpool came to a dramatic end late yesterday afternoon.

After a retirement of four hours and seven minutes, the jury disagreed.

Mr Justice Oliver ordered that Charles Connolly and George Kelly, 26-year-old labourers, should be kept in custody and tried again. They were accused of the murder of Leonard Thomas, manager of the cinema, on March 19 last year.

It was the second time in three days that a murder trial jury failed to reach a verdict. On Thursday at the Old Bailey no decision could be reached in the case of Brian Donald Hume, charged with the murder of Stanley Setty. He was afterwards sentenced to 12 years for being an accessory after the fact.

The final act of yesterday's drama began at 11.8 a.m., when the jury filed out of court to consider their verdict.

One hour and 17 minutes later there was a stir in court. The atmosphere became tense. Counsel, officials and others hurried back.

But what had happened was that the jury were cold in their room and wanted their overcoats. They were allowed to collect them, and again left the court.

Then the sequence of events was—

1.38—Mr Ian Macaulay, Clerk of the Assize, enters the jury room.

2.1—He leaves.

2.6—He goes back again.

2.8—He leaves again.

2.12—Tea and biscuits sent in the jury.

2.30—Mr Macaulay visits jury again.

2.35—He emerges for the last time.

2.5—Elderly woman collapses in public gallery. Ambulance called.

2.15—Jury returns.

They wanted further information on a point in the evidence. When this had been given, the Judge asked if they thought it would help.

The foreman replied, "I don't think we will agree."

The Judge—If there is no chance of agreeing, it would be useless to keep you here.

THE TWO MRS BABCOCKS

TWO women—one British and one American—each claiming to be the widow of Colonel William T. Babcock, U.S. Deputy Commandant in Berlin, stood at the graveside when he was buried in Arlington National Cemetery, Washington, yesterday.

It was the British woman who received the honours prescribed for the widow.

Colonel Babcock, aged 52, died on Monday.

One Mrs Babcock, a British subject, was on the plane which brought the body. The other from New London, Connecticut, met the plane.

"I am the real Mrs Babcock," she said. "He has been married to me for nearly 32 years."

DEFEATIST SATURDAY NIGHT GLOOM

—SAYS MR WEBB

Labour's reply to Mr Churchill's radio speech a week ago was made last night in a Party political broadcast by Mr Maurice Webb, chairman of the Parliamentary Labour Party.

He described the whole outlook of Mr Churchill and his Party as "unreal, dangerously unreal," and declared it is an outlook which is a grotesque distortion of the facts.

"We are not a nation almost beaten to its knees," he said. "We are not in dire straits, facing imminent calamity. And that is my reply to the defeatist Saturday night gloom of the Tory leader.

"Just take a look at Britain to-day. Bear in mind we have had to face crippling shortages, our reserves were never so small.

"But the plain truth is—we are doing it—Britain is at work to-day. There's a stir in the air. Business is on the move. It is just humming with activity. More jobs—more output—more purchasing power—never was there such a high degree of useful work being done as is being done to-day.

"It's pawnshops which are closed nowadays.

"Look at our countryside. Never did the farmer and farm worker have such good rewards for their work—and enjoy such long-term security of a good living.

"It is true that the inevitable post-war demand for goods has played a large part in keeping the wheels turning. Any Government, after such a long war would have inherited the benefits of a sellers' market.

"It would, therefore, be wrong to claim that Government action is the sole cause. But the remarkable thing is the way in which we in Britain have gone on keeping full employment and increasing production long after the sellers' market had faded out."

Railways To Cut Down Staffs

Further cuts are to be made in manpower on the railways.

This was indicated last night by Sir Cyril Hurcomb, chairman of the British Transport Commission. He was addressing the Permanent Way Institution in London.

"It is easy to talk about reducing the cost of running the railways, but far more difficult to do it," he said. "We have already been able to bring economies about, including a substantial reduction in staff, but the proper upkeep and safe operation of the country's railway system, representing an investment of about £1000 million, necessitates a certain minimum of expenditure which no manipulation of figures can conjure away.

"We must make further economies in money and in manpower.

Chapter 1
Just Brilliant

MANKIND, and womankind, are good at solving problems. It is the defining trait that separated our ancestors from the other monkeys swinging about the trees, wondering if there was any merit in rumours that there was something to be gained from walking on their hind legs. We make tools.

Sunday Post readers identified problems. And solved them. Then they wrote to the paper to share the knowledge they'd found.

IT STOPS THAT DOOR RATTLING—If a bedroom door rattles on windy nights, it can be silenced by stretching a rubber band between the two knobs. This cushions the door.—Miss Rose Parkhill, 74 Bushmills Road, Coleraine, County Derry, wins a pair of towels.

PEPPER—On country walks, carry a small quantity of white pepper in your pocket. It helps to keep midges and other pests away.—Miss Agnes McIntyre, Langrew, Cambeltown, Argyll.

CAP-SAVER—When taking the cap off a bottle which you wish to reseal, place a coin on top of the cap before applying the bottle opener. This prevents the cap being dented and enables you to reseal the bottle.—Mrs W. A. Allan, General Deliver, Innisfail, Alberta, Canada.

ADHESIVE TAPE—When the end has become stuck on itself, hold the roll of tape over the steam of a kettle for a few seconds. The end then unwinds freely.—Mrs J. Little, Lintz Green, 50 Kethers Street, Motherwell.

AIR REFRESHER—Next time you make chips, cut an onion in half and place it on the plate rack above the cooker. You'll find it an effective air-refresher.—Mrs I. Anderson, 36 Waverley Park, Bonnyrigg.

BROKEN BULB—If a blown electric light bulb breaks off in the socket when you're trying to remove it, use a large cork. Press the cork into the base of the bulb and unscrew it.—Miss A. Livingstone, 107 Argyle Street, Belfast.

DOOR STOP—A log, selected for its shape and size, makes a decorative door stop when it has been stripped and painted or polished.—Mrs H. Bloor, Smithy Cottage, Cultoquhey, Crieff.

PICNIC TIME—A card table with shortened legs is grand for picnics. Cut off the legs to about 12 inches and sharpen the ends so that they can be pushed into the ground.—Mrs K. Bodman, 7 Glebe Terrace, Rothesay.

SAVE THE SWEEPER—Fasten a small magnet to the front of the carpet sweeper by means of adhesive tape. This picks up any metal particles, such as pins or hair grips, and prevents damage to the sweeper.—James Scott, William Street, Tayport.

SUEDE HANDBAGS—When using a suede handbag, carry a polythene bag inside. This comes in handy to protect the handbag if you're caught in the rain.—Mrs E. Campbell, 7 Thornwood Road, Partick.

★ TOP TIP ★

QUICK FIX FOR LEAKING PIPES—If you've a burst water pipe, melt candle ends in a small jar and dip in some strips of cloth. Wrap these firmly round the leak. As the water hardens the wax, it forms a watertight bandage till the plumber arrives.—Miss A. Yelland, 21 Meersbrook Road, Sheffield, wins a pair of towels.

HANDY FILLER—If you haven't a funnel to fill a small-necked bottle, use a clean egg shell. Make a little hole with a thick needle, then pour the liquid through.—Mrs J. Nairn, Flass, Gordon.

DENT REMOVER—Put table tennis balls that are dented into a bowl and pour boiling water over them. This takes the dents out.—Mrs K. Hunter, 2 Abbey Park Place, Dunfermline.

NO SPILLS—After opening a tin of soup, etc, squeeze the sides to form a spout. Contents pour more easily without spilling.—Mrs M. Kelsey, 23 Gartons Road, Barmulloch, Glasgow.

★ TOP TIP ★

A KNOTTY PROBLEM—A knot in string or laces which cannot be easily loosened should be hammered gently. Then insert the point of a darning needle and prise open.—Mrs E. Beaton, 85 Brockburn Road, Glasgow.

CORK RAISER—If a cork gets pushed into a bottle, tie a small button on to a piece of string and lower into the bottle. Raise the cork to neck of bottle with the aid of a knitting needle. Pull up button and string, and the cork comes up and out along with them.—Mrs I. M. Eggie, 8 Caledonian Terrace, Kirtlebridge.

MANICURE HELP—I keep a plastic lemon in my manicure box. The juice, used while manicuring, removes stains from the fingers and softens the cuticle. The container is spill-proof.—Mrs J. Paterson, 26 Craiglockhart Road North, Edinburgh.

TIME SAVER—If you upset a box of buttons or pins, scoop them up with the edge of a postcard. Much quicker than picking up by hand.—Mrs Caldwell, 51 Colinslee Drive, Paisley.

HANDY FILTER—The tinfoil top off a milk bottle, with a few holes punched in it, will make a handy food filter for an easily-choked sink.—Christina Reid, Conicavel Club House. Darnaway, Forres.

HANDY HOLDERS—Drinking straws, cut to size, are excellent holders for small flowers in bowls. They keep them erect and allow the water to get to the stems.—Mrs H. Smith, 969 Aikenhead Road, Glasgow.

TIN-OPENING—When opening a tin, commence at the joint of the tin and the opener runs smoothly.—Mrs Helen S. Armstrong, 2 George Square, Greenock.

KEEPS CLEAN—When taking off a woollen jumper, put a large handkerchief over your face to prevent the jumper being soiled with cosmetics.—Miss J. Riddle, 24 Milton Road West, Portobello.

Mother does know best...

More than ever she looks for good *value*, and not at price alone . . . for fine tissue that's smooth and soft and safe . . . for the hygiene and protection that only Izal Germicide gives.

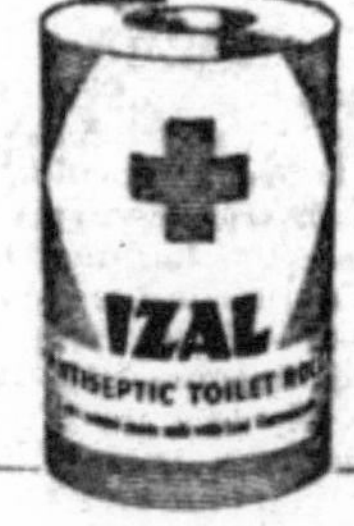

CLEARS THE AIR—To clear a room of tobacco smoke after a party, place a basin of water on the floor and close the door. In a short time the room will be quite clear.—Mrs McComisky, Harvieston Gardens, Gorebridge, Midlothian.

NO SPILLS—When baby's learning to feed himself, get two or three double-sided suction grips for fixing his plate to the tray on his high chair.—Mrs H. Turck, 5 Hazelbourne Road, Balham, London.

TIES—When I take off my tie, I roll it up tightly and put it in the corner of a drawer till next I need it. This takes out all creases as efficiently as a tie press.—T. Malcolm Auld, 26 Norman Avenue, New Silksworth, near Sunderland.

REHEATING PIE—When reheating either meat or fruit pie, put the dish right into a paper bag, fold over, and pin in end. The pie heats through without spoiling the crust.—Miss M. Cattanach, Craiglea, Newtonmore.

GIVES THAT PROFESSIONAL LOOK—The gold leaf numbering above my door was gradually being washed away. I bought two birthday cards with gold numbers for the age group, trimmed them neatly, and pasted them on the glass. Now my number looks quite professionally done.—Mrs Cook, 76 Colinton Road, Edinburgh.

CLOTHES PEGS—New clothes pegs should be popped into cold water and brought to the boil. Allow to cool and dry before using. They won't snap or break so easily.—Mrs E. McKinstra, 78 Killoch Drive, Knightswood, Glasgow.

BIN LID—To prevent your bin lid blowing away on a windy night, place it upside down on your bin. This prevents the wind getting under the rim.—Mrs H. M. Young, Reid's Buildings, High Street, Banchory.

A GOOD WAY TO GET RID OF FLIES—Take a piece of sponge, cover with boiling water, then squeeze the water out. Sprinkle a few drops of lavender oil over the sponge, and hang it in a suitable place. Flies detest this smell.—Mrs H. Brown, 33 Morar Street, Methill, wins this week's guinea.

NEW CAKE TINS—Always bake new cake tins in the oven until discoloured before using them. They absorb the heat better and cook well underneath. A shiny cake tin baffles heat.—Miss L Wilkie, 33 Sciennes Road, Edinburgh.

THIMBLES—If your thimble is too big, wrap a piece of adhesive tape round your finger to ensure a firm grip.—Mrs M, Wilson, 129 Dunottar Avenue, Shawhead, Coatbridge.

ALWAYS FRESH—To retain freshness in a teapot not constantly in use, place a teaspoonful of dry tea inside it.—Mrs W. Shepherd, 16 Arduthie Road, Stonehaven.

EASY TO THREAD—When sewing with a fine needle, dip the end of the thread in nail varnish to make threading easier.—Miss C. Scott, 21 Rosebery Avenue, South Queensferry, West Lothian.

NO DRIP—While waiting for a dripping tap to be fixed, the annoying noise can be stopped by tying a piece of string on the end of the tap so that the water can slide down the string.—Mrs C. Hogg, 11 Wilson Street, Cowdenbeath.

TWO-PURPOSE APRON—If you have an old plastic mack, cut a suitable piece to sew on the underside of your afternoon apron. This turns it into a useful dual-purpose garment—one side for washing up, the other for normal use.—Mrs A. Wade, 101 Westcliff Park Drive, Southend-on-Sea.

QUICK DISPOSAL—If you knock a pail or bowl of water over, the quickest and easiest way to get it up is to brush the water into a dust pan.—Mrs L. Gradwell, 91 Hulton Lane, Bolton.

★ TOP TIP ★

TINNED MEAT—Run hot water over a tin of meat before opening it. This melts the jelly and the meat slides out easily.—Mrs E. Blake, 46 Seamore Street, Glasgow, wins a pair of towels.

FIRST AID—Use large screw top jars to store lint, cotton wool and other first-aid necessities. You can see at a glance what you require in an emergency, and you can be sure the contents are clean.—Mrs Shepherd, Birkhill, by Dundee.

LIGHT SAVER—I often found my family forgot to turn off the bathroom light. We drilled a small hole in the top of the door panel and inserted a clear glass marble. Now it's easy to see if the light has been left on.—Mrs W. Bateman, Roseleigh, Popes Lane, Warboys, Huntingdon.

RUBBER GLOVES—To slip rubber gloves on easily, put a pair of old nylon gloves on first.—Mrs G. M. Webster, 146 Blenheim Place, Aberdeen.

★ TOP TIP ★

THERE WON'T BE A PLEAT OUT OF PLACE—Never fold a pleated skirt or spread it in a drawer. Roll the waist firmly from one side to the other. Cut the foot from an old clean silk stocking and draw the leg like a glove over the skirt. Put a piece of elastic round top and hang in the wardrobe.—Mrs Jean McAvoy, 4 Fullerton Terrace, Paisley, wins this week's guinea.

NO MIX-UP—When my little boy started school, I sewed bright red patches next to his name tabs on his coat, cap, etc. As he cannot yet read, this has helped him to recognise his own clothes quickly. So far, he has not lost anything.—Mrs M. P. Deveria, 41 Dorchester Avenue, Glasgow.

CORKS—Boil a cork for five minutes and it can be made to fit almost any bottle.—Isabella A. Webster, Hazeldene, Oldmeldrum.

BURNT FOOD—If anything in a saucepan becomes a little burnt, stand the pan in a basin of cold water immediately. This will remove the burnt taste and save a meal.—Mrs Drysdale, 78 Southhouse Broadway, Liberton, Edinburgh.

BROLLIES—Write your name and address on adhesive tape and fix it to the stick of your umbrella inside near the top. Lost umbrellas can then be returned to their owners.—Mrs McNulty, 186 Burnhouse Street, Maryhill, Glasgow.

NEW CAKE—New cake usually crumbles when cut with a knife. Use ordinary cotton thread as a cutter. Work the thread, saw-fashion, through the cake. It will be a clean cut job.—Mrs Priestley, c/o 25 Ramsay Road, Kirkcaldy.

★ TOP TIP ★

IT'LL PAY YOU TO DO THIS JOB AT NIGHT—Always put polish on boots or shoes at night and leaving polishing until morning. This feeds and preserves the leather, and gives a better shine.—Mrs Miller, 189 Childwall Road, Liverpool., wins a pair of towels.

MUFFLE IT—Sleep is often disturbed by the loud ticking of an alarm clock. Stand the clock on a cork mat. This makes it less noisy.—Mrs Dall, 3 Stenhouse Street West, Edinburgh.

DOUBLE USE—To remove dirt and dust from between floorboards after taking up carpets or lino, go over the cracks with your sink plunger. This sucks out the dirt, and it's then easy to sweep up.—Mrs E. A. M. Gear, 2 The Flats, Woodgreen, Witney.

NEW LIFE—Give your limp measuring tape a new lease of life by placing it between two sheets of waxed paper and press with a slightly hot iron. It will be stiff and much easier to use.—Mrs A. Hynd, 2 Lorne Place, Edinburgh.

CLEANING TIME—When spring cleaning, fix a wooden box to the top of the step-ladder to save brushes, dusters, &c., from falling off.—Mrs I. MacDonough, 24 Brooklyn Drive, Whitby, Ellesmere Port.

CLEAN—Use combs to clean brushes, and brushes to clean combs.—Mrs C. Thomson, 117 Sleigh Drive, Edinburgh.

SPACE-SAVING—If you have limited shelf space for household linen and towels, roll them up instead of folding. You store a lot more, and it's simpler to pull out a single article as needed.—Mrs M. Boswell, 12 Peter Street, Workington.

HOT PLATES—An easy and hygienic way of heating plates before a meal is to place them in a bowl of boiling water for a few seconds before using.—Mrs E. Muers. 19 Cecil Street, Sunderland.

BUTTONS—Buttons on pyjamas seem to pull off easily, often removing part of the fabric. Try sewing them on with wool instead of thread, which is apt to cut into the material.—Mrs Alexander. 40 Mill Lane, Whitburn, Sunderland.

FLORAL BUDS — If you want the buds in any floral arrangement to remain closed, brush the tips with egg white. —Mrs Henderson, 11 Earl Street, Glasgow.

CLEAN DISHES—When stacking away dishes that are not in everyday use, place them in Cellophane bags. They never get dusty and are always ready for use.—Mrs J. Ewan, 74 Lamington Road, Glasgow.

KEEPS FOOD HOT—Instead of putting food into the oven to keep hot for latecomers, cover it with a lid or plate and set it over a saucepan of hot water. This keeps the food hot, and at the same time prevents it from drying up.—Mrs E. Roach, 6 Cairnswell Place, Cumbernauld.

POLO NECKS—When wearing a polo-necked or roll collar jersey wear a piece of elastic, like a garter, where the collar turns over. The collar then fits snugly to the neck and is prevented from stretching and sagging.—Mrs M. Caldwell, 51 Colinslee Drive, Paisley.

MARK FREE—To prevent rain marks on leather handbags polish lightly with light shoe cream.—Mrs D. Wilson, 14C Forth Street, Alloa.

HAT TRIMMING—To save unpicking the ribbon bows from your hat when creased with rain, heat an old tablespoon and press the bowl of it inside the bows till all the creases disappear.—Mrs A. G. Forsyth, 46 Macindoe Crescent, Kirkcaldy.

SPLENDO
is delicious!

FOR SANDWICHES
ON TOAST
ON BISCUITS

Here's an exciting new delicacy that everyone will love. Splendo makes ideal sandwiches for office and school lunches—tasty snacks for tea or supper. And remember—a little Splendo goes a very long way. Use sparingly.

SPLENDO
It's meaty and economical
Spread it thinly

AN OXO LIMITED PRODUCT

TIME SAVER—Before opening tins of fruit or soup tear off the label first, as it usually sticks to the tin-opener.—Mrs J. Barnetson, Rose Cottage, Castletown, by Thurso.

SPACE SAVER—If you have several handbags, fix screw-nails at the back of your dressing-table to hang about four bags on. This gives more drawer space.—J. Farquhar, 52 Auchmill Road, Bucksburn, Aberdeen.

BLOUSES—To avoid tearing the material in doing up the little hook under the collar of blouses, embroider the "eye" in a slightly different shade of cotton. You then see it easily in the mirror.—Mrs M. Caldwell, 51 Colinslee Drive, Paisley.

SALT—Store packet salt in the airing cupboard instead of the pantry. It keeps nice and dry.—Miss A. Wilson, 109 Ashdown Road, Farringdon, Sunderland.

TIME-SAVER—Mark your sheets in each corner, D for double, and S for single. This saves unfolding when you want to know the size.—Mrs Birchall, 6 Primrose Terrace, Mill Hill, Blackburn.

VACUUM BAG—Sometimes it's difficult to remove dust from a vacuum cleaner bag without actually washing it. Try emptying a cupful of moist tea leaves into the bag, and shaking it well. Dust clings to the leaves and shakes out with them.—Mrs D. Chapman, 67 Polmuir Road, Humbedon, Sunderland.

NO STEAMY WALLS—A folded cloth placed on top of a saucepan lid when food is boiling, absorbs a lot of moisture. This prevents kitchenette walls, etc., being steamed up. —Mrs D. McBain, Ord Cottage, Feshie Bridge, Kincraig.

★ TOP TIP ★

NO MORE DUST WHEN YOU EMPTY THE VACUUM—Empty the contents of the vacuum bag on to wet paper. Dust and dirt don't rise, and the air is kept clean.—Mrs N. Weatherstone, 90 Queen Alexandra Road West, North Shields, wins a pair of towels.

CLEAN LABELS—A thin coat of clear nail varnish over medicine bottle labels keeps them clean and readable.—E. Dalgleish, 91 Parkfoot, High Station Road, Falkirk.

A SIMPLE REMEDY FOR AN ANNOYING HABIT—Bath and other towels have an annoying habit of slipping off the rails. This can be prevented by slipping a few rubber bands on the towel rail.—J.B. Dawson, 49 Stonyhurst Street, Possilpark, Glasgow, wins this week's guinea.

EXTRA SHELF—Pull out kitchen table drawer halfway and set tray or board on it. This provides an extra shelf to put ingredients on while baking, and the lot can be carried back to larder together when finished with.—Mrs M. Hay, 25 Hall Dene Close, Bushy Hill, Guildford, Surrey.

HANDY SPONGE—Keep a moist rubber sponge on your kitchen table when baking or cooking. It's handy to wipe sticky fingers on, and saves washing the hands so often.—R. Harris, 8 Dunholm Drive, Giffnock.

NO CHIPPED CHINA—Save rubber rings from jars and lids. Placed between saucers and plates of your best china they help to prevent chipping and cracks.—N. Kennedy, 4 Burn Road, Inverness.

FIRMLY HELD—When threading wears on your fountain pen or propelling pencil, insert a piece of silver paper in the holder. Then the top stays firm.—Mrs MacGregor Allan, 119 Kingsknowe Road North, Edinburgh.

ALWAYS READY—After using adhesive tape, roll the end round a spent matchstick. This makes it always ready for use and there's no difficulty in restarting the roll.—Mrs R. Smith, 90 Seedhill Road, Paisley.

The Sunday Post

Morning Special

PRINTED AND PUBLISHED EVERY SUNDAY MORNING.

No. 2343. [REGISTERED AT THE GENERAL POST OFFICE AS A NEWSPAPER] SUNDAY, JULY 23, 1950. RADIO—Page 4 PRICE TWOPENCE.

AMERICA WARNED—LONG WAR EXPECTED

Not Ready Yet For Offensive

IT may be mid-autumn or even spring before U.S. forces can launch a major counter-offensive in Korea.

This was stated by a leading Defence Department official in Washington last night. He cautioned Americans against hoping for a swift victory.

The public should not be discouraged or alarmed to find another setback occurring soon, he added. This was expected as part of the general pattern of resisting steadily while inflicting on the enemy the heaviest losses possible in a time-gaining manœuvre.

Meanwhile the build-up of American strength was proceeding. Bigger, harder-hitting medium tanks were on the way to replace the outgunned, outclassed light tanks which had been damaged by Communist armour.

Also en route were stepped-up shipments of the new tank killer—super-bazookas.

The official said that at no time had there been any division among military planners. Plans had changed because the Korean picture had changed.

At the outset, it was agreed to use only naval and air action, hoping this would give the South Korean ground forces enough support to expel the Communist invaders. But it soon became obvious this was not enough, and the decision to send in a division from the four in Japan under General MacArthur's command was reached.

This, too, had to be revised, and elements of the 1st and 25th Divisions landed north of Pusan this week.

Meanwhile, help was started from America. A part of the 1st Marine Division, with its own air support, steamed out of the west coast. The Army's 2nd Infantry Division prepared to sail, as well as smaller units from other Army divisions.

Trouble On Border

The Yugoslav Government has rejected Bulgarian allegations of illegal acts by Yugoslav frontier guards against Bulgarian farmers.

This was announced by the official Yugoslav News Agency yesterday.

Clerk Of Works Wins The Amateur

W. C. Gibson, Prestwick St Cuthbert's, 35-year-old ex-joiner, and now clerk of works at Prestwick Airport, yesterday won the Scottish Amateur Golf Championship at Prestwick.

He defeated Major David Blair, Nairn, by 2 and 1 in the 36-hole final.

"Gammie," as he is known to hundreds of Ayrshire golf fans, was one down at the end of the first round. He didn't take the lead until the thirty-fourth hole. Then he won the next hole to finish the game.

It was a dour struggle for him. Major Blair, the ex-Army champion, began firm favourite, but the local man, with his gallery of loyal fans, finally wore out the Major and took the trophy.

A week-end golfer, Gibson was a championship semi-finalist in 1939. He was chosen for the international series that year, but the games were not played because of the war.

Guards Surround Leopold's Bedroom

KING LEOPOLD went to bed in the Royal Palace in Brussels last night ringed by an army of police and guards.

Belgium remained calm, despite political predictions of bloodshed and industrial paralysis.

King Leopold had returned after six years of exile to a capital blue with fear of trouble between the bitterly-opposed supporters and opponents of the monarch.

[illegible]

He later presided over a Crown Council which was boycotted by three Liberal and nine Socialist Ministers of State.

[illegible]

They blew whistles (the Belgian Socialist Party bought up fifty thousand whistles to drown cheers on the King's home-coming), chanted "Leopold to the gallows," "Abdication," sang the "Marseillaise," and halted traffic through several important thoroughfares.

TOP: Cuddling his machine-gun, Private Zeilo Acadilla, from Honolulu, jolts northward in a railway truck towards the front. With him is his mascot—a doll.

BOTTOM—An American 155 mm. howitzer camouflaged among the scrub-covered hills of Korea, challenges the advancing Reds.

REDS PLAN NEXT MOVE IN EUROPE

Leading Communists from 17 countries met in Berlin yesterday.

Cominform tactics in the next phase of the East-West struggle were outlined.

The question of the remilitarisation of East Germany was said to top the agenda. The Polish and Soviet Communist Party representatives took a leading part in the discussions.

A second move reported to be under discussion is a wide-scale disruption of ports and docks along the West European coastline this winter.

DEARER EGGS

EGGS are 6d a dozen dearer to-day.

The increase was announced last night by the Minister of Food, and applies to wholesale and retail maximum prices of all eggs.

Perth Roadman Found Dead

[illegible]

Mr Mackenzie King Seriously Ill

[illegible]

TO-DAY'S WEATHER

[illegible]

BIG RED OFFENSIVE LIKELY TO-DAY

AS dusk fell over Korea's western front last night, after two days of uneasy quiet, American troops dug in south-east of Taejon.

They were waiting tensely for a big Communist offensive expected this morning.

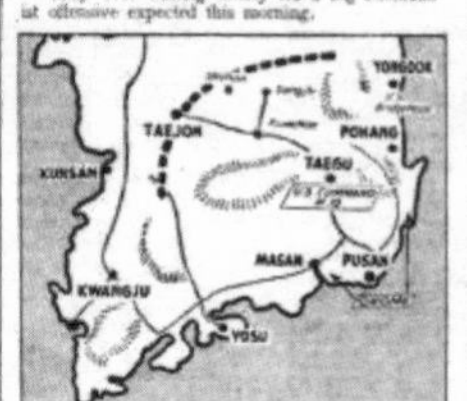

The morale of the G.I.s has lifted steadily since they were hammered out of Taejon on Thursday.

On the **EAST** sector, American troops, fresh from their sea landing earlier in the week, joined South Koreans in a push up the east coast after the recapture of Yongdok, 25 miles north of their beach head.

Among the mountains in the **CENTRE** of the peninsula, American troops and South Koreans stand fast. But North Koreans were rushing up reinforcements of men and armour in a bid to smash their way south to **Kumchon**.

Kumchon is the advanced supply centre, halfway between **Taejon** and **Taegu**, now the Americans' main forward base.

On the **WEST** coast, two Communist columns drove south to make their deepest penetration yet. They reached points only 60 miles from the south coast.

They are now halfway between **Kunsan** and **Kwangju**.

North Korean air activity increased. Fifteen Yak fighter-bombers, biggest concentration the Communists had yet mustered, hit an advanced American airstrip in a sneak raid.

This was the second sneak raid within four days. Seven Yaks swooped low over **Ulchon** two days ago and bombed and strafed American positions.

American jets caught them and shot down three.

Despite heavy rain yesterday, American jets and Mustangs poured bombs and rockets into targets inside Taejon and roads leading out of the city.

Many stragglers from the battle of Taejon continue to find their way back to their units through the rugged mountains.

Meat — Brighter News

The Uruguay Government has instructed meat-packing houses to resume frozen meat shipments to Britain as soon as the meat-packing workers' strike is settled.

While long British-Argentine discussions have been clouded by such obstacles as Argentine commercial debts and the decrease of Argentine purchases from Britain, no such difficulties have occurred in British-Uruguayan relations.

There are signs that Uruguay will be able to provide a big part of Britain's meat deficiency in the event of a complete stoppage of Argentine meat.

Uruguay shipments may reach 50 per cent. of the Argentine volume.

HE DISCOVERED VALENTINO

Mr Rex Ingram, producer of silent film days, has died in Hollywood at the age of 58.

He was the man behind "The Four Horsemen of the Apocalypse," the original "Prisoner of Zenda" and "The Garden of Allah."

He "discovered" Rudolph Valentino and Ramon Novarro.

Chapter 2
Thrift, The Measure Of A Household

IT was the holy grail of the housewife. To be thrifty wasn't only pressingly necessary in those austere days, but also the sign of being clever, resourceful and of running a good household.

The Sunday Post gave an award, a pair of towels, sometimes half a guinea or even a guinea to the top tip of the week, and thrifty Pass It Ons were regarded as the prize-winning tip more often than any other type.

These tips tell of hard times. Making ends meet could be difficult. But people were so proud of their ability to find ways to cope that they shared them with the world.

Here's to the heroic thrifty housewives of the 1950s.

TOWELS LAST LONGER THIS WAY—When the dish towels you are using get rather bare, stitch two together with strong thread. The two-in-one lasts much longer.—Mrs J. Scott, Isleview, Allanfearn, Inverness, wins a pair of towels.

NO CUTS—To prevent cutting the cloth when removing buttons from old clothes, place a fork under the buttons.—Mrs E. McIntosh, Janitor's House, Cauldeen School, Mackay Road, Inverness, wins a pair of towels.

TEA-WISE—Don't discard "empty" tea packets without unfolding the bottom. About a teaspoonful of tea is generally tucked away inside the folds.—Miss Betty Forrest, 16 Primrose Street, Glasgow.

ALL YOU NEED—When making a cup of tea for yourself and your husband, measure out just two cupfuls of water to boil in the kettle. That's all you need. It saves gas.—Mrs I. Taylor, 54 Roseangle, Dundee.

ROASTING—When roasting, turn off the oven gas 15 minutes before the meat is ready to come out. The heat of the oven will finish the cooking.—Miss A. Wilson, Recreation Grounds, Fulwell Road, Sunderland.

CHEAP CASE—I needed a pencil case so I made one myself. I simply cut the bottom off an old handbag and fixed a zip to the opening.—Mary Paxton, Grueldykes, Duns.

SADDLE COVER—Skirts and trousers don't become shiny through cycling if you fix an old beret on the saddle.—Mrs J. Brown, 12 King's Place, Rosyth.

CRISP BISCUITS—I always tape up my biscuit tin lid after use. I find this keeps the biscuits fresh and crisp to the very end.—J. Robertson, Carlisle.

OLD INTO NEW—If you have a dingy glass vase, don't throw it out. Give it a coat of brown oak varnish and it will look like glowing amber.—Mrs M. Sharp, 54 Main Street, Leith.

TWO FROM ONE—When a sweeping becomes worn in the middle or at ends, cut head in half and insert handles in the two ends. Then you've two useful hearth brushes.—Mrs Aitken, 102 Stenhouse Street, Cowdenbeath.

HANDY CLEANER—Having run out of steel wool, I used a tinfoil milk top to clean my pots. It proved most effective. I ran a thread through a dozen tops and now have a handy cleaner.—Mrs J. Thomson, 27 Park Crescent, Bonnyrigg.

★ TOP TIP ★

NEW LIFE FOR AN OLD SHOVEL—When the front edge of a shovel begins to wear and becomes jagged, there's no need to throw it away. Just trim off the jagged edge with a hammer and cold chisel. The shovel, though shortened, is still quite serviceable.—W. Finlay, c/o Campbell, 119 Warrender Park Road, Edinburgh, wins a pair of towels.

PLACE MATS—Buy a cheap contemporary cushion cover in a gay colour. Out of it, for a few pence each, you can make four lovely place mats. Have them fringed or machine stitched. And there's enough material left over to make four wine-glass mats and two book-markers. Not bad for 5s 11d.—Mrs M. Rutherford, Shangri-La, Lenzie Road, Kirkintilloch, wins a pair of towels.

THRIFTY COOKING—One fewer gas ring is needed if you fill a saucepan lid with potatoes and tie a cloth over them. Put the lid on the pan in which other vegetables are being cooked.—M. Whiteside, 83 Aitkenhead Avenue, Coatbridge, wins a pair of towels.

BIND THE SEAMS—A good way to double the life of children's gym knickers is to machine a strip of binding down all seams.—Mrs Wilderspin, 19 Ivanhoe, Monkseaton, Northumberland.

SMOOTH EDGE—The lip of one of my wine glasses got chipped. I rubbed the part with glass paper and so smoothed the sharp edge that it can now be used quite safely.—Mrs Andrew, 69 Battlefield Avenue, Langside, Glasgow.

PLASTIC GOODS—My plastic brush had a split in the handle. I smoothed it out with a hot iron. Now it is as good as new.—Mrs C. Campbell, 41 Roman Avenue, Drumchapel, Glasgow.

SCRUBBING BRUSHES LAST LONGER THIS WAY—Scrubbing brushes last twice as long if they are put to dry bristles downwards. When turned the other way the water soaks into the wood and rots the bristles.—Mrs Boswell, 12 Peter Street, Workington, wins a pair of towels.

QUICK COOKING—If you remove the centre from potatoes with an apple corer they bake or roast in half the time—Mrs E. Muers, 19 Cecil Street, Sunderland.

CONDENSED MILK—On opening a tin of condensed milk, pour the contents into a glass jar with a screw top. The milk keeps better and the jar is cleaner to handle than a messy, encrusted tin.—Mrs N. Inglis, 24 India Street, Montrose.

DRIP MATS—The lids and bases of round boxes which contain cheese portions make useful drip mats. Use them for milk bottles, sauce bottles, etc., on pantry shelves.—Mrs A. Howe, 14 Parade, Berwick-on Tweed.

NO MORE TOWELS CUT BY RAZOR BLADES—Save your towels by making your menfolk a book of blotting paper in which to dry their razor blades after shaving.—Miss E. Barron, 7 Blackhall Road, Inverurie, wins a pair of towels.

NO STRAIN—Very often the handle of a saucepan breaks. To avoid this, when cleaning the pan, hold by the side and not by the handle.—Mrs M. Boswell, 12 Peter Street, Workington.

★ TOP TIP ★

GUARD AGAINST RUST—Household containers (tin kettles, oil stoves, etc) should either be dried thoroughly or left filled with the liquid used, otherwise the life of the container is cut short through rust.—Mrs T. A. Muirhead, 186 Copland Road, Glasgow, wins a pair of towels.

BROLLY COVER—A man's old neck tie makes a novel umbrella cover. Cut off the length required, and slip in the umbrella from the wide end. Sew on a press fastener at the top.—Mrs Doris Gardiner, 40 Cromarty Gardens, Clarkston, Glasgow.

CHAIR BACKS—A discarded table or sideboard runner can be made into lovely chair backs. Just cut in half and sew on fringed cord.—Mrs E. Sorbie, 25 Camnethan Street, Stonehouse.

CHOKERS—Thread your choker necklace on a double thread of shirring elastic. It will last for months and "gives" with movement.—Mrs M. Salisbury, 249 Morningside Road, Edinburgh.

FUR FABRIC COATS—If your coat looks a little the worse for winter weather, go over with an electric vacuum cleaner. Using a small nozzle, gently run over the whole coat, paying special attention to the neckline and pockets. The pile of the fabric is raised and any dirt sucked away. It gives the coat a new look.—H. G. Jack, 12 Robert Street, Newport-on-Tay.

CHANGE TO HAND—I find it a good plan to keep a 10s or £1 note ready to exchange for shillings when the gas man calls. In this way I never really run short.—Mrs Richard, c/o 3 Meadow Vale, Cromwell Road, Burntisland.

GOOD REPAIR—I had a plastic basin which split at the bottom and was leaking. I cut a piece of plastic from the outer rim and, using the gas pistol to heat it, I melted it and allowed it to run into the split, which was sealed up completely. The basin is as good as new.—Mrs Gordon, 56 Wall Street, Camelon, Falkirk.

LONGER LIFE—Socks will last much longer if toes and heels are reinforced by darning before wearing.—Mrs J. Wales, 92 Cardross Street, Glasgow.

LONGER WEAR—Work a few rows of machine stitching round the end of men's shirt cuffs. They will wear much longer, besides having a very neat finish.—Miss M. Morton, 88 Balhousie Street, Perth.

A WAY TO USE UP OLD FROCKS—Discarded summer frocks make nice tea aprons. Use front or back of skirt, put in a few pleats, and attach to a waistband made from other remnants. Add a pocket.—Mrs E. Leckie, 15 Balgair Street, Possilpark, Glasgow, wins a pair of towels.

★ TOP TIP ★

SURPRISING WHAT YOU CAN DO WITH AN OLD PLASTIC COAT—There are uses for practically all the material in an old plastic coat. Make the back into a wash-day apron, using the coat belt as tapes. The pockets make good sponge and face-cloth bags or ration-book cases. Use sleeves for pulling over a child's pantaloons.—Mrs H. Thomson, 49 Hayocks Road, Stevenston, wins a pair of towels.

SAVES GAS—Cut carrots and turnips into cubes, tie in a muslin bag, and put in the same pot as the potatoes. They will all be ready at the same time, and are easy to serve.—Mrs Symington, 11 Windyedge Crescent, Glasgow.

BUTTONS—Pretty buttons are expensive, but you can have many changes at little cost if you buy some plain glass buttons and paint the backs with any pretty colours you fancy.—Mrs Neish, c/o 409 Warbreck Drive, Blackpool.

LEATHER GLOVES—Try adhesive tape to mend leather gloves. Warm the tape and place under the tear. Then gently pull the damaged edges together until the sides meet. It's quicker, and makes a neater job than sewing.—Mrs J. Cunningham, Park View, Blackford.

PIPE SMOKERS—When you refill your pipe, put the ash from the previous smoke on top of the fresh tobacco. The pipe lights with only one match, and burns more evenly.—J. Jackson, Carlisle.

DRESS COVER—Before discarding that old coat, take out the lining, wash and iron it. It makes a nice dust cover for your best dress.—Mrs E. Locke, 15 Balgair Street, Possilpark, Glasgow.

STAYS PUT—Adhesive dressing or tape will stay put much longer if the corners are rounded off instead of being cut straight.—Mrs G. Bremner, 13 Erskine Street, Aberdeen.

POLISHING—Instead of shaking out the polish put a clean rag on top of the bottle or tin and shake upwards. Much less polish is used.—Mrs Wray, 65 Percy Park Road, Tynemouth.

COMFY SLIPPERS—If your bedroom slippers have become wide, stitch a strip of foam rubber round the inside. It has a firm grip and is also comfortable.—Mrs J. Fraser, Fern Siding, Careston, By Brechin.

HANDY CUSHIONS—Foam rubber (sold at 3s 6d a sheet) shaped and fitted with loose covers, makes ideal cushions for kitchen chairs.—Mrs Bell, Springfield, Ord, Berwick-upon-Tweed.

GIVES LONG LIFE—Before using a new nylon pot scrubber sew it firmly through the centre with strands of nylon from the old scrubber. This prolongs its life.—Mrs D. Rutherford, 65 Morton Street, Joppa.

CHEAP BATH MAT—Buy a dozen various-coloured, good-sized face cloths. Sew them together, using an old towel as a foundation. They make a serviceable and inexpensive bath mat.—Miss N. Mitchell, Clark's Buildings, Carnock, Dunfermline.

★ TOP TIP ★

HELPS TO KEEP THE MILK FRESH—When I have any milk left over at night I drop in a pinch of bicarbonate of soda, and the milk is fresh for next day. If out at work all day, do as soon as milk arrives in the morning.—Mrs E. Adair, 99 Malcolm Street, Heaton, Newcastle-on-Tyne, wins a pair of towels.

SLIPPERS—Felt slippers tend to wear through quickly at the toes. Stick adhesive tape inside the toes of the slippers while they are still new. You will have no further trouble. —Mrs M. Miller, 130 Brackenbrae Avenue, Bishopbriggs, Glasgow.

FIRM AGAIN—My leather shopping bag became soft through much use. I cut two pieces of stout cardboard to fit sides of bag and fixed them inside. The bag is now quite firm.—Mrs H. Wells, 4 Martin Avenue, Dumfries.

ADDED STRENGTH—The handles of a folding shopping bag often break when the rest of the bag is still quite good. To obviate this, when you get a new shopping bag, reinforce the handles by sewing on nylon tape.—Miss S. Cooper, 29 Parksway, Pendlebury, Lancs.

GOOD POLISHERS—When lambswool-lined slippers become too shabby for further use, open them down the back of the heel and turn inside out. They make ideal polishers for furniture and floors.—Mrs Miller, 189 Childwall Road, Liverpool.

HANDY WORKBAG—To make a useful workbag out of an old lampshade, fix a piece of stout cardboard to the narrow end and cover the whole shade with flowered chintz. Make cover longer than the frame, and draw it at top with cord threaded through the hem.—Mrs Baird, 40 Lochinver Drive, Glasgow.

CHAMOIS—To make further use of an old chamois, cut it into strips 12 inches long and half an inch wide. Tie strips together in the middle, then trim them even all round. This will last a few months longer.—Mrs Arroll, 35 Courthill, Roseneath, by Helensburgh.

TAKES THE STRAIN—If your lingerie has fragile shoulder straps, a good idea is to unpick the stitching at the back, cut off about an inch, and replace with a piece of elastic the same width. This greatly reduces the strain on the garment and lengthens its life.—Miss H. M. Grant, 29 Gordon Road, Aberdeen.

PRAM BRAKE—When the tyres of a pram begin to wear, making the foot-brake less effective, put a piece of rubber hosepipe over the parts of the brake which rest against the wheels. This saves the danger of the pram "running away".—Mrs Kathleen E. Maleshead, 123 Vardar Avenue, Clarkston, Renfrewshire.

RUBBER GLOVES—After wearing rubber gloves, peel them off and leave them outside in. Next time they're put on they'll be worn on opposite hands. They last longer this way, as the right hand usually wears more quickly than the left.—Mrs Russell, 12 Howieshill Road, Cambuslang.

★ TOP TIP ★

EVEN WEAR—When making the beds I change the order of the blankets each day, putting the first last, second first, and so on. I also put them top to bottom. This prevents the sides of the top blanket wearing thin or becoming frayed through being tucked in at the same place.—Mrs H. Blount, 5 Hazelbourne Road, Balham, London.

PLASTIC BASINS—Never put ammonia or bleaching liquids into plastic bowls. They damage the smooth skin at the bottom of the basin, leaving it rough. I find that rubbing the bowl with fine sandpaper helps to take away the roughness.—Mrs E. Cameron, 10 May Terrace, Giffnock.

NEAT MENDING—If you tear an overall you can get a good-sized patch from under the pocket. Stitch a piece of another material in place. It doesn't show.—Miss M. D. MacGregor, Sutherland Cottage, Keir Street, Dunblane.

WINTER BOOTS—If the wool lining at the heel of winter boots wears away buy a piece of chiropodists' adhesive felt, cut to shape, and fix securely in place.—Mrs M. Craig, 14 Northfield Terrace, Edinburgh.

SAVES TWO BUYINGS—Instead of buying cot blankets, buy a single blanket and double it. When the growing child needs a single bed, the single blanket is of more use.—Mrs McDonough, Cullicudden Road, Conon.

IRON FLEX—The flex of the electric iron lasts longer if kept suspended from a hook instead of winding it round the iron when not in use.—Mrs Temple, 8 Nelson Street, Hendon, Sunderland.

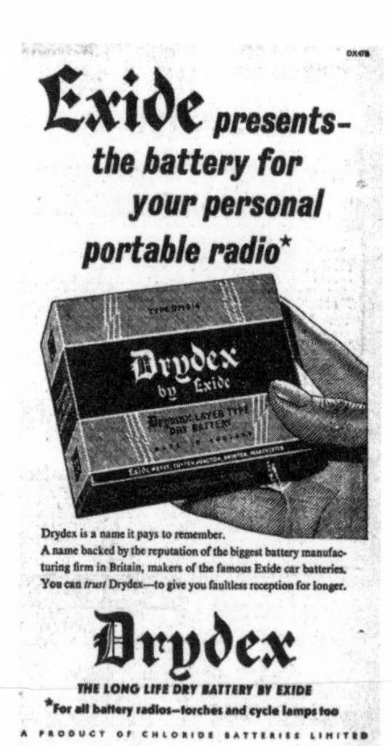

HOLIDAY CASES—Re-line a shabby case with self-adhesive plastic material. Clean the outside with furniture cream and shine the locks with chrome polish. The case takes on a new look.—Mrs M. P. Deveria, 39 Upper Cavehill Road, Belfast.

WASHING UP WATER—When baking, place an enamel bowl or saucepan of cold water in the oven. The water will be lovely and hot for washing up, and is a time and fuel saver.—Mrs D. J. Maxwell, 12 Stockwell Road, Blackwell, Carlisle.

WINDOW CLEANER—When your bottle of window cleaner gets low and starts to thicken, add a little methylated spirits. This helps to use it all up and also gives an extra shine to the windows.—Miss M. Purves, Bank House, The Square, Cockburnspath.

FOR BAKED POTATOES—When baking potatoes, put them on a wire pastry tray. The tray, being raised on small feet, allows the heat to circulate evenly, and the potatoes need no turning.—Mrs Sievewright, 6 Castle Sreet, Turriff.

NEW USE FOR AN OLD SHIRT—I use the tails of old shirts made in nice materials to make cushion covers. Strips cut from sleeves are set in to make frills.—Mrs Alexander, 556 Strathmartine Road, Dundee, wins a pair of towels.

SUBSTITUTE—Get a card of fuse wire (5 or 10 amp). With two No. 10 knitting needles, cast on 20 stitches with the wire and knit a square. Knit another square the same size with odd pieces of fine string. Join the two squares together. The result is a pad for purposes where steel wool was used before.—M. Stephen, Doonieshill, Nigg, Aberdeenshire.

COLOURFUL KNIVES—Brighten discoloured knife handles with a thin coat of Chinese lacquer, which can be bought in several colours.—Mrs E. Batley, 3 Tudor Terrace, Consett, Co. Durham.

ELECTRIC KETTLE—After pouring boiling water from an electric kettle never leave any below the element. Always fill up with cold water. This helps to keep a kettle in good condition. —Mrs H. Millar, 247 Kingsacre Road, Rutherglen, Glasgow

AFTER TEN YEARS THEY'RE AS GOOD AS NEW—After 10 years of hard wearing my bathroom rubber mats are still like new. I never wash them. I clean them once a week with a little black boot polish, then polish them up.—Mrs P. Murray, 5 Upper Wellheads, Limekilns, wins a pair of towels.

THE SUNDAY POST, NOVEMBER 18, 1951.

The Sunday Post

Morning Special

PRINTED AND PUBLISHED EVERY SUNDAY MORNING.

No. 2412. [REGISTERED AT THE GENERAL POST OFFICE AS A NEWSPAPER.] SUNDAY, NOVEMBER 18, 1951. Radio—Page 4. PRICE 2½d.

CHEERING CROWDS BREAK THROUGH POLICE CORDONS TWICE

REMARKABLE SCENES AS THE PRINCESS COMES HOME

PRINCESS Elizabeth, back from her triumphant tour of Canada, stepped from a train at Euston yesterday, went down almost to her knees and hugged her son, Prince Charles.

Then his father, the Duke of Edinburgh, grinned happily at the young Prince, and ruffled his neatly-parted hair.

This was more than the home-coming of the heir to the throne. It was a touching, affectionate reunion of mother, father and son.

There was a happy reunion too, as the Princess and Duke greeted the Queen and Princess Margaret.

Then they drove to Buckingham Palace, amid remarkable scenes of welcome, to see the King and 15-month-old Princess Anne.

After a 40-minute stay they left for Clarence House—again through [illegible] happy crowds. The family were home again.

During the 26 minutes he spent on the red-carpeted platform at Euston, Prince Charles captured the hearts of the huge crowds.

[illegible]

Watchful Eye

The Queen [illegible] kept a watchful eye over her grandson. [illegible]

[illegible]

"It's Mother!"

[illegible]

Princess Elizabeth stepped out the moment the train had stopped, kissed the Queen warmly on both cheeks, embraced her and then dropped almost to her knees to hug Prince Charles.

[illegible]

(Continued on Back Page.)

[illegible]

Power Board Chief Sees Lawyer

COLONEL WILFRED MARK LAPPER, £4000-a-year chairman of the Yorkshire Electricity Board, was seen by his solicitor yesterday afternoon in Leeds Prison.

The solicitor (Mr Malcolm D. Featherstone) said later that no definite decision about an appeal by the colonel, sentenced to six months' imprisonment for exceeding authorised expenditure on the board's headquarters at Scarcroft, and doing work not in accordance with the plans—would be taken until to-morrow.

He has 13 days in which to give notice of appeal.

Attempt To Bribe Scots Footballer

A SENSATION was caused in Scottish football circles last night when it became known that an attempt had been made to bribe an Airdrie football player.

[illegible]

Malaya's Blackest Week

Malaya last night ended its blackest week with a total of at least 78 people killed or wounded in [illegible].

[illegible]

British Troops Aid Flood Victims

[illegible]

Peace-Before-Xmas Plan —Korea Reds Reply To-day

FIRST Communist reaction to the Korean "peace before Christmas" offer is favourable.

"It seems to be in accordance with our principles," they said yesterday.

The Allied plan—put forward in the expectation that the Communists will accept—agrees to the Reds' proposal that a demilitarised zone should be based on the present battle-line.

But it sets the condition that all other points of the armistice must be fully agreed within 30 days, if this line is to stand.

Till now, the Allies have refused to fix a provisional ceasefire line before other armistice terms are discussed, because they feared the Communists might drag out negotiations when free from military pressure.

Other armistice points to be settled in the 30 days are:—

1—Exchange of prisoners.

2—Guarantees against the ceasefire agreement being used as a cover for [illegible].

3—A system of inspection to ensure these agreements being carried out.

Lieut.-Col. Howard Levie, Allied spokesman, said the United Nations [illegible] "thrown the ball" to the Communists. "Our proposal was made in the expectation it would be accepted. We don't see any reason why the Communists shouldn't accept it."

The official Communist reply is expected at to-day's truce session.

U.S. Oil For Persians

THE U.S. steamer, Steel Architect, left the Persian port of Khorramshahr yesterday after unloading 1750 tons of lubricating oil and 145 tons of grease from America for the National Iranian Oil Company.

The ship was reported going to Bandar Shahpur with 800 tons of military supplies for Persia.

An earlier consignment arrived at Khorramshahr recently in the steamer American Robin, and was shipped by the Commerce Oil Company of America to the National Iranian Company. Smaller shipments from the Cities Service Oil Company and the Petrola Oil Company, both of America, were addressed to Teheran.

The National Iranian Oil Company was formed by the Persian Government to succeed the nationalised Anglo-Iranian Oil Company.

21 FIREMEN HURT IN BLAZE

ONE of the biggest blazes seen in East London since the war was fought by 175 firemen last night.

They had 30 engines and three 100-foot ladders.

Six firemen were taken to hospital seriously hurt. 15 more were treated on the spot for injuries.

The fire occurred in the Highway, Stepney, at the large premises of Messrs John Brandon Ltd. [illegible]

A large part of the [illegible]

[illegible] flames were going through the roofs. Early this morning the fire was under control.

TO-DAY'S WEATHER

[illegible]

Chapter 3
The Art Of Cleaning

THERE was no insult more grave than for the neighbours to say: "She keeps a dirty hoose".

The women, and they are almost exclusively women, who wrote in with tips were cleaning demons who scoured, scraped and scrubbed their homes. Dirt was a challenge, grime was an enemy, dust was a sin.

Many of their husbands, sons and fathers would have been employed in heavy industries such as steel-making, mining and ship-building, so they brought grit, soot and dust home. But this was never complained about in the tips readers sent, it was merely a fact of life. It was dealing with it that was the job.

Ladies of the clean and polished 1950s, we salute you.

FRUIT JUICE—When fruit juice is spilled on a tablecloth, dip a piece of bread in cold water and put it over the stain immediately. The stain soon disappears.—Mrs R. Davidson, 16 Woodlands Crescent, Turriff.

IT CLEANS GAS FIRES IN A JIFFY—After a certain amount of use, gas fires sometimes take on a dingy appearance. When the fire is cold sprinkle salt over it, then light. The salt burns off, taking the grime with it.—Miss M. Williams, 19 Wrenbury Street, Holt Road, Edgehill, Lancs., wins a pair of towels.

AN EASY WAY TO CLEAN THE BATH—Try cleaning the bath with a long-handled brush (an old, soft-haired sweeping brush is ideal). The job is done in half the time, and not so back-breaking either.—Miss J. Lindsay, 22 Tower Street, Portobello, wins a pair of towels.

WOODWORK—When scrubbing white woodwork use cold water and a nylon pot cleaner with a light sprinkling of abrasive. Hot water makes the woodwork yellow.—Miss D. Bulmer, 90 High Street, North Berwick.

ASH TRAYS—To remove nicotine stains from ashtrays or other china, rub over with a cork dipped in damp salt.—Mrs J. McKenzie, 179 Earl Street, Glasgow.

PRESERVES WHITE ENAMEL—Polish white enamelled paintwork with furniture cream occasionally. It forms a skin which preserves the paintwork and makes it easier to keep clean.—J. Simpson, Parkneuk, Carmyllie, Arbroath.

WATER SPOTS—Water spots on a French polished table are easily removed with Vaseline. Use a piece of cotton wool and rub briskly round and round over the spot.—Mrs Carmichael, 19 Westland Drive, Scotstoun, Glasgow.

SPOTTY WINDOWS—I got this tip from a garage man. To clean a smeary windscreen or window, wet it, then rub with a penny. Chamois in the usual way.—J. Wilson, Denton Holme, Carlisle.

NO CLOGGING—To clean a pepper pot lid, there's nothing like drawing a darning needle, with white thread, through the holes.—Miss R. Lock, 84 Watermoor Road, Cirencester.

SHINY—After washing mirrors, picture-glass or even tumblers allow them to dry partly then polish with clean blotting paper. A perfect polish results with the minimum of work.—Mrs W. Young "New Corner", 4 City Road, Brechin.

SILVER TEAPOT—As this is used only on occasions, dry well after use. Put clean, old linen napkin inside and turn pot upside down so that spout can drain overnight. Next day put pot away with a lump of sugar in it and there's no danger of any musty smell.—Mrs J. Hill, 53 Calder Street, Alloa.

KNIFE HANDLES—If the ivory handles of your knives are turning yellow, rub them with a cut lemon, wash them in soapy water and dry immediately. This will clean the handles, and should be repeated at intervals to keep them white.—Mrs M. Nicholson, 16 Lyle Crescent, Bishopton, Renfrewshire.

CLEAN BATH—However badly stained and water-lined baths may be, they are quickly cleaned with salt and paraffin. Saturate a cloth with the oil, dip in fine salt, and rub the bath well. Afterwards rinse with cold (not hot) water to take away smell of paraffin.—Mrs Thomson, 121 St Vincent Street, Glasgow.

FRYING PAN—To clean a frying pan that has been used for herring or onions, wash it well with hot water and soda. Dry and sprinkle a little oatmeal into the pan. Place over heat for a few minutes to brown the meal. Shake out and wipe with a dishcloth. All smell and taste will have gone.—Mrs C. Burr, Primrose Cottage, Udny Green, Udny, Aberdeenshire.

NO DRIPS—When washing windows or high woodwork, tie a piece of towelling round the wrists to keep water from running down the arms.—M. J. Hill, 122 Younger Street, Alloa.

CARRY ALL—A two-tier tea trolley is handy at spring-cleaning time. It can be taken from room to room with all cleaning equipment.—Miss J. Christine, 7 Harbour Street, Creetown, Dumfries & Galloway.

SPECS—Use ordinary eau de cologne to clean spectacles. It quickly removes spots and grease from both lenses and frames. And keeps them from steaming up.—Miss A. Wilson, Welfare Grounds, Fulwell Road, Sunderland.

LEATHER FURNITURE—Keep free from cracks by polishing regularly with a cream made from 1 part vinegar and 2 parts linseed oil. Bottle, and shake until creamy.—Mrs Aird, 39 Brown Crescent, Thornton, Fife.

MAKES DUSTING EASY—Instead of laboriously dusting round ornate legs or tables and chairs, I slip an old woollen mitt on my hand and work in all the corners with my fingers. The job's done in a fraction of the time.—Mrs E. C. Duthie, 6 Raeburn Place, Aberdeen.

★ TOP TIP ★

A TIP FOR LIGHT SHOES—To keep pastel-coloured leather shoes looking like new, take out dirty marks and scratches with a soft rubber.—Mrs E. Cowan, 91 Queensferry Rd., Rosyth, wins a pair of towels.

CLEAN JOB—When I do distempering or whitewashing I put on an old pair of socks over my shoes to keep my shoes and stockings clean. They're also handy for rubbing wet spots off the floor.—Mrs E. Dainty, 48 Honor Avenue, Goldthorn Park, Wolverhampton.

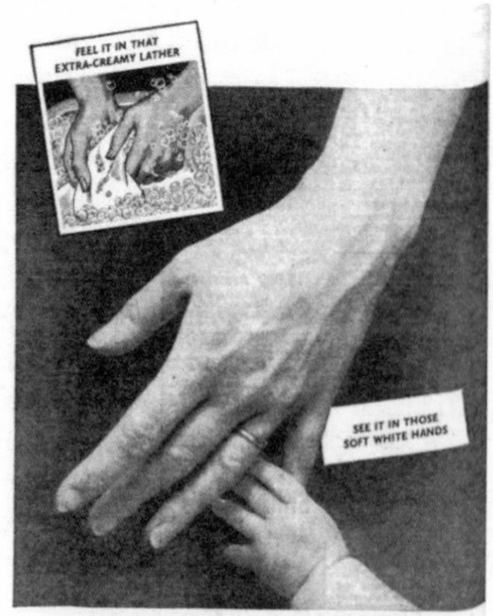

DIRTY JOBS—If you wear an overall for doing the chores, it's a good idea to fasten the cuffs by looping a small elastic band through the buttonhole and round the button. The sleeves can then be pulled up and down without unfastening the cuffs—helpful when doing a wet or dirty job.—Mrs D. Goodall, 8 Rowan Drive, Woodley, Reading.

FELT FEET—If you find it hard work to pull out and push back beds after making them, glue a piece of underfelt to the bottom of each leg, then moisten with light oil. Beds are then moved easily.—A. A. Mitchell, 5 North Shore Street, Campbeltown.

VASES—To prevent ugly stains forming in glass flower vases press a ball of cotton wool into the bottom before pouring in water. Renew the cotton wool each time you change the water.—Miss L. Sinclair, 35 Lorne Street, Edinburgh.

DOORPLATES—To clean doorplates without messing up the surrounding wood, cut a frame the size of the plate in heavy cardboard. Slip it over the plate when cleaning.—Mrs G. Stewart, 5 West Mount Street, Aberdeen.

MOP HEAD—Never discard a beret. Thread string through the double part of the brim and slip it over the head of a polishing mop. It does a good job, and when soiled it's easily removed and washed.—Mrs E. Harris, 51 Downs Road, Walmer, Kent.

SOOT WASHING OFF IN A JIFFY—Before cleaning flues, rub hands and arms with a good lather of soap, and allow to dry. This prevents soot getting into pores, and it's washed off in a twinkling.—Mrs B. Henderson, 28 Sandwell Street, Buckhaven, wins a pair of towels.

PAINTWORK—When washing paintwork, it is easier to use two squares of foam sponge instead of cloths, one to wash and the other to dry off. They get into corners better and need only half the pressure.—Mrs S. I. Patterson, 22 Greystoke Gardens, Newcastle.

STICKY CARDS—When playing cards become soiled and sticky give them a light rub with furniture cream, and polish well. They deal easily afterwards.—Rose Ferrier, Tannadice, Forfar.

KITCHEN CLOTHS—The cotton net bags in which onions are sold make excellent washing-up cloths, if they are first bleached.—Mrs H. W. Torrance, 21 St Lawrence Street, Dunfermline.

SCUFFED TOE CAPS—Toe caps of boots and shoes often get scuffed and don't take on a polish very well. Paint over the cap with a thin coating of glue size solution and, when dry, apply polish. This gives a shine to the leather.—T. Campbell, 340 Caledonia Road, Glasgow.

SCRATCHES—Surface scratches on a polished table can be helped by rubbing lightly with a cork dipped in camphorated oil. When oil has worked in, polish in usual way.—G. Kitchener, 70 Dean Street, Swindon, Wilts.

ECONOMICAL POLISH—To polish my furniture I use a saucer of slightly heated olive oil rubbed over evenly and then polished. Result, a beautiful shine and any scratches are completely camouflaged.—Mrs Laing, Pinewood Cottage, Corsiehill, Perth.

HANDY CARRIER—When spring cleaning, I find it a great help to put all my polishes, dusters, brushes, etc., in a basket and carry it around with me from room to room. It saves a lot of running here and there.—Mrs M. McGathan, Tummel Bridge, Pitlochry.

EASILY CLEANED—If the juice from apples runs over the oven while cooking, shake salt on it. This causes the juice to burn to a crisp so that it can be easily removed.—Miss I. Parkhill, 74 Bushmills Road, Coleraine, Northern Ireland.

CISTERNS—Have your cistern cleaned out every year by a plumber. You'll be surprised at what collects at the bottom, no matter how well covered it is.—Mrs J. M. Bean, 39 Corstorphine Road, Edinburgh.

DOGS' HAIR—A strip of foam rubber tacked to the reverse side of a sweeping brush will pick up dog hairs when passed lightly over the carpet.—Mrs D. Bowen, 17 Victoria Place, Brechin.

BRIGHTENER—Tortoise-shell dressing-table sets with backs that have become dull can be made to look bright again by rubbing with a little olive oil. Then polish with a soft cloth.—Vera Smith, 24 Meadowside, Inverbervie.

BEST TIME TO CLEAN THE OVEN—Wash the outside of your oven while you have something baking inside. The job takes half the time if done while the oven is hot. As soon as baking is removed, rub over the inside.—Mrs E. Beaton, 85 Brockburn Road, Glasgow, wins a pair of towels.

PLASTICWARE—Wash new plastic egg cups and spoons with cold water to keep them a good colour and avoid cracks.—Mrs A. G. Forsyth, 46 MacIndoe Crescent, Kirkcaldy.

OMELETTE PAN—An omelette pan should never be washed, but rubbed clean with kitchen paper and a little salt whilst still warm.—T. Helyar, Garden House. Milton of Campsie.

HANDY HOLDER—A plastic string bag makes an excellent holder for dusters, polish, &c. Hung up in the cleaning cupboard you see at a glance what you require.—Mrs White, 127 Glencairn Road, Ayr.

BATH CLEANER—Powdered borax sprinkled on a damp cloth is a quick, efficient cleaner for porcelain baths and the like.—Mrs Smith, Forester's Cottage, Arbuthnott, Fordoun.

EASIER POLISHING—When washing dusters, don't rinse out the soap. You will find the soap deposit brings up a nice polish on your furniture.—Mrs C. Preston, 410 Shieldhall Road, Glasgow.

BRUSHES—Next time you buy a new banister brush, nail a fold of thick cloth round wooden part. There's no fear of chipping woodwork when brushing down stairs.—Mrs Robertson, Dundee.

EASY DUSTING—When spring cleaning, if you varnish the flat tops of your hall and bedroom wardrobes dusting becomes much easier.—Mrs N. Shennan, 47 Thrushcraig Crescent, Paisley.

FOR FLUFF—Keep a small, wide-toothed comb beside your electric cleaning equipment. It is invaluable for freeing the brushes of fluff and dust.—Mrs J. McNally, 19 Ross Avenue, Inverness.

MOPS—When changing your mop head, it's easier to screw in a cup hook than to hammer in a nail. The hook can be used for hanging it.—Mrs B. Jack, 89 Greenfield Street, Govan, Glasgow.

GAS STOVES—While the stove is still hot after cooking, rub over with a paste of bicarbonate of soda and water. Leave for an hour (longer if very dirty), then wipe over with a damp cloth. Result—a perfectly clean stove.—Mrs A. Ford, 10 Sandown Road, Purewell, Christchurch.

WINE STAINS—Should wine get spilled on your tablecloth, sprinkle at once with powdered starch and leave on for two hours. Shake powder off, wash in cold water, and the stains disappear.—Mrs Martin, 43 Auldhill Crescent, Bridgend, Linlithgow.

★ TOP TIP ★

NOW SCRATCHES ON THE FURNITURE WON'T SHOW—I had a few scratches on my oak sideboard. I rubbed in some dark tan shoe polish a couple of times, then polished with furniture cream. Now not a scratch is visible. But this treatment is only advisable for good furniture with a heavy polish.—Mrs Helen Barton, 75 Redhall Drive, Edinburgh, wins a pair of towels.

EASILY KEPT—To eliminate daily scrubbing of the strip of wood across the threshold, cover with adhesive plastic material. A wipe with a damp cloth is all that is required to keep it clean. —Mrs K. Leishman, 10 Wardlaw Place, Edinburgh.

BRIGHTER CHROME—To keep chrome taps, ornaments, etc., bright and shining, a duster dipped in dry flour works wonders.—Mrs M. H. MacLeod, 370 Auchmill, Bucksburn, Aberdeen.

CAGE CLEANLINESS—The tray of a bird's cage is easy to clean if you stick on a piece of adhesive material. It also keeps the cage from getting rusty.—Mrs K. Milne, 154 Gartocher Road, Springboig, Glasgow.

CLEAN BATH—Just before stepping into the bath, sprinkle a very small quantity of detergent into the water. On emptying, no tide mark is left on the bath.—Miss M. S. Graham, 9 Hampden Terrace, Mount Florida, Glasgow, wins a pair of towels.

CHROMIUM PLATING—Taps and door knobs become dull in damp weather and do not always respond to rubbing with a duster. If rubbed occasionally with a paraffin rag, they never lose their attractive gleam.—Mrs Brass, 17 Clermiston Gardens, Edinburgh.

MUD STAINS—Umbrellas should be allowed to dry thoroughly before being brushed off with a stiff brush. If mud stains are obstinate, sponge with a little warm water to which a few drops of ammonia have been added.—Mrs Robertson, Greenock.

★ TOP TIP ★

EASIER CLEANING—If you use an embossed plastic table-cloth, try sponging it down with a nylon pan scrubber dipped in warm water. Stains and particles of food caught in the embossing disappear. Wipe dry with clean cloth.—Mrs Boswell, 12 Peter Street, Workington, wins a pair of towels.

HANDY CLEANER-A small piece of foam rubber glued on to the knob of a long knitting needle, and kept by the kitchen sink, is handy for removing marks inside bottles and small-necked jars, etc.—Mrs J. Clark, 37 Clydesdale Road, Mossend, Bellshill.

CHAIR SEATS—The plastic covers, sold for the underside of bird cages, make ideal covers for loose chair seats. They are spongeable and cost very little.—Mrs M. Kelman, Netherton, Baiquhain, Inverbervie.

OLD LOOFAH—Don't throw away that old loofah. Use it for cleaning the oven. It holds scouring powder better than a cloth and is easily cleaned afterwards.—Mrs B. Carmichael, Bay View, Ardrishaig.

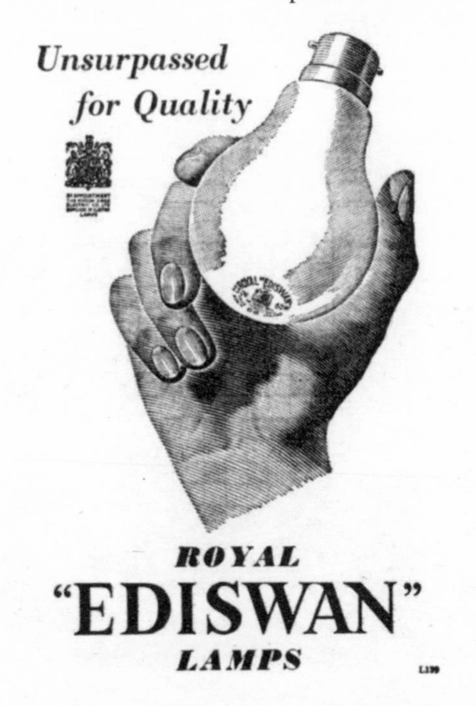

QUICK TIP—To clean silver chains and brooches, place article in the palm of the hand and rub with bicarbonate of soda. Brush off surplus powder with a soft brush then polish with a duster.—Miss M. Clark 33 Duddingston Road West, Portobello.

ASH TRAYS—When cleaning an ash tray, rub a little wax polish on it and you will then find the ash will not stick.—Mrs J. L. Young, 23 Swanston Grove, Fairmilehead, Edinburgh.

CLEAN STEPS—Cement steps can be kept clean with the starch left over from the washing. Add hot water to the starch, wash steps, and they're left clean and non-slippery.—Miss A. Smith, 23 The Loan, Selkirk.

DOYLEYS—To remove the stickiness on plastic doyleys after washing, rub them with a little dry starch or cornflour. They become silky smooth again.—Mrs M. Robertson, 7 Bellfield Avenue, Dundee.

HANDY CONTAINER—For dusters and polishes, machine together several plastic food bags. It keeps them tidy and it's washable.—Mrs Brenda Denham, 48 Portland Road, Carlton, Nottingham.

THE SUNDAY POST, APRIL 8, 1951.

The Sunday Post

Morning Special

PRINTED AND PUBLISHED EVERY SUNDAY MORNING.

No. 2380. [REGISTERED AT THE GENERAL POST OFFICE AS A NEWSPAPER.] SUNDAY, APRIL 8, 1951. RADIO—Page 4. PRICE TWOPENCE.

WHAT A TUMBLE!

TRUMAN ANGRY AT GENERAL'S "INDISCRETIONS"

MacArthur May Be Relieved Of Supreme Command

ALL Washington was discussing last night whether President Truman would relieve General MacArthur of his supreme command in the Korean war.

The President yesterday discussed the whole position with his Secretary of Defence, General George Marshall, and the chairman of the joint Chiefs of Staff, General Omar Bradley.

This followed a new outcrop of statements by General MacArthur last week, underlining disagreements between him, the Truman administration and the Allies regarding the conduct of the war and the U.S. Government's foreign policy.

General MacArthur's letter to Representative Joseph Martin particularly shocked many who are inclined to be sympathetic to the General, because it was so defiantly made to the Leader of the Opposition in the House of Representatives.

The scene at the first Grand National fence yesterday.

34 Horses Fall In A Fantastic Grand National

AT Aintree yesterday, in one of the most fantastic Grand Nationals ever, 34 of the 36 horses, including the heavily-backed entries, fell.

A long way behind, Derrinstown, who had fallen and had been remounted, finished third.

Winner Trained On Duck Eggs!

FORFAR MAN WINS £23,000

Hundreds Of Dundee Folk On Winner

Aberdeen Man Wins £1320

TO-DAY'S WEATHER

SINGERS TRAPPED IN WRECKED CAR

TWO well-known Aberdeen stage artistes, Miss Juliette M'Lean, 199 Forrest Avenue, and Mr Ronald Robb, 71 Great Western Road, were involved in a road accident in Kincardineshire early yesterday morning.

Miss M'Lean is in Aberdeen Royal Infirmary critically ill. Mr Robb escaped practically unhurt.

OUR COMMANDOS LAND BEYOND THE PARALLEL

AND STILL IT SNOWS!

NEW PRICES FOR BREAD

SAVINGS

Chapter 4
Staying Warm And Dry

THERE was more exposure to the elements in days gone by. Few working-class people had cars, so a lot of walking and waiting at bus stops was done. In winter (and in spring, autumn and summer) this could be a damp experience.

No one had a tumble dryer, many didn't even have a bath to fill with hot water. Very few houses had central heating, so cold days outside were also cold inside. All those stories about ice on the inside of bedroom windows are true. Blankets were heavy items that kept people alive while they were trying to keep them warm.

The ingenious Sunday Post readers turned their attention to these problems.

SOMETHING TO KEEP YOU WARMER IN BED—Now that cold nights are here, try sleeping with the eiderdown between top sheet and blankets. You'll be surprised at the extra warmth.—Mrs L. Burns, 55 Ann Street, Greenock, wins a pair of towels.

WARM FEET—Cartons made of corrugated cardboard make ideal insoles for boots and shoes. Cut insoles to shape and make sure the corrugations run across the sole. This allows air to circulate and keeps the feet warm.—Mrs R. Hay, 23 Commerce Street, Fraserburgh.

EXTRA WARMTH—If you want a dressing-gown to be extra warm, make a cummerbund or wide sash of the material and stitch in. It is surprising how much warmer the extra material round the waist makes the garment.—Mrs Stewart, 56 Dudhope Street, Dundee.

ALL OVER—Stand your stone hot-water bottle on end under the blankets, and the heat spreads through the bed. Lying flat, the bottle warms only one place.—Mrs S. Young, 63A Camberwell Road, London, wins a pair of towels.

WARM AND SAFE—Place a feather pillow at children's feet in bed. Then you're sure they've warmth without fear of burns from a too-hot bottle.—Miss Murdoch, 47 High Street, Bonnybridge.

TWO PAIRS—A pair of old nylon gloves, worn under fabric or unlined ones, keeps the hands warm during the coldest spell.—Mrs A. Macpherson, 18 Meadowpark Street, Glasgow.

FOR WARMTH—Stitch a piece of thin silk into the backs of fine woollen dresses. It gives that extra warmth and can be easily removed to freshen.—J. Farquhar, 52 Auchmill Road, Bucksburn, Aberdeen.

WARM HANDS—Going to the pit on very cold mornings I don't wear gloves. I just put a brown paper bag in each coat pocket and put my hands in the bags inside.—T. Campbell, 54 Park Avenue, Kirkintilloch.

FOR WARMTH—To keep baby warm, stitch a pocket in one of the blankets, then a hot water bottle is easily slipped in.—Mrs Watson, 23 Salisbury Road, Herne Bay.

KEEPS DRY—Some mackintoshes gape, allowing the bottom of skirt or coat to get wet, especially in windy weather. I cut up an old plastic cape and made an apron to tie on under my mack. This has proved very successful.—Mrs Watson, 43 Penley's Grove Street, York.

TANK TRICK—If you have a cold water tank in the attic, leave the trap door open during severe frost. Warm air from rooms below rises and helps to prevent burst pipes.—B. Clark, 11 Berelands Avenue, Prestwick.

★ TOP TIP ★

COSY COAT LINING—Remove pockets and buttons from outgrown blazers. Take out sleeves and cut off lapels and collar. Then neatly hem under the raw edges. It's a perfect lining to slip on under school trenchcoat or raincoat.—Mrs R. Nicoll, 4 Old Halkerton Road, Forfar, wins a pair of towels.

IT HELPS TO KEEP THE QUILT ON—If you are re-covering an eiderdown quilt, add 18 inches of the same material to one end. This allows a good tuck-in at the bottom and the eiderdown won't slip off during the night.—Mrs Hart, Arkleston Cottage, Paisley, wins a pair of towels.

★ TOP TIP ★

WHEN YOU CAN'T GET YOUR COAT DRIED—If you get your coat wet and drying space is limited, place coat on a hanger and hang outside the wardrobe. Fill a hot water bag and suspend it from the hanger inside the coat. This not only dries the coat, but also smooths creases.—A. E. McIntyre, 48 Longrow, Campbeltown, wins a pair of towels.

FROSTY MORNINGS—Before hanging out washing on frosty mornings, rub a little talcum powder on the backs of the hands and wrists. It prevents chafing.—Mrs M. Wilson, 36 Old Town, Broxburn.

MITTENS—When baby's fur-backed mittens are too small, cut out the leather palms and replace with new woollen palms, knitted a size larger. This makes mittens last at least another winter.—Mrs N. Gardner, Helena, Springside, Kilmarnock.

CONVECTORS—Owners of paraffin convectors should always keep paraffin in the tank. There is always a certain amount of moisture which can cause corrosion if tank is left empty.—Mrs Janet Paton, 7 Cross Street, Tayport.

FUR COATS—Before putting away your fur coat or fur-collared coat, wind an old silk scarf round the coat hanger hook, this prevents the fur being ruffled at the centre back of the neck.—Mrs J. Muir, c/o 8 Grossart Street, Salsburgh, North Lanarkshire.

STORING WOOLIES—Winter woollies should be stored during summer in clear plastic bags and sealed with Sellotape. The garments are kept airtight and mothproof.—Mrs Hill, 122 Younger Street, Alloa.

INNER JACKET—Make a plain jacket of terry towelling to wear under your rubber-lined mackintosh. It absorbs any moisture and helps to stop the rubber perishing.—Mrs E. Harris, 51 Downs Road, Walmer, Kent.

FLASK TEA—If tea has to be carried in a flask, it is better to carry tea bags. Fill the flask with boiling water and pop in a tea bag just before required. Let it infuse for a few minutes. This gives much fresher-tasted tea.—Mrs J. McLean, 86 Ralston Road, Campbeltown.

ATTRACTIVE—Floral or nursery-patterned wincyette makes attractive pillow-cases for children's beds. My children were delighted with theirs, and found them very cosy on cold nights.—Mrs E. Cruickshanks, 64 Chapelton Drive, West Calder.

HEAD HUGGER—When you wear a head scarf, slip an Alice band in between the folds and clip on to the head. Tie ends in usual way. The silkiest scarf doesn't slip off.—Mrs J. Lonie, 50 William Street, Tayport.

COLD COMFORT—Knit two sleeves from odd ounces of leftover wool. Thread elastic through the tops, and wear over short sleeves under your coat.—Margaret O. Bell, 18 Westlands, Sunderland.

EAR COMFORT—In winter stitch small powder puffs into baby's bonnet to give extra protection to the ears from cold winds.—G. Hadden, 3 Neville Terrace, Priestgate, Peterborough, Northants.

KEEPS DRY—To keep salt and pepper running freely in damp weather place an inverted tumbler over each container.—M. C. Toye, 14 Netherhill Road, Paisley.

COSY FOR BABY—A wool beret-type hat, sold with woolly sets, is cold for baby in winter. A good idea is to open half up the seam, hem the raw edges, turn back the headband, and add a chin strap. This makes a cosy helmet and keeps the set complete.—Mrs Falconer, Whitegates, Crowborough Hill, Crowborough, Sussex.

★ TOP TIP ★

DRY IN THE WETTEST WEATHER—When children's trench coats have lost their "proofing" through dry cleaning, etc., place a piece of plastic material between coat and lining across shoulders. I find this keeps them dry in the wettest weather.—Mrs M. Allan, 16 Stirling Terrace, Dundee, wins a pair of towels.

MORE HEAT FROM ELECTRIC FIRE AT NO EXTRA COST—Clean the reflector of your electric fire with metal polish, and the fire gives out much more heat. Always unplug the fire before doing the job.—Mrs A. Thomson, Pityoulish, Aviemore, wins a pair of towels.

COMFORT ON COLD NIGHTS—If blankets are too small to tuck in properly at sides, put one on the bed length-wise and place a second length-wise across the bed. This gives a good tuck-in at both sides and bottom of bed and prevents draughts.—Mrs L. Addison, 3 Teesdale Place, Cowpen, Blyth.

SALT—Put a cocktail stick through the top of the salt cellar. It's not only ornamental, but keeps the salt from going damp and blocking the aperture.—Mrs D. Scott, 186 High Street, Lochee, Dundee.

ELECTRIC BLANKET — To prevent an electric blanket from wrinkling up in bed, which tends to break the thin electric wires inside, sew on strips of tape to the four corners long enough to fasten to the end of bed or bed-spring.—Mrs J. Napier, 8 Burnside Lane, Hamilton.

LAGGING PIPES—When lagging outside pipes, bind strips from an old plastic mackintosh round the lagging to keep it intact and dry. It also stops the pipes from freezing as cold winds cannot penetrate.—Mrs A. Foster, 4 North Road, Tow Law, Bishop Auckland.

WATERPROOF MITTS—An old plastic mac can be used to make waterproof mittens for rainy or snowy days. Made big enough to cover woolly gloves, they keep children's hands warm and dry.—Mrs A. Bird, St Anne's, 101 Westcliff Park Drive, Westcliff-on-Sea.

SUNDAY POST JUNE 29, 1952

The Sunday Post

Morning Special

PRINTED AND PUBLISHED EVERY SUNDAY MORNING.

No. 2444. SUNDAY, JUNE 29, 1952. PRICE 2½d.

Radio and TV—Page 4

She Was A Picture Of Loveliness

WHEN the Queen began her engagements yesterday by visiting Huntly House Museum in the Canongate, she presented a lovely picture.

As she stepped from her car there was a gasp of admiration from the crowds of women.

Although looking a little tired, the Queen was beautiful in a grey and black striped taffeta dress with flared skirt, blue mink cape, black picture-hat with back-folded brim, black patent open-toed shoes, black handbag and gloves, and three-strand rope of pearls and gold bracelet.

"What Tiny Hands She Had!"

Queen's Surprise For 75,000 At Holyrood

COMES FROM PALACE TO PLATFORM

EDINBURGH'S Royal Week came to a climax last night with a sunset ceremony at Holyrood Palace. From early evening crowds converged on the Palace. Despite a drizzle of rain, 75,000 gathered.

And the Queen gave them all a never-to-be-forgotten surprise.

Picture of Queen on Platform—Page 3.

FLYING SAUCER OVER MALTA

96-Year-Old Was On Parade

The Queen changed for her afternoon engagement, when she wore a white, close-fitting hat and a white wool taffeta, single-breasted, button-through full-length coat.

After 70 Years

"You Wear Well!"

Stole Gun To Blow Open Safe

Dundee Woman Found Dead In Bath

Dundee By-Election —July 17

Today's Weather

Chapter 5
Wash Day

IN the 1950s, washing wasn't as easy as selecting a wash-and-spin cycle on the plumbed-in, all-electric machine in the corner of your kitchen. There was a lot more to it.

Boiling, soaking and starching was involved, and sometimes you had to get some help to paddle the dirt out of the thicker blankets. Then you had to wait for "your" day on the green and hope the weather was kind.

Nowadays, night classes or several hours of instruction via YouTube (whatever that is) would be involved to learn all this. In the 1950s you learned by watching what your mother did. Who had learned by watching what her mother did.

PRESTO! AND THE SCORCH MARK WAS GONE—I was unfortunate to scorch my new camel coat when a squib went off. With my finger, I lightly rubbed plenty of bicarbonate of soda into the mark, and left the coat on a hanger overnight. Next morning I whipped it up gently with a clean clothes brush—and there wasn't a trace of the mark.—Mrs Jean Nicoll, 170 Dumbarton Road, Partick, wins a pair of towels.

GLOVES—When washing chamois or hogskin gloves, add only a drop of olive oil to the rinsing water to keep them soft.—Miss M. Kemp, 78 Union Street, Larkhall.

WATER SAVING—When doing the family wash, a lot of water is often required to get rid of lather after the first washing. Sprinkle some common salt over the lather and the suds disappear.—Mrs Sievewright, 6 Castle Street, Turriff.

BLANKETS—Brush blankets with a soft brush dipped in lavender talc after they've been laundered. Shake them before use. They're soft as new and fragrant.—Mrs C. Tindal, 25 Baldwin Avenue, Glasgow.

★ TOP TIP ★

TRY A BALLOON ON WASHING DAY!—I've always dried baby's bonnets on a toy balloon blown up to the right size. Dried this way, they retain their original shape and dry like new, with only the ribbons to be ironed.—Mrs M. Gellatly, 68 Ballindean Terrace, Douglas and Angus, Dundee, wins a pair of towels.

CORDUROY—To wash corduroy suits or slacks, fill a tub with warm, soapy water. Wash gently by lifting up and down in the soapy water, rinse thoroughly. Do not wring. Place garment on line and shake occasionally while drying.—Miss A. A. Mitchell, North Shore Street, Campbeltown.

DRESS SENSE—After washing a dress with an elastic waist, stuff the waist part with newspaper. This absorbs excess water in the elastic and the dress dries quicker.—Mrs A. G. Forsyth, 46 Macindoe Crescent, Kirkcaldy.

HOGSKIN GLOVES—Wash gloves in lukewarm water as though washing your hands, rub gently with soap, using nail brush. Remove from hands and hold gloves under running tap. Hang in cool place till they drip. Blow into each finger and keep rubbing skin while drying. Don't allow to harden. Then place under cushion and sit on them for a time.—Miss J. A. M., Aberdeen.

DRIP-DRY SHIRTS—I accidentally put a white drip-dry cotton shirt in bleach and it turned brown. I put it under the running, cold water tap, and then in a pan of cold water to which washing powder had been added. I boiled it slowly until it was restored to its usual whiteness.—Mrs M. Adamson, 4 Crookston Drive, Glasgow.

NEW BLANKETS—Before washing new blankets, I soak them overnight in cold water and oatmeal, using 3 oz. oatmeal to each pair. Wash them next day in usual way and shake out the oatmeal. I find my new blankets are not cloudy, but beautifully soft.—Mrs A. Peebles, Woods Hospital, Upper Largo.

VELVET—To bring up the pile on a velvet garment, place on a hanger and hang over the boiler while the clothes are gently boiling. All traces of marks disappear.—Mrs Myra Pringle, 7a Bowring Park Road, Liverpool.

GLOVES—If doeskin gloves become hard and dry after washing, steam the fingers over a boiling kettle for a few seconds. They become soft and pliable again and can be worked on to the hands quite easily.—Miss B. Mitchell, 5 North Shore Street, Campbeltown.

BLOT THE STAINS—Before removing stains from clothes, always put a clean piece of blotting paper under the material. It absorbs dirt and superfluous liquid.—Mrs Adams, 1 Hawthorn Avenue, Bearsden, Glasgow.

SILK MACS—Mud can be removed from silk mackintoshes by adding a teaspoonful of ammonia to a pint of fairly hot water. But don't do it too often in case of bleaching.—Miss A. Graham, 4 Liddell Road, Longtown, Cumberland.

STRAW HATS—Black and other dark-coloured straw hats can be cleaned by brushing in soapy water. Rinse in several waters. While straw is still damp, brush with the well-beaten white of an egg. Press into shape, and dry thoroughly.—Mrs Blacklaws, 42 Cameron Street, Stonehaven.

LIKE NEW—When I wash my boy's corduroy trousers I wring them, then brush them down with a small stiff nail brush. They dry just like new each time.—Mrs Fitzgerald, Aberdalgie Village, by Perth.

★ TOP TIP ★

IF YOUR SCRUBBING BOARD SKITES ABOUT THE TUB—Screw a small rubber door-stopper on bottom of each leg of your scrubbing board. This prevents the board slipping, and scratching tub. It also saves the legs from wearing.—Miss L. Murdoch, 47 High Street, Bonnybridge, wins a pair of towels.

FRESH COLLARS—If you wear white collars on dresses, sew press studs on the collar and dress neck facing. The collars are quickly adjusted or removed for washing.—Miss N. N. Leslie, 12 Northburn Avenue, Aberdeen.

Try the NEW
RINSO lather!
SEE-
'Fresh-air'
WHITE!
FEEL-
"Fresh-air"
SOFT!
SMELL-
"Fresh-air"
CLEAN!
RINSO for 'Fresh-air' washing
— dried indoors or out!

KEEP THAT GLAZE—To clean glazed chintz articles, lay on flat surface and quickly scrub with a soft brush, warm water and soap suds. Sponge with clean water and wipe dry with soft cloth. If the material requires pressing, do it with a warm iron on wrong side.—Miss Jane Connolly, Upper Locharwoods, Ruthwell, Dumfries.

CANDLEWICK CARE—A candlewick bedspread should be washed in mild suds, rinsed well, and hung in wind and sun until nearly dry. The wind fluffs it up again. Shake well, but do not iron. When aired, spread over the bed, and brush with a clean brush.—Miss Mary Ritchie, The Villa, Lonmay, Aberdeenshire.

SOCKS—To remove stains from children's socks caused by dye from shoes, damp the stained part and rub in a little dry baking soda, then wash in the usual way.—Mrs J. Kelly, 275 Dalmarnock Road, Glasgow.

HANDBAGS—To clean a white handbag, buy an ounce of light magnesia powder. Rub in generously with a clean cloth, leave overnight, and brush out next day.—Mrs Crighton, 3 Ramsay Street, Montrose.

BLANKETS—When airing blankets and bedspreads hang them with their weight distributed over two lines. I find this prevents them stretching.—Mrs H. Smith, 14 John Street, Ruabon, near Wrexham.

NEW LOOK—Dissolve 1 dessertspoonful gelatine in 2½ quarts hot water. When thoroughly dissolved, use as final rinsing water for silk or cotton frocks. It gives that necessary "body" and makes them just like new.—Mrs Helen Smith, 9 Kelvingrove Street, Glasgow.

HANDY—I find a wire coat hanger and two spring clothes pegs ideal for hanging up skirts. On wash days, peg socks and hankies to hanger, then peg hanger to the line. It's easy to take in if it rains.—Mrs McLaren, 19 Northfield Road, Dunipace, Denny.

IT'S EASY—When putting out the washing, hang a pillow-case last, with open end at top. When taking in the clothes it's ideal for holding socks and other small items.—Mrs Helen MacKenzie, 6 Corrie Gardens, Muir of Ord.

CARE OF FELTS—If your felt hat has become spoiled with rain, hold it over the steam of a boiling kettle until all spots have disappeared. Allow to dry thoroughly. Soak a piece of clean flannel in methylated spirits and come over the hat, working the shag of the pile.—Mrs Lindsay, Dundee.

★ TOP TIP ★

CLOTHES SOAKING—It is a mistake to soak clothes in hot water and leave until water is cold. Cloth fibres expand in warm water and contract in cold, and in this way hold the dirt. Make suds in cold water if soaking for any length of time.—Mrs J. Allan, 40 Kincorth Place, Aberdeen, wins a pair of towels.

MARK THE SPOTS—Soiled places on blankets are difficult to find once they're into the suds. Before immersing mark each spot with rustless safety pin, and remove them as each mark receives attention.—Mrs C. Gray, 18 Lippiatt Road, Otahuhu, Auckland, New Zealand.

PROPS—Always paint clothes props. It preserves the wood, they're easy to keep clean and, if clothes flap against them, there's no harm done.—Mrs O. Campion, 12 East Mount, Malton, Yorks.

DUSTY POCKETS—To remove dust and fluff from the inside of pockets of heavy overcoats, use the long, narrow gadget of the vacuum sweeper.—Mrs Johnston, 63 Port Dundas Road, Glasgow.

BLANKET WASHING—When washing blankets I tried out my rubber sink plunger. It worked well, for the suction brought out the dirt immediately and my blankets never looked nicer.—Mrs R. McKay, 9 High Street, Dollar.

CURTAIN CARE—If in doubt as to whether heavy curtains should be washed, wet a handkerchief or piece of white cotton, lay on the corner of a curtain, and run a hot iron over it. If the curtain "bleeds" it is safer to have them dry-cleaned.—Mrs Ganrow, 11 Stocket Parade, Aberdeen.

CARDIGANS—Before washing cardigans, catch-stitch buttonholes together so that they won't stretch.—Mrs M. McCallum, 88 Longrow, Campbeltown.

BLANKETS—Add a few drops olive oil to rinsing water when washing blankets. This replaces natural oil lost in washing.—Mrs I. Anderson, 36 Waverley Park, Bonnyrigg.

MUD MARKS—Mud splashes on trousers are easily removed when dry by using a rubber suede brush.—Mrs M. Miller, 42 Rossend Terrace, Burntisland.

WHITENER—To whiten unbleached sheets, pillow cases, etc., add a small packet of Epsom salts when boiling. Rinse well in several waters before hanging out. The articles will be beautifully white.—Mrs M. Robson, 32 Whitehall Place, Aberdeen.

NAVY BLUE—When washing children's navy school clothes, I add a strong solution of laundry blue to the rinsing water. This helps to prevent that purple-greyish shade which some navies go with repeated washing.—Mrs S. Docherty, 127 Crewe Road West, Edinburgh.

BLEACHING — When bleaching sheets and pillow-cases, add a small quantity of bath salts to the final rinsing wafer. This gets rid of the smell of the bleach and leaves the articles pleasantly perfumed.—Mrs Margaret B. Griffith, 119 Menock Road, Glasgow.

★ TOP TIP ★

MAKES LAMPSHADES LOOK LIKE NEW—Having washed my lampshades successfully in soapy water, and hung them out to dry, I was disappointed at the still-matted look of the tassels on the fringe. Laying the tassels on the edge of the kitchen table. I beat them gently with the edge of a wooden spoon and they came up like new.—Mrs I. B. Watson, 70 Breckhill Road, Woodthorpe, Nottingham, wins a pair of towels.

PLEATED SKIRTS—Permanently pleated skirts are apt to splay when they have been washed. To avoid this, place a loose rubber band round skirt centre and hang up to dry as usual.—Mrs Marion Murray. 91 Curling Crescent. Glasgow.

NO TANGLE—Avoid a tangle in the washing machine by attaching the sleeve buttons of men's shirts to the front buttonholes.—Miss M. Birnie, 17 High Street, Sandhaven, by Fraserburgh.

BLANKETS—After washing and airing blankets, hang them on the line and beat lightly. This raises the wool and fluffs it up. They feel and look like new afterwards.—Mrs Murdoch, 7 Ogilvie Terrace, Edinburgh.

CHAMOIS GLOVES—To keep chamois gloves like new, wash in tepid water, rub and rinse well. Place them on the hands, rub in a little olive oil and washing soap. Squeeze out thoroughly and hang out to dry. I've kept my gloves for years doing this. Don't use hot water.—Mrs Eggie, Caledonian Terrace, Kirtlebridge.

WOOLLIES—I have found by experience the finest way to dry woollies is to use a deck chair. Open the chair to its flattest angle, and over the full length of canvas spread a dry towel. Over the towel pat into shape sweaters, etc. If the garment is a heavy one, change the towel after an interval.—Mrs A. Dell, 74 Davyholme Road East, Stretford, Manchester.

LOOSE COVERS—Before putting loose covers on settee and chairs, put cushions into large plastic or polythene bags. Cover backs and arms with plastic or polythene, then anything spilt only damages the loose covers.—Mrs P. Connell, Fulton Cottage, Blackford, wins a pair of towels.

COTTON SKIRTS—After washing cotton skirts, rinse in warm water, adding one tablespoon plastic starch. Don't wring, but hang out to dry and iron while damp and your skirt has a glazed, fresh finish.—Miss Laura Bremner, 2A Manse Terrace, Turriff.

TAKES STRAIN AWAY—When washing a hand-knitted garment, lift it from the water in a plastic colander. This allows water to drain through, takes the weight and prevents stretching. Particularly useful for double knitteds.—Miss M. J. Martin, 34 Balgarvie Crescent, Cupar.

★ TOP TIP ★

OIL AND GREASE—Overalls and working clothes often get stained with oil and grease. They should be washed before they're used, and starched with a thin starch to prevent oil from soaking in. After use, soak the overalls in warm water containing a little ammonia, and the grease will come out easily.—W. Moodie, 11 Park Street, Motherwell, wins this week's half-guinea.

Let's be honest—we don't only want our whites to *be* clean, we want everyone to *see* they're clean. That's why to a mother—whiteness matters

So it's easy to understand why far more women use Persil for all their family whites. It washes whiter—you can see it does! And that means *cleaner*. All dirt vanishes when Persil's special oxygen bubbles get going.

A woman chooses Persil to *keep* family coloured things bright, woollens and fine things soft as new.

And in washing machines ...

For best results use Persil in your washing machine! it's best *in* it and safe *for* it!

Hands matter, too!

Persil is so much *kinder* to hands and nails. You can feel it is!

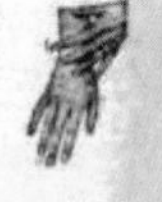

Boil or no boil, Persil beats the lot! Best in your washing machine, too!

Persil washes whiter!

—and that means CLEANER!

PLEATED SKIRTS—Before washing a permanently pleated skirt, tack front and back skirt bands together. The skirt doesn't droop when hung up to dry.—Mrs J. Henderson, 261 Ayr Road, Newton Means.

WHITE LINEN—To keep stored linen white, dye an old pillow-case deep blue, and keep the linen in it.—Mrs C. Bowie, 154 New Row, Dunfermline.

BLACKS—When washing black material, do the last rinsing in very blue water. This keeps the black from getting a rusty tinge.—Mrs J. Jennings, 29 Avonbeg Street, Belfast.

DRIP HOLDER—When drying a drip-dry shirt, etc., indoors, hang on a coat-hanger and place in large Polythene bag, leaving space at bottom for water to gather. Hang in an out-of-the-way place. When garments are free of drips, remove from bag and dry off in usual way.—Mrs G. Sutherland, 24 Glover Street, Craigie, Perth.

CORDED TROUSERS—After washing corded velvet trousers, take an ordinary scrubbing brush and brush downwards with it once or twice while they are still wet. This takes all creases out and leaves the ridges in the cord as good as new.—Mrs Symington, 11 Windyedge Crescent, Glasgow.

PEGGING CLOTHES—When pegging clothes on a line, fold the first corner one way over the line and the other corner the opposite way. This holds washing firmly, even in high winds.—Mrs N. Hope, 37 Twirlees Terrace, Hawick, wins a pair of towels.

WOOLLIES—Woollen garments put into a pillow case when spin-drying prevents them becoming fuzzy.—Mrs C. Charles, 239 Fintry Drive, Dundee.

HANDS—Keep a jar filled with oatmeal at the kitchen sink. After drying the hands in cold water, rub them well with the oatmeal. This helps to dry the hands thoroughly and prevents hacks or chaps.—Miss Hay, 40 Keir Hardie Street, Methil.

★ TOP TIP ★

THEN YOU WON'T HAVE TO DO THE WASHING TWICE—To prevent clothes props from slipping, especially on damp grass, hammer a nail half-way into the bottom of the prop. This enables it to remain firm as the head of the nail grips the ground.—Mrs R. Black, 105 Burnside Street, Motherwell, wins this week's guinea.

FOLD SOCKS—It's always better to fold men's socks rather than rolling them when putting away. Rolling stretches the tops and causes them to fall down when worn.—Mrs Hugh Brown, 33 Morar Street, Methil.

PILLOWS—To keep feather pillows soft and fluffy, place them in front of a fire for about twenty minutes, turning them once or twice. The heat fluffs up the feathers and keeps the pillows like new.—Mrs M. Cunningham, School House, Harthill.

KILT HANGER—By pressing in a drawing pin at either end of a coat hanger, my kilt can hang properly by the two loops from the waistband. The vest and jacket fit neatly on top and the outfit is neatly stored.—Donald S. Wylie, 7 Crosslees Road, Thornliebank, Glasgow.

WASHDAY HINT—Save old pyjama cords and use them instead of pegs for vests, sleeveless blouses, short-sleeved dresses, etc. Garments dry quicker this way and there aren't any peg marks.—Mrs Margaret Hood, 95 Dumbarton Road, Clydebank.

SHIRT CUFFS—My husband's shirt cuffs became very grubby in the office. With having to scrub them before putting them in the washing machine, they soon began to wear. Now he wears a pair of white plastic cuffs over his shirt cuffs. They lie neatly under jacket sleeves and are easily kept clean.—Mrs Rhoda Evans, 143 Millbrae Terrace, Chryston, Glasgow, wins a pair of towels.

A NEW WAY TO CLEAN COATS AND HATS—I've a light tweed coat which I clean regularly with Fuller's Earth. Sprinkle a little over the coat, brush firmly, then brush it out. It removes stains and marks. Light felt hats can be cleaned in the same way.—H. M. MacNiven, 63 East Claremont Street, Edinburgh, wins a pair of towels.

Sunday Post, May 31, 1953.

The Sunday Post

PRINTED AND PUBLISHED EVERY SUNDAY MORNING.

Morning Special

No. 2492. [REGISTERED AT THE GENERAL POST OFFICE AS A NEWSPAPER] SUNDAY, MAY 31, 1953. Radio and TV—Page 4 PRICE 2½d.

PRINCES, PRINCESSES, SHEIKS, STATESMEN ARRIVE

LONDON OVERWHELMED!

[illegible] didn't dampen the enthusiasm of the crowds outside the Palace in the slightest.

A section of the huge crowd outside Buckingham Palace, where Royal cars were halted.

The Duke of Edinburgh, Crown Princess Marthe of Norway and Princess Astrid, her daughter. With Crown Prince Olav, the Royal visitors stepped ashore from a launch at Westminster. They arrived from Norway in the Royal Yacht Norge.

The Duke of Edinburgh greeting the party which travelled with the Sheik of Kuwait yesterday.

'Come Closer!' Shout To Prince Charles

YESTERDAY was London's most astonishing pre-Coronation day yet.

The crowds were the biggest ever.

So enormous were the afternoon and evening throngs in the West End, Whitehall way and at Buckingham Palace, that the Scotland Yard crowd plan began yesterday, instead of tomorrow night as intended.

This meant that Central London's traffic was directed from a special control room at the Yard, where minute-by-minute radio flashes told of the state of the roads.

The world's biggest two-way queue filed past Westminster Abbey. It went on for hours.

Last night it was estimated that the crowds had passed Westminster Abbey at about 60,000 an hour.

Outside the Palace gates, the crowd formed a solid human barrier half-way across the road.

Twice in 30 minutes Royal cars from the Palace were forced to a standstill by the mass.

One car gave up the attempt. Police cleared a path behind it. The car reversed, and then sped to a third gate, through which it escaped.

In the evening, several hundreds of the 20,000 throng at the gates got a thrill when Prince Charles and Princess Anne appeared at a second floor window.

A little boy in the cheering crowd yelled—"Come closer!"

Prince Charles scrambled higher up and pressed his nose hard against the pane.

Cheer followed cheer, and then sank to a long-drawn "Oh" as a nurse appeared and took the Royal children away.

At about 9.30 p.m., when foreign dignitaries were leaving Buckingham Palace, the crowd surged forward and blocked the road outside the Palace. At one time, about 200 cars were brought to a standstill around the Victoria Memorial, all queuing bumper to bumper.

Uniformed police and motor-cycle patrol men tried to clear a way. Eventually a lane was formed through the crowd from the Palace to the Mall.

In Trafalgar Square, so many coins were chinking into the two hats of a pavement artist that he put out a third hat—the one he had been wearing!

BY rail, road, sea and air they came yesterday — overseas Royalty, statesmen and soldiers.

(Continued On Page 2).

Eden To Fly To U.S. For Third Operation

MR EDEN is to fly to Boston, U.S.A., on Friday for an "imperative" operation.

It is to be performed by Dr Richard Cattell, of the Lahey Clinic.

After a bulletin, signed by five doctors, had been issued last night, the Foreign Office stated Mr Eden would fly to Boston in an aircraft of the Royal Canadian Air Force.

President Eisenhower offered to send his own aircraft for Mr Eden if it was needed.

Mrs Eden will fly with her husband. He will be accompanied by Mr Guy Blackburn, one of his doctors. Mr Basil Hume, who performed the two previous operations on Mr Eden, has also been invited to be present at the operation.

The medical bulletin issued by the five doctors stated: "Mr Eden has made excellent progress during the past weeks in so far as his general condition is concerned. The main bile duct, however, has not healed, so that a further operation has become imperative. On our advice, Mr Eden has agreed to travel to Boston, in order that Dr Richard Cattell, who saw him recently in London, may perform the operation."

The bulletin was signed by Dr Rossdale, Sir Horace Evans, Mr Basil Hume, Sir Gordon Gordon-Taylor, Mr Guy Blackburn.

Mr Eden entered the London clinic on April 8, suffering from chronic inflammation of the gall bladder.

On April 12, he underwent an operation for gallstones. A second operation was performed on April 29, to remove fluid causing jaundice.

On May 19, it was stated that Dr Cattell, a specialist in this condition, had seen Mr Eden when he was in London to lecture at the Royal College of Surgeons.

Peer Dresses Up For The Children

Weather On The Great Day

THE weather, up to and including Coronation Day, is likely to be rather cool, said the forecasters yesterday.

It will probably be changeable, with rain or showers at times, but there will be bright intervals.

TWENTY-TWO seats in Westminster Abbey have been found to give no view of the Coronation ceremony. So the Earl Marshal's office has allocated them to a number of blind people, who will be able to hear the ceremony perfectly.

Chapter 6
The Fascination Of The Wringer

THE invention and proliferation of the electrically-powered spin dryer meant the death of one of the most recognisable implements of the 1950s kitchen, the wringer.

It was a necessary, and fascinating, piece of equipment that was a magnet for small boys to experiment with, but at the same time a gadget to be feared thanks to the scare-tales of squashed fingers.

There isn't a child of the 1950s who didn't experiment with putting slices of bread through the wringer (when Mum wasn't around) or various belongings of younger brothers and sisters.

The ever-washing housewife also had to master the intricacies of ropes and pulleys that made indoor drying possible.

WRINGER ROLLERS—When finished washing, run a piece of polythene between the rollers to prevent them sticking together.—Mrs S. Everitt, Heather View, Waskerley, Consett.

EIDERDOWNS—Prepare plenty warm soapy water when washing an eiderdown. Wash by kneading and squeezing. After rinsing thoroughly, put through the wringer and shake. Continue to frequently shake vigorously during drying, to separate the down. When almost dry, beat with a light carpet beater. This fluffs up the down and any creases in the cover usually disappear. Thorough airing is essential.—Mrs Reid, 20 Lindsay Drive, Glasgow.

However well you wash your clothes, the final results still depend on the wringing. And only Acme wringing makes it certain that washday after washday your clothes will be as clean, crisp and sparkling as ever you could desire. Five million women already know this. Whether they use a washing machine, sink or tub, they all say . . . .

However you wash–

you should have

ACME wringing

ACME WRINGERS LIMITED DAVID STREET GLASGOW SE

PILLOWCASES—When putting pillowcases, bolster cases, etc., through the wringer, avoid a build-up of water in the closed end by putting that end through first.—Mrs G. More, Almar Cottages, Glencraig, Lochgelly.

PULLEY ROPE—When renewing a pulley rope, bind the ends with sticky tape. They then go through pulley wheels and holes in pulley without fraying.—Mrs M. D. Cameron, 83 Broxburn Road, Glasgow.

STICKY ROLLERS—If the rollers of your washing machine wringer stick, stitch a strap of linen round the top roller and they run smoothly.—Mrs E. Bew, 14 Dunmore Avenue, Seaburn, Sunderland.

SAVES THE LINO—Metal wringer stands sometimes score the linoleum. To avoid this, get four rubber door stops the size nearest to diameter of stand leg, and insert them in the bottom of the legs.—Mrs Mary Smith, 27 Ibrox Street, Ibrox, Glasgow.

PULLEY ROPE—To prevent rope from wearing, take a small piece of flat rubber, make a hole in centre, and then cut from one edge to hole. Insert it above knot of rope, which runs to castor on ceiling. This will keep rope clear of edge of castor wheel.—Mrs M. McMillan, 4 Myrtle Street, Glasgow.

CLOTHES LINE—A new clothes line has a tendency to tangle. Prevent this by boiling the line for 15 minutes before using.—Miss I. Morris, Fosterton, Thornton.

BUTTONS—To prevent buttons breaking when putting a garment through the wringer, keep all buttons on top of the article, and when they come near the rollers, press them well down on the garment with the finger.—Mrs Hay, 65 Capelrig Street, Thornliebank, Glasgow.

★ TOP TIP ★

SAFER PULLEY ROPES—Home accidents are sometimes caused by pulley ropes breaking. This can be prevented by tying on a piece of round hardwood, about three inches long by half-inch in diameter, above the knot. On lowering the pulley, the wood acts as a buffer and prevents the rope being frayed by the metal wheels.—W. A. Cameron, 19 David Street, Kirkcaldy, wins a pair of towels.

CLOTHES ROPE—To successfully wash a clothes rope, lock one end in the wringer and pull on it. Then scrub. It can be done bit by bit, and wrung through at the same time.—Mrs Shenken, 30 Braemar Street, Glasgow.

PULLEY ROPES—To prevent a pulley rope from fraying through wear and tear, give it a coating of candle wax. Fix a strong ring to the hauling-up end of the rope. When the pulley is fully raised, attach the ring to the wall hook. This takes the strain off.—Mrs Susan Martean, 154 Glasgow Street, Ardrossan.

JUMPER CARE—Putting jumpers through the wringer may ruin them. Instead, put them into a colander and press the moisture out gently with the fingers.—Miss N. Lawrie, 21 Craigentinny Avenue North, Edinburgh.

WOOLLIES—A rolling pin is useful when washing sweaters and pullovers. Use it to roll out excess moisture, after putting the garment between towels.—Mrs E. Webb, 8 Catherine Street, Doncaster.

WASHING LINGERIE—When I wash my fine lingerie in the washing machine I sew it inside an old pillowcase, then put it in the machine. And I put it through the wringer while it is still in the pillowcase. This prevents the garments being torn.—Mrs Robertson, Househillmuir Road, Glasgow.

DRYING—When clothes have to be dried indoors because of bad weather, don't subject them to too much heat. All materials are weakened by excessive heat. Putting them on top of a radiator or an oven, or too near a gas or electric fire, can be very harmful.—Mrs I. Nicol, Gordondale, Port Elphinstone, Inverurie.

★ TOP TIP ★

HANDY TO HAVE ON WASH-DAY—To avoid using stretcher clothes props, which usually fall in windy weather, my husband fixed a pulley on top of one of the clothes poles. This allows the line to be lowered. When the washing has been hung up, the line is made taut and tied off on a spike fixed lower on the pole. The pulley is the type used for window sash cords.—Mrs Farrel, Rosemouth, Wanlockhead, Abington, wins a pair of towels.

No thanks

Mum,

no breakfast

WHO'D BE A MOTHER? You've no sooner said goodbye to winter than spring starts breaking up the happy home. Here's Janet off her food again. But this year I know what to do about it. Go quickly young woman, and help yourself to the Andrews. I'll not have my family under the weather.

Mum knows the answer to these change-of-season upsets. A morning glass of Andrews. This cooling, fizzy laxative does a four-fold job. Cleanses and freshens the mouth. Soothes and settles the stomach. Tones up the liver. Keeps the system as regular as clockwork. Take a glass of pleasant-tasting Andrews next time you need a little help.

ANDREWS

LIVER SALT

¼ lb. tin 1/6d · ½ lb. tin 2/6d

WET WASHDAYS—On wet washdays I open my dining table out to full length and spread a sheet or large table cloth over it, leaving the washing on it all night. It's dry in the morning.—Mrs H. Smith, 14 John Street, Ruabon.

CLOTHES LINE—When putting up a plastic clothes line, first tie two or three loose knots in it at intervals. Then articles that need to be dried on coat hangers don't slide up and down if the hanger hook is slipped through a knot.—Mrs Hawthorne, 97 Riversdale Road, Collier Row, Romford.

FOR LONGER LIFE—When buying a new clothes line, rub it over with a lump of beeswax warmed a little before using. This protects the rope from the weather and makes it last for years.—Miss Wilson, 109 Ashdown Road, Farringdon, Sunderland, wins a pair of towels.

THE SUNDAY POST JUNE 7 1953

The Sunday Post

Morning Special

PRINTED AND PUBLISHED EVERY SUNDAY MORNING.

No. 2493. [illegible] SUNDAY, JUNE 7, 1953. Radio and TV—Page 4 PRICE 2½d.

ARISE, SIR JOHN AND SIR EDMUND!

EVERST: THE QUEEN HONOURS HER HEROES

AT LONG LAST, IT WAS SIR GORDON'S DAY

The Queen shakes hands with Gordon Richards at Epsom yesterday. Gordon put Pinza first past the post four lengths ahead of the Queen's horse, Aureole.

MR EDMUND HILLARY, who, with Sherpa Tensing, conquered Mount Everest, and Colonel John Hunt, leader of the expedition, are to be knighted by the Queen. This was announced last night from 10 Downing Street.

The statement said the Queen approved that the honour of knighthood be conferred upon Colonel Hunt and that Mr Hillary be appointed a Knight Commander of the Order of the British Empire.

"It is also Her Majesty's desire to recognise the achievement of Sherpa Tensing. Since he is not a British subject, this requires consultation, and no immediate announcement can be made."

The British Government is already in consultation with the Government of Nepal concerning the honour to Sherpa Tensing.

Mrs Hunt, speaking on the phone from her home, told a reporter, "I hardly know what to say. I am delighted.

"I think I know what my husband's reaction will be. He will look upon it as an honour to the whole expedition."

Mrs Hunt, who is 39, is a former Wimbledon tennis player. She is also well-known as a Himalayan climber. She married Colonel Hunt in 1936 and still has a practical interest in climbing.

Commenting on the award to Mr Hillary, the Prime Minister of New Zealand, Mr Holland, who is in London, said, "The news that the Queen has conferred this high honour upon Mr Hillary will be received in New Zealand with the greatest pleasure and satisfaction."

Mr Hillary, 33-year-old bee-keeper, of Auckland, New Zealand, is 6 ft. 4 in. tall.

British and Indian mountaineering circles in New Delhi welcomed the Knighthood awards.

There was general approval of the Queen's intention to honour Tensing. One Indian comment was "What a pity he could not be Sir Tiger Tensing."

The expedition is expected at Katmandu on June 20.

EVEREST LEADER MAY VISIT DUNDEE

MR [illegible] G. FORBES, [illegible] Road, West Ferry, has invited the head of the Everest expedition, Colonel Hunt, to Dundee for a visit.

Mr Forbes met Colonel Hunt while he was on service at N.A.T.O. headquarters, Fontainebleau.

This photograph of Colonel Hunt in ski-ing kit was taken by Mr Forbes.

And Epsom Looked SO Different!

Mrs [illegible] Fordham, Ceylon-born wife of Australian jockey Ted Fordham, watching the racing.

Three Nigerians study their race-cards.

A Great Derby

WHAT a memorable Derby it was!

Gordon Richards, [illegible] Knight of the Turf, [illegible] crowned his riding career and achieved his life's ambition.

He won the Derby for the first time. It was his [illegible] attempt.

Gordon rode Pinza past the post four lengths ahead of the Queen's colt Aureole to the cheers of the biggest crowd that Epsom has known.

Then came another honour for Gordon—congratulations from the Queen, the Duke of Edinburgh, the Queen Mother and Princess Margaret, who received him in the Royal box.

They were obviously pleased that Gordon had won—despite the fact that Aureole had been beaten.

"Her Majesty said how delighted she was," Gordon told a reporter afterwards.

Of the race he said, "I have seldom had an easier winner."

And to a suggestion that he might retire at the end of the season, he replied, "I shall not know until about Goodwood time or September."

Thousands of people burst into a roar of cheering as the Queen and Duke of Edinburgh headed the procession of Royal visitors.

In open cars, they drove slowly down the finishing straight, past the crowded rails to the grandstand.

The thunderous wave of cheering rolled across the Downs.

There were more cheers as the Queen and Duke, with the Queen Mother, Princess Margaret and other members of the Royal Family, came to the rail of the box.

CONTINUED ON PAGE 2.

Today's Weather

MODERATE south-west to west winds. Cloudy with fine intervals. Occasional [illegible]. Normal temperatures.

Pilot Saved

A U.S. amphibious aircraft saved a British Sabre jet pilot who baled out into the sea 1000 yards off the North Korean coast.

Thousands at Abbey

THOUSANDS queued patiently yesterday to see Westminster Abbey in its post-Coronation splendour.

Chapter 7
Ironing Discipline

THE multi-temperature, steam-scooshing, water-sprinkling irons of today are a far cry from the ironing tools of old. It took skill, experience and a little ingenuity, not just the press of a button, in those days.

IF YOU EVER SCORCH HIS SHIRT WITH THE IRON—Spread a starch and cold water paste over the mark. Dry in the sun, then brush. (If mark doesn't yield to this treatment, boil shirt again).—Mrs A. E. Shapland, 257 Turnpike Road, Fitchburg, Mass., USA, who wins first prize.

EFFECTIVE—When ironing puffed sleeves on a child's dress, cover a darning mushroom with soft, clean material, and iron over it.—Joan Evans, 112 Albert Grove, Ruabon, Denbighshire.

TOWELS—Never iron towels. It flattens the pile and reduces absorbency. Soak new towels in cold water before using.—Mrs McWilliam, Tomdargie, Derculish, Strathtay.

IRONING TIP—When ironing, slip off shoes and stand on a cushion. Any amount of ironing can be done without fatigue.—Mrs D. McMillan, 167 Garrioch Road, Glasgow.

COLLARS—When ironing collars, both stiff and soft, place a small round cake tin into a warm oven and put the collars in as soon as they are ironed. This keeps them a round shape and stiffens them.—Mrs S. Moore, 122 John Street, Workington, Cumbria.

TIME SAVER—Fold soiled linen when you put it aside. You'll find this a big help when preparing your bundles for the laundryman.—Lena M. Innes, Royal Hospital for Sick Children, Edinburgh.

A GOOD IDEA FOR WASHING DAY—On washday, before clothes become too dry, roll them up and pop into a polythene bag. They will keep damp until you're ready to iron them.—E. J. Greenock, 323 Curtis Avenue, Glasgow, wins a pair of towels.

COLLARS—When washing men's semi-stiff collars, do not wring, but just drip-dry. They need very little ironing.—Mrs A. Wyles, 31 Baldwin Crescent, Kirkcaldy.

WRINKLE FREE—When ironing, place a sheet of newspaper between the blanket and ironing sheet and the sheet keeps free of wrinkles.—Mrs Borland, 924 Tollcross Road, Glasgow.

NOVEL SUBSTITUTE—If no sleeve-board is available when ironing a blouse, wrap a piece of flannel round the rolling pin and use that instead.—Mrs Priestley, c/o 25 Ramsay Road, Kirkcaldy.

PRESSING—Use brown paper instead of a damp cloth when pressing knitted work, especially if it has a pattern that should stand out. If carefully done, the "spring" will be left in the work and a flat look avoided.—Mrs M. Priestley, c/o 25 Ramsay Road, Kirkcaldy.

CANDLEWICK CARE—A candlewick bedspread should be washed in mild suds, rinsed well, and hung in wind and sun until nearly dry. The wind fluffs it up again. Shake well, but do not iron. When aired, spread over the bed, and brush with a clean brush.—Miss Mary Ritchie, The Villa, Lonmay, Aberdeenshire.

RAYON—If a rayon garment becomes too dry for ironing, re-wet it completely. Sprinkled water makes it spotty.—Mrs T. Penman, 105 Halbeath Road, Dunfermline.

SWEET SMELLING— Sprinkle cologne on your ironing board and allow to dry before ironing blouses and delicate underwear. The heat of the iron makes them sweetly fragrant until they are washed again.—Miss Helen Smith, 18 Bank Street, Glasgow.

RUGS—To keep wool rugs in shape after washing, go over them on the wrong side with a hot iron when damp, only pressing lightly on the edges.—Gladys Ritchie, 22 Tayside Street, Carnoustie.

★ TOP TIP ★

IT SAVES A LOT OF IRONING—Hang out your nylon undies dripping wet. You'll be surprised how little ironing they need. It's wringing, especially by hand, that makes creases.—M. Whiteside, 83 Aitkenhead Avenue, Coatbridge, wins a pair of towels.

SHIRT IRONING—When ironing shirt cuffs and collars, always iron on the wrong side first. When doing the right side they are then very smooth and free from creases.—Mrs E. McLean, 34 Victoria Avenue, Whitley Bay.

★ TOP TIP ★

STORING LINEN—When storing bed or table linen for any length of time, take it out periodically and refold on different lines. This prevents those stubborn fold marks which are so hard to remove.—Mrs S. B. Guy, 121 Hint Road, Harthill, wins a pair of towels.

PREVENT THESE AWKWARD MOMENTS WHEN IRONING—Starched articles sometimes stick to the iron. To prevent this, add a very little glycerine to the starch when making it up.—Mrs J. McArthur, 43 Walker Drive, South Queensferry, wins a pair of towels.

SOAP CARTONS—Keep empty soap cartons. When ironing, open one out flat and rub iron along soapy side of carton now and again. The iron runs smoothly and gives a nice gloss to linen.—Mrs Wren, 80 Orchard Park Avenue, Giffnock, Glasgow.

SILK DRESSES—Before ironing a silky material dress for the first time, iron on an inside seam to test whether it takes a hot iron or a medium one. This may save the dress being ruined.—Mrs C. Gibson, Mark Holm, Victoria Place, Stranraer.

HOW TO MAKE LINEN LAST LONGER—Household linen will wear much longer if, after ironing, it is folded by hand instead of having the crease pressed into it.—Mrs H. Allan, 9 Commerce Street, Aberdeen.

STARCH—When making starch for men's collars, drop a piece of soap into the warm starch for a few minutes. Remove soap, and starch in the usual way. Collars will iron more easily and have a glossier finish.—Mrs J. Halley, 77 Whitecrook Street, Clydebank.

COLLARS—If collars are too dry for ironing, hold them in steam of a boiling kettle for a few minutes. This dampens them just enough.—Miss A. Wilson, Welfare Grounds, Fulwell Road, Sunderland.

SCARVES—After ironing scarves, especially chiffon, roll them round a newspaper scroll-wise. They remain uncrushed until required.—Mrs S. Cunningham, 23 Willoughby Road, North Shields.

CREPE—Crepe material nearly always irons flat. To preserve the crinkle, iron over a turkish towel.—Mrs A. McNaught, 24 Wilson Street, Airdrie.

PLEATED SKIRTS—When ironing a child's pleated skirt, slip a folded newspaper inside and pin the pleats to the paper. The skirt can then be pressed without creasing the other side.—Mary Addison, 29 Ewing Street, Cowdenbeath.

GLOVES—Fabric or net gloves, put through a thin permanent starch, last twice as long. Don't iron, but press between two clean sheets of paper.—Mrs Marion Murray, 91 Curling Crescent, Glasgow.

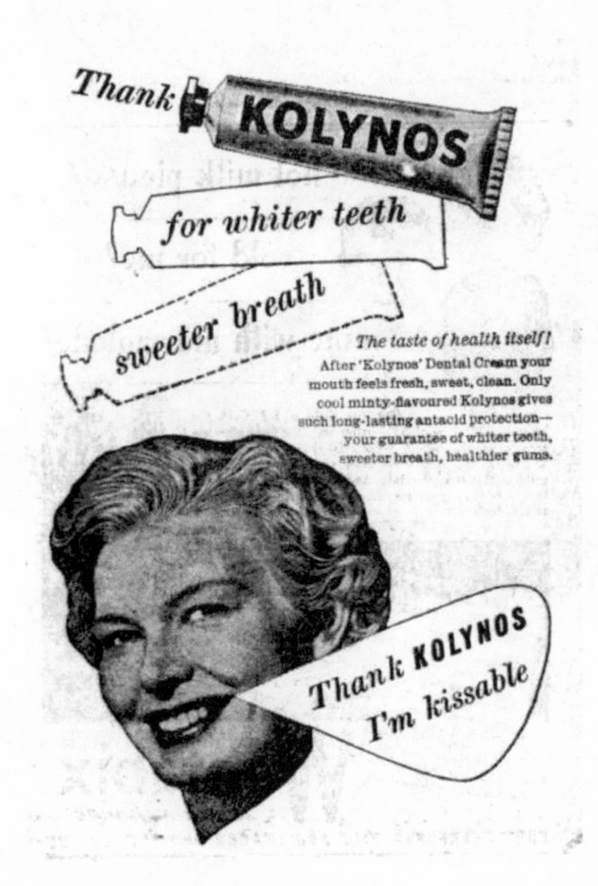

Knock off for PUNCH!
PUNCH
PUNCH
FRY'S MILK PUNCH 3D
3d
-it's a treat to eat!

CLEAN PAD— A large plastic bag pulled over the ironing board keeps the pad clean between ironing sessions.—Mrs A. Black, 25 Spencer Place, Kirkcaldy.

WHEN IRONING TABLE LINEN—Always iron the way of the thread. Otherwise, instead of the linen being smooth and flat, it will look bumpy and will not lie flat on the table.—Mrs L. Gilfillan, Bromwell Cottage, Wallacestone, Falkirk, wins a pair of towels.

TABLECLOTHS—Before putting away ironed table-cloths, roll them round a clean newspaper. When taken out for use, there are no wrinkles.—Mrs A. Craven, sen., 289 Links Street, Kirkcaldy.

COLLARS—Before ironing soft collars, squeeze them through sweet milk. Stretch and put a layer of fine cotton over them. Iron with a moderate iron, remove cloth and iron until collar is glossy. The collar will be like new and will keep clean for a long time.—Mrs M. Jeffrey, 27 Moyne Road, Glasgow.

CURTAINS—To prevent tearing when ironing lace curtains. Use the broad end of the iron instead of the pointed end.—Mrs P. Atkinson, 26 King Street, Pelaw-on-Tyne, Gateshead.

IRONS—If the letters on the temperature indicator of your electric iron have worn off, rub a piece of white chalk over them. They show up clearly again.—Mrs E. Cleary, 53 West King Street, Helensburgh.

IRONING BOARD—To prevent the asbestos pad on the ironing board from crumbling with heat, tack on a square of household aluminium foil.—Miss Pamela Prentice, 44 Comely Bank Street, Edinburgh.

★ TOP TIP ★

A HANDY THING TO USE AT IRONING TIME—To avoid scorching clothes while ironing, keep a scrap pad at the end of the ironing board. Make it from pieces of satin, cotton, crepe, rayon and other material. Try the iron on the appropriate scrap, and you are able to tell immediately if the iron is too hot.—Mrs P. Martin, 120 Graham Street, Airdrie, wins a pair of towels.

The Sunday Post

Morning Special

PRINTED AND PUBLISHED EVERY SUNDAY MORNING.

No. 2521. SUNDAY, DECEMBER 20, 1953. Radio and TV—Page 4 PRICE 2½d.

SIR WINSTON SHOWING SIGNS OF STRAIN

PREMIER MAY RETIRE IN NEW YEAR

By A Parliamentary Correspondent

THE resignation of Sir Winston Churchill as Prime Minister is expected early in the New Year.

Many Conservative M.P.s think that, although Sir Winston is mentally as alert as ever, he has been showing in recent weeks more signs of physical tiredness.

He has become, in many ways, "the old man."

It is understood his closest friends have been suggesting to him for some time that he should take life easier.

Sir Winston is turning to the view that he cannot hope to carry on the Premiership and leadership of the Conservative Party until the normal end of the Conservative Government. So he may prepare the way for his successor, almost certain to be Foreign Secretary Anthony Eden.

This will involve several changes in the hierarchy of the Government, but no General Election.

If Sir Winston's resignation should come in the absence of the Queen, he will advise the Regency Council, who will then send for the successor nominated by Sir Winston.

Yesterday's picture—Sir Winston, arm in sling, leaves 10 Downing Street to spend the week-end at Chartwell. (See report page 3.)

Torchbearers Guard Queen As She Sleeps

FOUR hundred men and women from Queen Salote's island kingdom, carrying flaming torches, mounted guard last night outside the Royal Palace while the Queen and the Duke of Edinburgh slept.

BILLY STEEL'S SECRET

The Bandsmen Went Fishing

BABY DIES IN AIR CRASH

DAME FLORA IS BACK

SAVINGS

Today's Weather

Consolation Prize

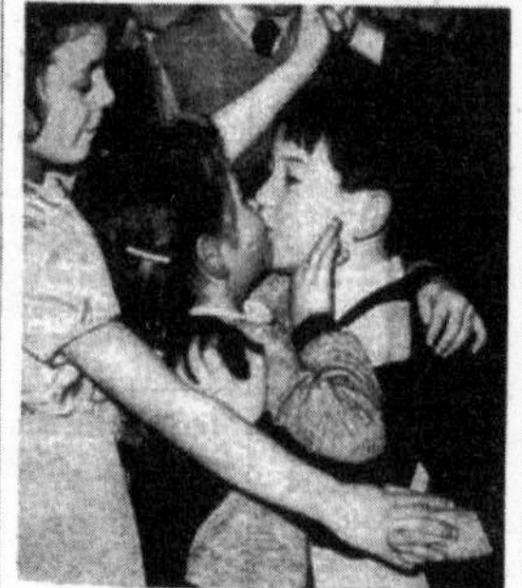

Caroline Richardson and Robert Ross, both aged four, exchange a party kiss after being caught at "The Grand Old Duke of York." The party was for children of the staff of Highland House, Perth,

Brake Crashes 80 Ft. Into Ravine

FOUR people had an amazing escape from death yesterday afternoon when a shooting brake left the Blairgowrie-Bridge of Cally road and careered 80 feet down into Craighall Den, through which flows the River Ericht.

CAIRO TALKS

DIPLOMATIC talks between representatives of Britain, Egypt, the United States and India were held in Cairo yesterday.

Canberra Does It Again

AN R.A.F. Canberra bomber touched down at London Airport yesterday to set up a new record for the 6000-mile journey from Cape Town.

Chapter 8
Uncredited Inventions

I AM convinced there was a cadre of so-called inventors who would surreptitiously read The Sunday Post's Pass It On tips, disappear into their workshops for a few hours, then get straight on to the Patent Office with "their" wonderful invention.

Bags for flowers, oven gloves, safety plugs, hot water tank insulation...even sell-by dates. Sunday Post readers thought of them first, and they changed the world.

IT MAKES A HANDY RACK FOR KITCHEN GADGETS—A piece of wooden garden trellis makes an ideal rack for kitchen gadgets. Enamel to match the kitchen, and screw small hooks into it to hold the articles. Attach to kitchen wall.—Miss M. Mills, 76 Ronald Street, Coatbridge, wins a pair of towels.

FOR SAFETY—Guard all electric points near the floor or within children's reach, as any child could thrust a hairpin or clip into a point with disastrous results. Buy spare plugs to cover the points when not in use.—Mrs M. Hood, 7 Kelvin Street, Largs.

SPLASH MAT—To prevent grease splashes marking kitchenette wallpaper behind the cooker, slit a large polythene bag and secure with Sellotape. It can be washed down easily.—Mrs T. Wilson, 27 Essenside Avenue, Drumchapel, Glasgow.

FLOWERS—When carrying cut flowers, place a polythene bag over the ends of the stems. It keeps them fresh and prevents stains on gloves or clothing from wet paper.—Miss I. Stevens, 9 Main Street, Larbert.

FOR PLANTS—A sprinkler top on a bottle of water makes an excellent watering can for pot plants and bulb bowls—Mrs J. H. Dubrey, Guildrynoch, Waterfoot, Renfrewshire.

HANDY HOLDER—A cutlery box with partitions, set on its side in the kitchen cupboard, makes an ideal set of shelves for holding spice boxes, essence bottles, etc. They are seen at a glance.—Miss K. Imlach, The Elms, Dufftown.

POCKETS—Before discarding an old garment, keep the pockets. Sew one at each end of a piece of strong material. Slip a hand in each when dealing with hot plates.—Miss Isa Morris, Fosterton, Thornton.

DOG'S DISH—Glue a rubber ring to the bottom of the dog's dish. This prevents it sliding about the floor at meals.—Miss Isa Morris, Fosterton, Thornton.

Danger—MAGPIES at work!

Few works and farms are without a Magpie—hoarding things that ought to go with the rest of the scrap. Things he honestly thinks will 'come in useful—sometime'. Search them out! Rummage around for them. Get them into the scrap merchant's hands. They're useful *now*—as raw material for the nations needs.

This appeal is directed to works and farms only. Transport and other facilities may make it possible to widen this later to cover household and other light iron and steel scrap.

BAKING HINT—I find it excellent to use a torch when looking into the oven to check the progress of baking. The contents can be clearly seen, and the door need only be opened a chink.—Miss M. M. Birrell, 96 Kinnell Avenue, Glasgow.

★ TOP TIP ★

THE BATHROOM—To "de-steam" and cool a bathroom quickly, let the cold water run hard as you empty the bath. Leave it running for a little after all the hot water has run off.—Mrs H. Christison, 38 Gairn Terrace, Aberdeen, wins a pair of towels.

PLASTIC COAT CARRIER—With a yard of one inch wide elastic, turn each end in to form a loop at both ends and stitch firmly. Leave about eight inches in the centre to form the handle. Fold the raincoat and push it through both loops, and you have a handy carrier.—Miss J. M. Towns, 9 Crimon Place, Aberdeen.

PEDAL BIN—Place an open carrier bag or large paper bag inside a pedal bin. All you have to do is lift out bag when full, and there's no messy bin to wash.—Mrs Simpson, 97 Ashdale Drive, Mosspark, Glasgow.

CAKE CARRIER—When buying small cakes, I take a cake box with divisions made from pieces of card-board — one down the middle and two across slotted to make six squares. This enables me to carry home cream cakes and meringues whole.—Mrs M. Caldwell, 15 Briery Side, Kilbirnie.

OUT OF THE WAY—If your washing machine is of the moveable type and you have difficulty with the flex, get two white stick-on hooks. Fix them about 8 inches apart on the opposite side to the draining tube, then coil the flex neatly round them.—Mrs Lily Devlin, 95 Millbrae Road, Langside, Glasgow.

NON-SLIP—To prevent the ironing board slithering all over the floor, my husband attached four small rubber door stops to the feet.—Eileen Riley, Park Cottage, Blairgowrie.

WATCH IT—When cooking soup, stew or a steam pudding that needs a long time, replace the pot lid with a Pyrex plate. You can see how the contents are cooking without taking off the lid.—Mrs E. Anderson, 56 South Tay Street, Dundee.

PICNIC TIME—Sew four press-studs to your travelling rug, and with these attach a square of plastic or other waterproof material. This makes the rug damp-proof on grass or sand.—Mrs M. Ladnit, 24 Laurel Avenue, Dalmuir West, Glasgow.

CLEAN PAPER—To keep wallpaper clean round light switches, use a plastic table mat six inches in diameter. Cut the centre out the size of the switch and press it over. No glue is required, it stays put.—Mrs E. McAdam, 15 Hillhead Crescent, Motherwell.

IDEAL COVER—When hanging a coat or dress on a hanger, turn a paper carrier upside down and put the hanger hook through it. This makes an ideal dust sheet for clothes in the wardrobe.—Mrs William Laird, 16 Slatefield Street, Glasgow.

CLEAN STEP—Leave a wooden box on the doorstep for your milk bottles, then they won't mark the doorstep or get knocked over.—Mrs S. Young, 63A Camberwell Road, London.

FOR SHOES—To make a handy container for shoes, double a strong piece of material, sew up the sides, then stitch into pockets, each with an opening at top. Put in shoes with heels uppermost. Attach a hook at either side and hang on back of cupboard door. —Mrs M. L. Campbell, 7 East Avenue, Renfrew.

HOT WATER—To make a hot water tank more effective, get enough corrugated cardboard to wrap twice round the tank. Cut in half and wrap one layer round with smooth side inwards and the other layer with smooth side outwards. Secure at top and bottom with strong cord. If desired, a piece may be cut to fit the top of the tank and tucked under the first layer.—Wm. G. Bowie, 57 Marchmont Road, Edinburgh.

BABY'S BOTTLE—A good way to sterilise baby's bottle is to place a funnel, large end downwards, in a saucepan of boiling water. Invert the bottle over the upturned stem so that the steam goes directly into the bottle and sterilises it in a few minutes.—Mrs Parker, Station House, Kelvinbridge, Glasgow.

DATE THEM—Before putting tinned foods in store cupboard write date of purchase on them so that they can be used in proper order.—Mrs T. Dow, 40 Turret Road, Glasgow.

OVEN TESTS—Place a sheet of white paper in the oven. If it turns brown in less than a minute the oven is too hot. When it becomes golden brown, the oven is suitable for pastry. When light brown, for pies, tarts, and small cakes. When dark yellow, for large pies and cakes. When light yellow, for puddings and biscuits.—Mrs J. Black, 32 Mill Road, Bathgate.

★ TOP TIP ★

IT'S THE VERY THING FOR COLD WASH DAYS—On cold wash days, peg small articles for drying to a length of broad cotton or tape. It only takes a minute to peg the lot on the line outside. If there's a sudden shower, they can be taken down in a jiffy.—Miss M. Chalmers, 30 Constitution Street, Inverurie, wins a pair of towels.

HANDY BASKET—The new shopping basket on wheels is a boon to the housewife. Not only for heavy shopping, but on wash days it can be used for putting out and taking in the clothes.—Mrs A. Varty, 5 George Street, Blackhill, Consett, County Durham.

SHOPPING LIST—To avoid searching for a shopping list with a full basket, write your list on a tag luggage label and tie to the handle of your basket.—Mrs B. Palmer, 78 Westbourne Road, Marsh, Huddersfield.

CLEAN CEILING—To prevent kitchen ceiling being discoloured or splashed with grease, place a sheet of tin or asbestos on top of cooker rack.—Mrs S. Cunningham, 23 Willoughby Road, North Shields.

HANDY FORK—An old fork with prongs bent upwards is handy for removing pickles from a jar.—Mrs A. Allan, 6 Hillneuk Avenue, Bearsden, Glasgow.

PICKLES—Sugar tongs are excellent for serving pickles, and save the bother of chasing them round the jar.—Miss Elizabeth Taylor, 24 Leven Street, Glasgow.

PREVENTS SPILLING—An opened packet of rice, cake mix, etc., often scatters all over the cupboard. To prevent this, seal with strip of Sellotape. It also keeps the contents fresh.—Mrs Alberta Walker, 26 Woodside Crescent, Halifax.

UMBRELLA CARRIER—When shopping or carrying luggage, an umbrella can be a nuisance. I have solved the problem by tying a loop of elastic to each end of the handle of a case, or to one of the handles of a shopping bag, and slipping the umbrella through the loops.—Miss A. Wood, 8 Jackson Street, Inverurie.

EMERGENCY TIP—I had an operation to my foot, but didn't have the type of cage used by hospitals so I covered a half-round fireguard with a towel, and used that instead. It has kept the weight of bedclothes off my foot, and proved a huge success.—Mrs H. Stewart, Dalnagairn, First Avenue, Bardsley, near Leeds.

REMAINS FAST—If you have no marking ink, use a ball-pointed pen for household linen, school clothes, &c. Press with a hot iron immediately after marking to set the ink. Names remain indelible in spite of repeated washings.—A. Docherty, 33 Barrie Avenue, Cresswell, Dumfries.

TRY-OUT PLAN—Before decorating a room, sketch it on paper and paint in your colour scheme. For the furniture, cut squares or oblongs of paper and arrange them on your sketch. You get many good ideas this way.—Mrs M. Thompson, 12 Davidson Street, Lancaster.

SHINY TAPS—To keep chromium fittings bright and free from water marks in bathroom or kitchenette (where there's steam), rub them with a cloth dipped in olive oil.—Mrs B. Hilton, 91 South Fredrick Street, South Shields.

HATS AND SHOES—When steaming felt hats or suede shoes to freshen them, attach a piece of rubber hose about six inches long to the spout of the kettle. The steam can be guided without fear of scalding the hands.—Mrs H. Smith, 14 John Street, Ruabon.

HANDY APRON—For bathing a baby, make a plastic apron lined on one side with terry towelling. It's warm for baby to sit on, and the plastic backing prevents moisture seeping through.—Mrs C. Piathowska, Beancross, Falkirk.

WELLINGTONS—Children's legs are sometimes sore and red with the tops of wellingtons. A good plan is to stitch pieces of velvet or other soft material round the top of the inside of the boots.—Mrs I. C. Campbell, 10 Mossgiel Avenue, Stirling.

HANDY BOOKMARK—I use an ordinary wire paper clip, clipped on the top of the page, and find it very serviceable. It's clean and hygienic.—Mrs A. Shand, 38 Milton Street, Monifieth.

DOOR DRAUGHTS—To prevent a draught from the bottom of a door, pad an old nylon stocking thickly with old cloth. Tie at the top. Cover the "sausage" with gay material and tie the top again. Place at the bottom of the door.—Miss P. B. Barnes, 3 Maritime Crescent, Easington, County Durham.

PLASTERING CRACKS—When you want to fill up cracks between bath and tiles or around wash basin, make a greaseproof "icing bag", fill with plaster or filler and work along into the cracks.—Mrs M. C. Bruce, 1 Pennine Avenue, Sundon Park, Luton.

HANDY HOLDERS—When your rubber hot water bottle is of no further use, cut the corners off diagonally and you've four useful kettle and pot holders.—Miss Goodwin, 10 Torphichen Place, Edinburgh.

HAT PIN TIDY—To make a useful holder for small hat-pins, use an empty pepper drum. Cover with fancy paper or bright material. Fill with fine sawdust and seal top. Pins are put through the holes in the top of the lid.—Mrs W. Hatcher, 3 Palmstead Road, Pennywell, Sunderland.

EASY JOB—If you are sanding a curved surface, make it easier by attaching the sandpaper to a foam sponge. The flexibility of the sponge conforms to the surface and distributes the pressure evenly.—M. Harper, Tulloch, Old Meldrum.

FRESH DAILY—An empty milk carton makes a fresh sink tidy every day. Pierce a few holes in the bottom for drainage. The carton is easily disposed of by burning in the fire at night.—Mrs A. Strathdee, 10 Backcroft, Dunblane.

★ TOP TIP ★

THIS SAVES MANY A NASTY FALL—Rugs on polished floors are apt to slip and cause accidents. A simple preventative is to sew five rubber rings on the underside. One ring at each corner and a ring in the centre, and the rug will stay put.—P. McLaren, 80 Warwick Street, Oxford, wins this week's guinea.

AS GOOD AS NEW—If your sheepskin paint roller becomes worn, strip off the sheepskin and re-cover with a strip of plastic foam.—A. Tompkins, Dundee.

CHEESE—To keep cheese from going hard and sweaty, put it (unwrapped) in a polythene bag immediately. It keeps moist and fresh.—Miss Edith Ross, 67 Arbroath Road, Dundee.

HANDY HOLDER—I fixed a tie rack on the inside of a cupboard door in the children's bedroom. I use it for hanging hair ribbons, school ties, dress girdles etc. They keep that newly-ironed look, and I can find whatever I want in a jiffy. It also saves drawer space.—Mrs M. Macfarlane, 9 Crags Crescent, Paisley.

UNDER CARPET—I put a large bundle of old newspapers to good use by fixing them, 12 sheets at a time, together with gummed paper, and laying them under my carpet. They make a lovely underpad, and help keep moths at bay.—Mrs I. Gillespie, 10 Glebe Street, East Kilbride.

FOR DRY SOAP—Use a plastic sponge instead of a soap dish. The soap drains immediately and lasts longer.—Mrs McLeary, 76 Loch Road, Kirkintilloch.

BRUSHES—Before using a new sweeping brush buy a length of rubber draught excluder and tack it round the edge of the brush. This serves as a buffer, and saves furniture and paintwork from scratches.—Mrs W. Mustard, 27 Seafield Street, Cullen.

CUP HANDLES—To prevent cracking cup and jug handles, cut some ordinary cycle valve tubing into small lengths and put it over your cup hooks. I have found this most effective.—Mrs McKay, 39 Easter Drylaw Place, Edinburgh.

COMFORT—A sheet of plastic foam, costing about three to four shillings, placed under the sheet at hip-level makes all the difference in night comfort to an aged person. The rough surface prevents it moving from the desired position and provides softness and buoyancy.—Mrs McDougall, 6 Dodhill Place, Glasgow.

HOLDERS—I lined two oval pieces of leather (as used for jacket elbows) with felt from old hats, and oversewed all round. They made grand kettle holders.—Mrs M. Purcell, Broats Cottages, Annan.

NO SMELL—Where there is a gas poker there is nearly always a smell of gas. After using the poker take it off the tube immediately and insert a cork in the end of the tube. It is the gas remaining in the tube that causes the smell.—M. H. Foguell, 42 Meadowhouse Road, Edinburgh.

SELF-CLOSING—To make a door close automatically, get a piece of rubber six inches long and half an inch wide. Close the door from the outside and fix one end of the rubber to the lintel and the other end to the door.—Mrs Alice Jordan, 55 Whitevale Street, Glasgow.

FOR CYCLISTS—To save trousers looking like frills round mutton chops after bicycle clips have been removed I bought three-quarter inch snap fasteners and sewed them inside trouser bottoms at the appropriate places. A sharp jerk and the trousers are tidy, with no ugly marks.—Mrs C. Clunas, 29 Tomnahurich Street, Inverness.

COAT LOOP—To make an unbreakable loop for ties inside a coat, buttonhole round a small curtain ring and sew it into position.—Mrs S. Moore, 122 John Street, Workington.

SPECTACLES—If your glasses keep slipping down, get a piece of bicycle valve tubing and cut two pieces 3/8 of an inch long. Put a piece on the end of each leg. This keeps the glasses secure.—M. L. Potts, 102 Fern Avenue, Jesmond, Newcastle-on-Tyne.

★ TOP TIP ★

KEEPS VEG FRESH—A good way to keep root vegetables fresh after buying is to plant them in the garden and water lightly every other day. If no garden space is available, a box of soil kept under the sink serves the same purpose.—Mrs M. B. Gibson, Strath House, By Avonbridge, wins a pair of towels.

LETTER HOLDER—A small, square plastic basket, such as is sold for clothes pegs, is easily fitted to the back of the door to catch letters corning through the letter-box. The baskets can be bought in different colours and do not mark the wall when door is opened.—Mrs Fender, Perth Street, Blairgowrie.

STOPPERS—Screw a cup-hook on the window ledge of your sink. This enables the stopper to drip and keeps it out of the way when working at the sink.—Miss Barbara Wilson, Littlegill, Auchenheath, Lanark.

LEMON SQUEEZER—If you haven't got a lemon squeezer, use an upturned eggcup on a saucer. The juice collects in the saucer while the pips are caught in the hollow bottom of the eggcup.—Mrs McMillan, 3 Cedar Street, Glasgow.

SAVES THE WALLS—To prevent kitchen chairs marking walls, cut pieces of old velvet or felt (same shape as back bar) and glue on firmly to the bar.—Mrs Troup, 8 Beechgrove Avenue, Aberdeen.

SINK MAT—Collect rubber rings from lids of fruit bottles, etc. (all same size if possible), and tie them together in mat form with strong cord. Keeps sink clean and prevents breakages.—Mrs H. Elliott, Kidd's House, Allenheads, Hexam, Northumberland.

OLD BROOM—When a broom has seen its best days, burn off any remaining bristles and bind over with old flannel or velvet. It makes an excellent floor polisher.—Mrs J. Sneddon, 58 Nora Street, High Barnes, Sunderland.

HANDY CORK—If you need a cork urgently and can't find one, peel a potato, cut from it a "cork" to fit bottle or flask. Wrap with greaseproof paper and fix.—Mrs Marion Tennant, Broomhall, Rathnew, Co. Wicklow.

HANDY TABLE—A wooden three-tier cake-stand makes an ideal emergency bedside table, especially if space is limited.—Mrs Penman, 105 Halbeath Road, Dunfermline.

SMALL CHOPPER—A handy chopper for parsley, herbs, peel, etc., is made by inserting a razor blade sideways in a good-sized cork. A cork with a metal top makes the best holder.—Mrs L. Wreghitt, 10 Railway Terrace, Holgate Road, York.

PREVENTS DAMAGE—To prevent bed ends damaging the walls, fix rubber stoppers to posts of bed meeting the skirting-board.—Mrs Helen C. Gray, 9 Cherrybank Road, Glasgow.

DRYING HINT—Screw four or five cup hooks into the open ends of the clothes horse. Hang small articles on the hooks, and there is space on the rails for the bigger garments.—Mrs J. Evans, 112 Albert Grove, Ruabon, Wrexham.

HANDY RACK—A toothbrush rack, fixed in the kitchen, holds lots of small gadgets in daily use, such as scissors, tin openers, etc.—Mrs E. Stewart, 231 Crowhill Street, Glasgow.

LIPSTICK HOLDER—Slip the clip off an old pen and fit it over your lipstick case. The lipstick can be clipped on the pocket of a handbag, and easily found when required.—Mrs H. Hutton, 68 Rose Street, Aberdeen.

HOOKS—When fitting bathroom rails or kitchen racks, use a hook instead of a screw for the lower hole of brackets. This is useful for dressing gowns in the bathroom and kitchen cloths in the kitchen.—Miss V. McCallum, McCallum, Street, Campbeltown.

BIRD SCARE—To keep the birds from eating your strawberries, place several toy windmills in the strawberry bed. The noise of them whirling scares the birds away.—Mrs V. Porter, 274 Killin Street, Glasgow.

★ TOP TIP ★

NO MORE CRASHES AT THE SINK—Cover an old picture frame with fine wire netting and stand it on the draining board. Articles will drain better, and there's no fear of them slipping and breaking.—Mrs J. Will, Council Houses, Silverhillock, Cornhill, Banff, wins a pair of towels.

HANDY—An old shoe horn makes a good trowel for pot plants. It's a handy size and makes transplanting easy.—Mrs McDonough, Cullicudden Road, Conon.

STRING BAGS—Make a plastic lining for your string bag, and you won't lose small parcels through the mesh.—Mrs J. G. Greig, 187 Albany Highway, Perth Road, Albany, West Australia.

HANDY RAIL—Remove knobs from kitchen table drawer and, in their place, fit a short rail for towels. It also serves as a handle.—Mrs Parker, 6 Bowman Flat, Larkhall.

TIDY DRAWER—A strip of elastic, tacked to the front inside your dressing table drawer, makes a handy holder for bottles of perfume, nail polish, lotions.—Mrs C. Campbell, Millburn Lodge, Dalserf.

PREVENTS STEAMING UP—For windscreens and inside windows in a car, here is a cheap and simple remedy to prevent steaming up. One application lasts for more than 48 hours. Put one ounce liquid detergent, one ounce glycerine and 10 ounces methylated spirit into a large clean bottle. It is important to shake well before using and it should be applied with a soft duster.—G. Clarke, Lothian Drive, Easthouses, Dalkeith.

★ TOP TIP ★

MAKE YOUR OWN MOTH-PROOF BAGS—For storing furs or winter coats, buy a role of Cellophane. Cut two sheets to required size. Place article to be stored between the sheets and seal edges with Cellophane tape. —Mrs C. Chambers, 1296 Maryhill Road, Glasgow, wins a pair of towels.

HANDY—Fix a magnet to the corner of your oven cloth. It adheres to the side of the cooker, and is always handy.—Mrs H. Adamson, 53 East Clyde Street, Helensburgh.

FIRM HOLD—Before putting a screw into a plaster wall make a hole with small drill, then pack with steel wool. When screw is put in it's held firmly.—I. Brereton, c/o 27 Halliburton Place, Galashiels.

BELT HANGER—Screw cup hooks into the underside of a heavy wooden coat hanger. Belts hang straight from the buckle without creases.—Mrs J. McLean, Carlisle.

PARAFFIN FILLER—If you've lamps or stoves to fill, keep a cheap tin kettle filled with paraffin. It's much easier than pouring the oil through a funnel.—Miss H. B. Tuck, 5 Hazelbourne Road, Balham, London.

EASY FASTENING—Use pipe cleaners to fasten the tops of polythene bags. They keep the bags tightly closed and are easier to use than rubber bands.—Mrs M. Jeffrey, 27 Moyne Road, Glasgow.

COOKER SWITCHES—Wall switches for electric cookers are usually in one colour. It is a good idea to have the switch in two different colours. For "off" show the original colour, for "on" show red. A glance across the room shows whether the cooker is on or off.—James Jack, Drumairlie, High Street West, Anstruther.

The Sunday Post

Morning Special

PRINTED AND PUBLISHED EVERY SUNDAY MORNING.

No. 2529. SUNDAY, FEBRUARY 14, 1954. Radio and TV—Page 4 PRICE 2½d.

LOVE LETTERS CLUE IN DOUBLE MURDER

"Sunday Post" Investigation

THE EFFECT OF SMOKING: WHAT THE DOCTORS BELIEVE

THE Government committee's findings on the relationship between smoking and lung cancer set all Britain talking yesterday.

In many surgeries, patients asked doctors what they thought of the report.

"The Sunday Post" made a wide canvass among smokers yesterday. We found that only 3 in 100 are considering cutting down.

We also asked specialists and doctors in London, Edinburgh, Dundee, Aberdeen and Glasgow for their views. Here they are:—

SPECIALIST SMOKES 20 A DAY

WOMAN DOCTOR'S VIEW

"MUST IRRITATE"

(CONTINUED ON PAGE 2.)

Victim May Have Had Secret Fear

THE field of inquiry in the Old Folk's Home double murder was widened last night.

New facts came to light as a squad of detectives sat at a table in Ealing, London, Police Station for hours reading letter after letter.

Love letters were among the pile of over 3000.

As each neatly-tied bundle was opened, the letters threw new light on the life, over a period of 20 years, of one of the victims, 42-year-old Mrs Isobel Chesney.

Some letters were yellowing with age. Many were in different handwritings. Foreign stamps were on some of the envelopes.

All were read with one thought in mind. Could any of them have a bearing on the crime which had horrified neighbours and elderly guests at the 16-roomed residence in staid, tree-lined Montpelier Road?

Pope To Broadcast

MOST of the population of the Bedfordshire town of Shefford were at the Parish Church of St Michael and All Angels yesterday to see the wedding of the 18-year-old Rackall twins to two U.S. airmen.

Dorothy Rackall was married to A/1C Adrian Wilkinson, of West Hamlin, West Virginia. Her sister, Shirley, was married to A/3C Orville Coulter, of Indianapolis, Indiana.

Jet Crashes Going Through Sound Barrier

A METEOR II jet crashed in a copse near Lower Beeding, near Horsham, Sussex, yesterday.

The pilot was killed.

Mr D. S. Homer, of Pipers Croft, Mapleshurst, Horsham, who was out with the Crawley and Horsham Hunt, said the plane dived over the hounds and exploded in the copse a quarter of a mile away.

"We Want Our Money Back," Shout Hundreds

NO! NO! NO! AND NO! AGAIN

Today's Weather

Windy. Dull with rain at times. Snow and sleet in places.

Chapter 9 Curtains, Blinds And Windows

POSSIBLY because they were the only part of the house a passer-by could see into, and therefore an advertisement for the house's inner cleanliness, a surprising number of 1950s tips were about curtains, blinds and windows.

The tips were for cleaning, washing and drying curtains and blinds. There were comparatively few intended just to make windows look attractive.

Windows in the 21st Century are more likely to be double-glazed but they still need cleaning and they still have curtains and blinds. A high proportion of the tips here will still be useful to the proud householder.

NO STEAMY WINDOWS NOW—If you're bothered with steamy windows, roll newspaper up loosely and a place on window-sill just inside curtains. The paper absorbs damp and keeps curtains and sill dry.—Mrs Brown, 225 Stoneyhurst Street, Glasgow, wins a pair of towels.

CURTAINS—It is a good plan when drying heavy curtains to thread the drying line through the hems. There are then no peg marks.—Miss M. MacGregor, Sutherland Cottage, Keir Street, Dunblane.

NO IRONING NOW—After curtains have been laundered, fold lengthwise and drape them over the bar of a coat hanger Hang in wardrobe or cupboard, and they're ready to put up without ironing out the folds.—Mrs Gray, 58 Erskine Street, Alva.

WINDOW LEATHER—Soak a new chamois in salt water before using. This prevents streaky windows.—Mrs R. French, 89 Drygate, Glasgow.

STRIPED CURTAINS—When washing striped curtains etc., hang out with the stripes running down. If colours aren't fast, the dyes will run down their own stripes instead of blurring into one another.—Mrs G. Lumley, 52 William Street, Tayport.

★ TOP TIP ★

TO KEEP THE HOUSE FRESH IN HOT WEATHER—Window sills washed with a weak solution of chloride of lime keeps out midges and gnats. This also helps to keep the air in the house fresh in warm weather.—Miss Janetta M. Stirrat, 1 Bankhead Drive, Bankhead, Rutherglen, wins this week's guinea.

VENETIAN BLINDS—Rub the laths of venetian blinds with a rag dipped in linseed oil. When dry it gives them a newly-varnished look and helps to preserve them.—Mrs C. Stevenson, 302 Linthaugh Road, Glasgow.

QUICK WORK—When making window curtains of plastic material, the top hem through which the curtain rod passes can be quickly made by sticking it down with adhesive plastic tape. Being transparent, the tape is not noticeable.—W. W. Reid, 11 Marchmont Street, Edinburgh.

NO MESS NOW—Window boxes are attractive, but messy in rainy weather. To prevent windows being spattered, scatter a layer of gravel over the top of the soil.—Mrs E. Annal, 47a Moodie Street, Dunfermline.

NOVEL BLIND-PULLS—Use plastic sewing thimbles, which come in various colours. Drill a hole in the top of each, insert the blind cord, and knot the end.—Mrs J. Parker, 193 Burnbrae Street, Balornock, Glasgow.

FOR SILK—When ironing taffeta or silk curtains, keep a piece of paper smeared with a little soap on the ironing board. Run the iron over this now and again, and it doesn't stick to the silk. It also prevents wrinkles, which are hard to remove.—Mrs A. McMillan, 201 Crossloan Road, Govan, Glasgow.

PERFECT SHAPE—When washing light-weight curtains, insert a rod through top and bottom hems. Tie one end to clothes line, and the curtains dry in perfect shape.—Mrs Donaldson, 109 Randolph Drive, Clarkston.

NET CURTAINS—Before washing net curtains, fold sides towards the centre and tack all round. Wash in usual way. Dry and iron with the threads still in. Result is a lovely straight edge.—J. Johnston, Woodhill, King Street, East Newport.

WET CURTAINS—Recently my curtains were soaked when ice on the window thawed. I fixed a piece of string across the window frame about four inches from the bottom. Curtains and blinds rest on the string – entirely clear of the window. No more wet curtains now.—Mrs Scott, 258 Ruchazie Road, Glasgow.

BLINDS—When putting up linen blinds, sew broad tape on to the top of the blind, then tack tape on to the roller. This prevents tearing blind when taking off for washing, etc.—Mrs I. Dawson, 144 Earlston Avenue, Glasgow.

CURTAIN FITTINGS—Metal curtain fittings and rings tend to lose their speed on the fixture unless periodically treated with a cloth slight moistened with sweet oil.—Mrs E. Macgregor, 30 Summertown Road, Glasgow.

MARK CURTAINS—When removing the hooks from curtains, mark each place with a ball-point pen or blue pencil. When the curtains have been washed the hooks are quickly replaced without having to count the spaces.—B. Clark, 96 Alexander Street, Airdrie.

STRAIGHT LINE—To make sure you are cutting straight when making curtains, draw out a weft thread. This leaves an open mark which is easy to follow.—Mrs G. Duff. 15 Ferries Crescent, Woodside, Aberdeen.

★ TOP TIP ★

IF YOU'RE CLEANING WINDOWS—A teaspoonful of borax in the water you wash windows with helps to keep flies away. It was used regularly as an insecticide before D.D.T. was produced.—Mrs N. Wilson, Durham, wins this week's guinea.

A MILLION BOY FRIENDS INVITED HOME!

CLEVER GIRL! SHE KNOWS WHAT'S ON THE MENU!
Batchelors CHICKEN NOODLE SOUP
IN A SPECIAL FLAVOUR-GUARDING FOIL ENVELOPE
MADE IN 7 MINUTES
Just empty the entire contents of envelope into 1½ pints boiling water, simmer for 7 minutes. It's glorious golden chicken soup full of tender, nourishing noodles (made from egg and refined wheat)!
oodles of NOODLES!
What a FLAVOUR!
taste the CHICKEN!
Batchelors
WONDERFUL
CHICKEN NOODLE SOUP
4 big helpings 1/- Come and get it!

NEW WINDOW SILL—To cover a badly-marked window ledge, I used a piece of hardboard cut to shape from a template of paper. I fixed it with plaster, then sized and sandpapered it, and painted it to match the window frame.—Mr G. Shakeshaft, 20 Clinton Place, Liverpool.

CURTAIN PELMET—To make it easier to put up and take down curtains from rail when a pelmet is used, fix hinges on the pelmet. Then you can swing it up out of the way.—I. A. Bowman, 31 Annette Street, Glasgow.

BLINDS STAPLE—To prevent blinds being torn and to keep cord straight, insert a small staple at the side of window frame and put cord through it. The cord will work more smoothly.—Mrs E. Wyse, 32 Orchard Street, Grangemouth.

LINEN BLINDS—To clean cream linen blinds, take a dry, clean nailbrush and dip it in powdered bathbrick. Scrub blind from side to side and then dust carefully with a clean dry duster.—C. F. Bell, 48 Ripon Drive, Glasgow.

SUNBLINDS—To keep sun blinds from blowing up, make a deep hem, keeping one end closed, and fill with silver sand. When laundering, empty sand into large pail so that it can be used again.—Mrs Murdoch, 57 New Dykes Road, Prestwick.

COOL—If your larder window faces the sun, rub it over with your washing blue bag. This will keep it much cooler.—D. Moncur, 39 Prospecthill Street, Greenock.

NO TROUBLE—When painting woodwork of windows, rub a bar of soap flat along all glass edges. Any paint which overlaps woodwork can be wiped off in a jiffy with the soap.—J. Brown, Glasgow.

CURTAINS—Before hemming net curtains, run a strip of three-inch bandage across them. Then fold over and hem in the usual way. Rods can be run through without tearing the net.—Mrs O'Gara, Strathclyde Street, Glasgow.

WINDOW SHINE—Before washing windows squeeze the blue bag into the water. It gives a lovely shine.—M. Downie, Eaglesfield, Lockerbie.

PERFECT SHINE—When cleaning windows, use a square of clean velvet for the final rub up. No hairs or fluff will be left, and the result is a lovely shine.—Mrs E. D. Malcolm, 150 Den Walk, Methil.

★ TOP TIP ★

CHEAP WAY TO CLEAN THE WINDOWS—For cleaning windows I buy a pint of methylated spirits and threepence-worth of whiting. Dilute whiting with a little water and fill up with meth. This lasts me six months. Cost 1s 9d.—I. H. Walker, 332 Charles Street, Bush Hill Park, Enfield, wins a pair of towels.

NO MORE TORN BLINDS—The cord is apt to mount the roller and tear a paper window blind when it's pulled up. To prevent this, fix a small ringscrew high on the window frame to guide the cord into the proper channel.—Frank Macnab, 1 Westerlea, Leslie.

CURTAIN RUNNERS—Rub curtain runners with metal polish. Furniture cream attracts dust, and is apt to clog the wheels.—Mrs F. Henderson, 3 Moat Drive, Edinburgh.

SASH WINDOWS—If your sash windows have become struck with the rains, give the wood slides a good rub over with wax floor polish. The sashes will then slide up and down easily.—Mrs C. F. Jardine, 39 Pentland Terrace, Edinburgh.

LINED CURTAINS—When lining curtains for windows which face the sun, buy patent fasteners on a tape (sold by the yard). Attach one tape to each curtain and the matching side to the lining. Then linings are easily detached for washing.—Mrs K. Hunter, 2 Abbey Park Place, Dunfermline.

WASH LEATHER—Before using a new wash leather, soak it overnight in cold water and salt, using one dessertspoonful of salt to each pint of water. Rinse next morning in clear water. This stops the smears sometimes left on glass when a new leather is used.—Miss W. Martin, 34 Balgarvie Crescent, Cupar.

RUST—I find this the best way to treat rusty iron window frames. Clean off rust, see frame is thoroughly dry, then apply red or white lead paint. Complete with one or two coats of required paint.—Mrs Mitchell, Aberdeen.

CURTAIN TIP—To save ironing net curtains after washing them, ask someone to help you pull them straight. Then fold them and put through the wringer. Shake them out and hang up right away.—Mrs E. J. Tasker, 43 Watermill Road, Fraserburgh.

CURTAINS—Try roller towelling for bathroom and kitchen curtains. It lasts long, looks attractive, absorbs steam, and shows no splashes. It hangs perfectly, and is non-shrinkable. It can be bought with a border matching the colour scheme or dyed to match.—Mrs E. A. M. Gear, 2 Warehouse Flats, Wood Green, Witney.

PLASTIC CURTAINS—When sewing plastic curtains, rub your machine's plate well with talcum powder. Also sprinkle some on teeth and foot of machine. This stops the plastic from sticking.—Mrs Tulloch, 25 Acacia Grove, South Shields, Co. Durham.

CURTAINS—If new curtains don't hang properly, simply machine down the selvedge, and that should do the trick.—Mrs McWilliam, 1047 Tollcross Road, Glasgow.

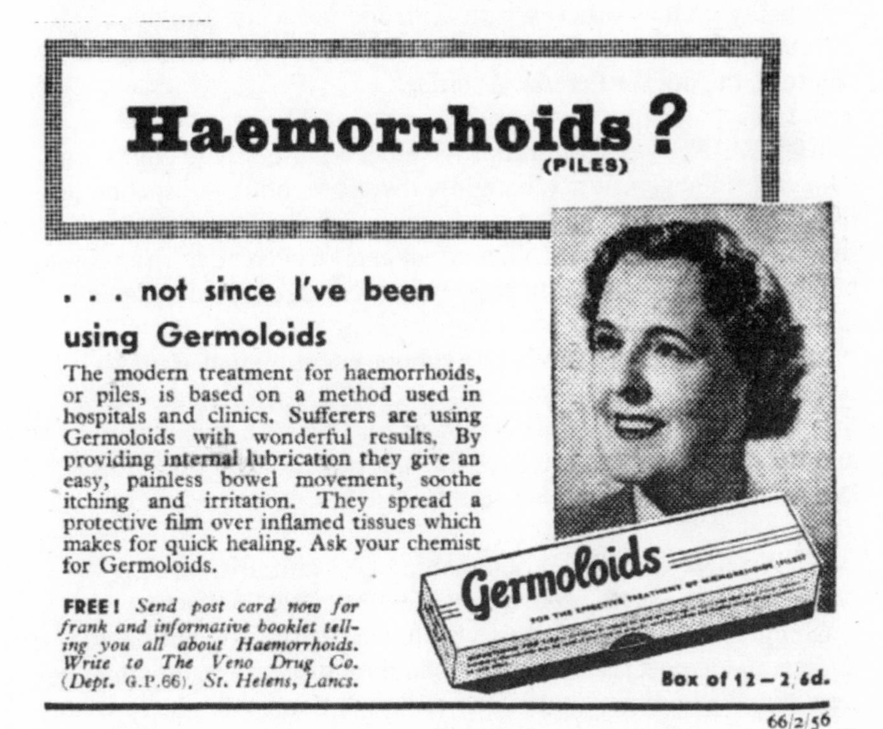

COLOURFUL—Add colour to your bathroom by making curtains from gay, turkish towelling. They also absorb the steam.—Mrs Cassidy, 73 Blackwell Road, Carlisle.

IRONING CURTAINS—When hanging curtains, always iron the top part first and put hooks in position. Then iron remainder. This avoids creases caused by hooking after the ironing. —Mrs J. Mitchell, 35 Cunningham Gardens, Falkirk.

★ TOP TIP ★

CURTAINS WASHED THIS WAY CAN LAST 18 YEARS—When washing net or brocade curtains, add a level tablespoonful of size, melted in boiling water, to the warm rinsing water. Iron when not quite dry – this gives the stiffness of new material. I've got curtains treated like this, still in good condition after being in constant use for 18 years.—Mrs Thomson, 52 White Street, Glasgow, wins a pair of towels.

CURTAIN CARE—If in doubt as to whether heavy curtains should be washed, wet a handkerchief or piece of white cotton, lay on the corner of a curtain, and run a hot iron over it. If the curtain "bleeds" it is safer to have them dry-cleaned.—Mrs Ganrow, 11 Stocket Parade, Aberdeen.

CURTAINS—After curtains have been washed, the edges are sometimes uneven. When hanging, therefore, hook the second last hook to the end eye and the last hook round the outside to the second eye. This gives a rolled effect and an even edge from top to bottom.—Miss M. B. Row 261 Muiryhall Street, Coatbridge.

KNEELING MAT—When a rubber kneeling mat starts to perish and becomes difficult to keep clean, cut two pieces of linoleum exactly the same size. Stick lino on each side and allow to dry under pressure. This makes the mat both durable and easily kept.—Mrs A. W. Keith, 8 South Bridge Street, St Andrews.

NEW CURTAINS—When making new curtains, turn up bottom hem to length required and feather stitch. After first washing curtains usually shrink a little. The stitching is easy to unpick and leaves no marks. You can then machine to length required.—Mrs P. E. Cantle, 181 Hilton Avenue, Aberdeen, wins a pair of towels.

WINTER CURTAINS—When laying away winter velour curtains, I roll them round a long pole (the handle from an old broom is ideal). This keeps them from creasing and they are ready to be hung up again in the autumn.—Mrs M. Coutts, 21 Rubislaw Park Crescent, Aberdeen.

SAVE THE DOOR—Make hem about three inches deep at bottom of door sun-blind. Fill with sand. This keeps curtain from blowing about and prevents paintwork being blistered by the sun.—Mrs D. Hardie, 6 Backmarch Crescent, Rosyth.

BLINDS—When windows are open, blinds often fly up and become wedged between roller and window-frame. To prevent this, sew a button at each corner of bottom hem at window side. This keeps the blind from over-winding and jamming.—Mrs J. Hill, 53 Calder Street, Alloa.

CURTAINS—Net curtains are best hung at the windows when wet. Then they always hang evenly.—Mrs D. K. Tolley, 84 Watermoor Road, Cirencester.

NO MORE WAVES—When making up new curtains turn in all selvedges and stitch down. This prevents that annoying wavy edge which often occurs after curtains have been washed.—Mrs Jean S. Murdoch, 28 Belmont Avenue, Eaglesfield, by Lockerbie.

WAX POLISH HINTS—A rub of wax polish on curtain rods means smoother travelling for curtains. It also makes sliding clothes-hangers work better. Ashtrays, too, when smeared with wax are easier to clean and smell fresher.—Mrs G. Barr, 221 Carlisle Road, Ferniegair, Hamilton.

ON FOGGY NIGHTS—Make a filter of butter muslin or other fine material. Tack this over the open part of the window. It keeps the fog out and lets fresh air in.—Mrs E. Dempster, 263 Chirnside Road, Glasgow, S.W.2.

CURTAINS—When you have several rooms curtained with the same material, the curtains often vary in length. I find it saves time and bother to mark each curtain with an initial—F for front room, B for bedroom, etc., so that they are easily paired after laundering.—Mrs A. M. Coe, 14 Hendon Road, Lower Edmonton, London.

ah!
BLUE RIBAND
BLUE RIBAND
GRAY DUNN
CRISP WAFER
FULL CREAM MILK CHOCOLATE
AND DELICIOUS SWEETMEAT
ALL FOR 2½D
MADE BY THE MAKERS OF CARAMEL WAFER, GLENOATA AND CHOCOLATE JOY
GRAY DUNN

STORING CURTAINS—After curtains have been laundered, put them over the bar of a coat hanger and keep than in a wardrobe until needed. This saves drawer space and keeps them unwrinkled.—Mrs J. MacGregor, 15 Dunchurch Road, Paisley.

OLD PEG—Make good use of old spring clothes pegs by using wooden parts as window wedges, etc.—Mrs C. McCreadie, 21 Princes Street, Ayr.

DRIPPING WINDOWS—If you have to contend with dripping windows in winter buy a sheet of foam rubber, cut it in strips to fit and place on the window sills.—Mrs H. W. Johnson, 48 Lamarisk Road, South Ockenden, Romford.

SPOTS AND SMEARS—To remove spots and smears of paint from windows, fittings and hands after decorating, use nail polish remover. Cotton wool twisted round a stick and immersed in polish remover reaches the most awkward corners and removes the paint immediately.—Mrs E. M. Stark, 10 Park Avenue, Stirling.

DRAUGHT PROOF—To keep out draughts from metal windows. I seal them with thin rolls of Plasticine. It is easily removed and can be re-used the following winter.—Mrs A. Hudson, Budle Cottages, Bamburgh.

PREVENTS THOSE AWKWARD TEARS—When making net curtains, get a length of white tape 1½ inches wide, double it and sew it on to the top of the hem. Slip the rod through this tape. There is no fear of tearing the curtains when inserting or taking out the rod.—Mrs W. Scott, 16 Townhead Road, Newton Mearns, Renfrewshire, wins this week's half-guinea.

THE SUNDAY POST JULY 4, 1954

The Sunday Post

Morning Special

PRINTED AND PUBLISHED EVERY SUNDAY MORNING.

No. 2549. | SUNDAY, JULY 4, 1954. | Radio and TV—Page 4 | PRICE 2½d.

RUMP STEAK AT 7s 6d A LB. IN LONDON!

THE BATTLE OF THE BEEF PRICES IS ON

BEEF will cost anything from 8d to 1s 6d a pound more tomorrow. This was the forecast of Scottish butchers yesterday.

But butchers are determined to bring the prices down as soon as possible. "A few weeks should see a substantial fall," said a leading East of Scotland butcher last night.

"The panic-buying and high prices of the past few days frighten us. But as more cattle come forward in July and August, and the public and butchers possibly hold off buying, prices will drop."

Dundee's new meat prices will be decided today.

Mr W. K. Fitzgerald, president of Dundee and District Master Butchers' Association, said last night he estimated that best frying steak will be selling at 4s 10d per lb., an increase of 1s 4d.

He believes there will also be an increase of 1s 4d per lb. for best stewing steak—from 3s 2d to 4s 6d.

Panic-Buying

Many butchers in the West yesterday said it was panic that sent the prices sky-high. They claimed it was a buying authority that started the meat scramble.

This offered the farmers 20 per cent. more for their beef than the Government had paid. Many farmers accepted.

When other carcases were brought to the meat markets all over the country, bargaining began at this inflated level.

Up and up went the prices. One butcher said: "They properly set the heather on fire in the market."

Some small men had to withdraw from the bargaining. They couldn't afford to pay the inflated prices and risk heavy losses. They said they'd stick to sausages rather than take steak at 5s a pound.

Prices Forecast

Hundreds of cattle were slaughtered. Hundreds more were turned away. Killing was continued in Glasgow, Dundee and other places yesterday—an unusual thing for a Saturday.

A Glasgow butcher forecast: Shoulder steak 5s 6d, rump 4s, fillet 4s. Another butcher said his prices would be at least 6d dearer.

[illegible]

A leading **Arbroath** butcher said: "I cannot see a rise of less than 1s and I wouldn't be a bit surprised if it's 2s 6d. But in three or four weeks the market will ease."

"Free meat" was on sale in **Aberdeen** yesterday. The average price was up by about 6d a pound.

Mr D. Clark, president of Dunfermline and District Retail Butchers' Association, said, "I don't anticipate there will be an increase of above 8d to 10d in the pound."

The Association's secretary, Mr James Mills, said he was starting tomorrow with an average increase of 6d a pound.

"There's a chance that we might have to raise it a little above that, but I'd say the maximum would be about 10d."

"Fantastic"

Most butchers at Smithfield Market, heart of the London meat trade, yesterday thought prices of meat would be high at first.

The representative of one firm said, "Rump steaks may be as much as 7s 6d or 7s 6d a pound. But if people hold off buying, prices may well drop again even before the end of the week."

In Manchester some prices being paid by the trade were described as "fantastic."

We're Eating More!

THREE years ago, we in Britain were eating [illegible] tons of meat a week.

NOW we eat over 30,000 tons—an increase of nearly [illegible] per cent.

[illegible]

THESE figures were given yesterday by Dr Charles Hill, Parliamentary Secretary to the Food Ministry.

Dundee Express Stopped In Nick Of Time

PROMPT action by a signalman last night prevented a serious accident at Arlesey (Beds) [illegible].

A goods train was derailed, blocking the down main line from King's Cross just before the Dundee express from King's Cross was due.

[illegible]

EXPLOSION DANGER

[illegible]

Today's Weather

Changeable, with rain or showers at times in most places, but also bright intervals.

Dustman—And 399 Others—At Guinness Wedding

The dustman toasts the bride

The Princess Weds—In Just One Shoe!

PRINCESS Marie-Gabrielle von Urach Wurttemberg yesterday wed the Hon. Desmond Walter Guinness, 22-year-old younger son of Lord Moyne—wearing only one of her shoes.

As the 21-year-old bride walked up the aisle at the start of the service in the cathedral at Christ Church, Oxford, she lost one shoe.

She hesitated, and then went on. The shoe was taken to her at the end of the service.

It was Oxford's biggest society wedding of the year. 400 guests attended the service in the flower-decked cathedral.

One of them was Mr Patrick ("Paddy") O'Reilly, a 60-year-old Dublin dustman, who was invited by mistake after sending a letter of congratulation on reading of the forthcoming marriage.

As he walked alone through the massive outer doors into the quadrangle, Paddy said, "I'm very glad to be here, though it all seems very strange for a working man."

Paddy had hired a morning suit and top hat for the occasion. He had sent the bride a piece of shamrock, and in his own button-hole sported a white carnation.

As he walked across the quadrangle, he was joined by Lord Moyne, who went with him into the cathedral.

Paddy said—"The Guinnesses are a fine family—always were very democratic."

The bride is the daughter of Prince Albrecht von Urach, Count of Wurttemberg. Lord Moyne is vice-chairman of Arthur Guinness, Son & Co., the brewers.

The best man was the Hon. Jonathan Guinness, the bridegroom's 24-year-old elder brother.

There were five bridesmaids, three of them small children.

Because of showery weather, the reception was held in the Great Hall of the College, instead of in the gardens as planned.

There were strawberries and cream, champagne and two barrels of stout for the guests.

Pole Found Dead After Attacking Wife

THE body of Jerzy Zagrodnik, a Polish textile worker at Almondbank, has been recovered from a loch in Glenisla.

His wife, mother-in-law and child are living in Glenisla.

Two years ago Mr Zagrodnik figured in a prolonged legal action in which he sought custody of his daughter, Mary Beatrice, who is now six.

Sheriff Prain, Perth, granted him custody, but this was overturned by the Court of Session after his wife, Esther, appealed.

Mr Zagrodnik was allowed to see Mary Beatrice every Sunday between 10 and 4 and every Monday between 10 and 3. He was also allowed to have her for certain holiday periods.

He had travelled every week-end to see his daughter.

Mrs Zagrodnik told a reporter last night—

"He came by taxi on Friday afternoon. I was putting Mary to bed upstairs when I heard a thud and a strange noise coming from downstairs.

"I ran down and he was at the living-room door with a chisel in his hand. My mother had been hit on the head. He slashed my hand, then my ear. All this time I was screaming for help and he suddenly left me and ran out the door."

Mrs Zagrodnik staggered out into the road still shouting for help. Seventeen-year-old James Miller, who lives in the next house, ran for the police, while his mother tended the women's wounds until a doctor arrived from Kirriemuir.

Mrs Zagrodnik had several stitches put in her hand and ear. Her 68-year-old mother, Mrs Beatrice Fyfe, had a scalp wound.

Dumbock — The Two Men Work On

THE two men who refused to down tools and continued to work at Dumback No. 1 mine, Harthill—Peter Woodhead and John Somerville—went to their work yesterday undisturbed.

Chapter 10
The Coal Fire

A LOT of homes had coal fires. The heat they provided was wonderful on a cold day, and for small boys (and girls) being allowed to light the paper and kindling was an adventure.

But a roaring fire drew air in the room up the chimney, which meant air had to be replaced somehow. This was known as a draught—and it was no fun to sit in a draught.

Coal fires also meant a lot of work to break up and bring in the coal, and clean out the grate in the morning.

IF YOU'RE BOTHERED WITH A SMOKY FIRE—To prevent the fire from smoking on a damp day, set it in the usual way, put a handful of paper or shavings on top of the coal. Light this and let it burn away before lighting the fire. This produces a current of hot air in the chimney which draws the smoke up.—Mrs William McCutcheon, High Dowalton, Sorbie, Wigtown, wins this week's guinea.

FREE LIGHTERS—Don't throw away old linoleum. Cut it into strips, keep in a box, and you have a good supply of firelighters.—Mrs M. Eadie, 227 Mosspark Drive, Glasgow.

SOOTY HANDS—After working with soot, always rinse hands with cold water first. Hot water opens the pores and makes the soot more difficult to remove.—Mrs S. B. Guy, 121 Hirst Road, Harthill, wins a pair of towels.

TAKE CARE—When putting hair-combings in the fire, make sure they burn. Otherwise they stick to the chimney and gather deposits of soot.—J. Royan, 166 Butterbiggins Road, Glasgow.

EVEN TEMPERATURE—Before replenishing a fire in a sick room, draw glowing red coals to one side, and pack in fresh fuel at the other side. This does not cause the same chilly atmosphere as putting fuel on top of fire.—Mrs W. R. Robertson, Moffat Mills, Airdrie.

FIRE-LIGHTING—When lighting a fire, place two kindling sticks crosswise before putting in the paper. This prevents the paper clogging the air from under the bars. The fire burns quicker when the air flows in.—Mrs P. Barty, 21 Hill Street, Broughty Ferry.

WHEN YOU'RE CLEANING OUT THE FIREPLACE—When clearing ash from the fireplace, place your bucket inside the fireplace and shovel the ashes into it. The draught draws all the floating ash up the chimney.—Mrs R. Wylie, 300 Househillmuir Road, Glasgow, wins this week's guinea.

DRAUGHT EXCLUDERS—When making sausage-shaped draught excluders for doors use plastic for outer covering (sleeves from old plastic coats are ideal). They're kept dust free by wiping with a damp cloth.—Mrs McLellan, 74 Darnley Street, Glasgow.

SOOT DESTROYER—If a strong solution of salt and water is thrown over the coals periodically, less soot will collect in the flues and chimney. The fire, too, will burn clear and bright.—Mrs Johnston, 63 Port Dundas Road, Glasgow.

INTERIOR FIRES—Some interior fires are slow to kindle. A sure and easy way is to push two sheets of newspaper under the fire after it has been set and light from the bottom. It never fails.—Marie Campbell, 17 Drakemire Road, Glasgow.

COAL-SAVING—Before going to bed make a hole in the centre of the fire. The flames will die down, leaving the coal for kindling next morning.—Mrs J. McGrath, Holyoake, Hurlford, Kilmarnock.

★ TOP TIP ★

AN ONION DID THE TRICK—When breaking coal I got a small particle in my eye, which gave me great pain. Nothing would remove it. I cut an onion and held it up. It made my eye water so much that the particle was washed away and I got instant relief.—Mrs E. MacKinnon, 1591 London Road, Glasgow, wins a pair of towels.

HELPS TO SPIN OUT THE COAL—Before taking your next delivery of coal, spread a thick layer of coal dust and coke on the bunker floor. Damp it and when coal is put on top the dross sticks to the coke, which burns like coal.—Mrs I. J. Douglas, East Barns, Dunbar, wins a pair of towels.

COAL BUNKER—Re. last week's hint about damping coal dust and coke to help spin out the coal ration. If the bunker floor is wood, and just a little too much water is used, there's a danger of starting rot in the timber.—Property Agent.

GLOVES—When making household gloves, line them with plastic. This keeps coal dust from going through, and has the added advantage of being washable inside.—Mary Kyles, 326 Victoria Road, Glasgow.

POWER CUTS—When power cuts send you hurrying to place an aluminium pot on the fire, first smear the outside of the pot with damp soap. This forms a skin to which the carbon sticks, and washing the pot later is the work of a minute.—Mrs H. A. Wishart, 23 Woodbank Crescent, Clarkston, Glasgow.

COAL BREAKING—When breaking coal, use a chisel under the hammer. The coal breaks evenly, and no pieces scatter about. —Mrs C. Thomson, c/o Duncan, 117 Sleigh Drive, Edinburgh.

CHIMNEY FIRE—Soak newspapers in water and put them on top of the fire. The steam draws the fire in chimney and puts it out.—Mrs D. Buchanan, Hill Cottage, Brightons, By Falkirk.

SAVES COAL—Place a piece of well damped cardboard flat on a. low fire. Put dross (also well-damped) on top. It will cake and burn like a solid piece of coal and won't choke the fire.—Miss L. Murdoch, 47 High Street, Bonnybridge.

★ TOP TIP ★

MAKES YOUR FIRE GO MUCH FURTHER—A briquette placed at each side of the fireplace when the fire is being set results in a nice glow. Less coal is needed. When the fire needs replenishing, don't disturb the briquettes. What is left of them can be broken up and used to help kindle the fire next morning.—Mrs H. MacBride, 50 King Street, Crieff, wins a pair of towels.

LONG LIFE—Next time you buy a coal pail, fix a sixpenny sandwich tin in the bottom. The pail lasts much longer as the bottom always wears out first.—Miss L Murdoch, 47 High Street, Bonnybridge.

GOOD COAL BOX—A new use for an old bread bin. Paint or enamel it any colour desired, and use as coal or log box.—Mrs B. Forbes, 41 Guthrie Street, Dundee.

★ TOP TIP ★

NO RATTLING DOORS—Cut a piece of cork the exact thickness required to make the door fit firmly when closed. Fix it to the frame a little above the lock with glue. It stops a draughty rattle. Paint it the same colour as the door and it will not be noticed.—Mrs Lees, 364 Easter Road, Edinburgh, wins a pair of towels.

REVIVES FIRE—A medium-sized tin, with both ends removed, revives a dying fire in a few minutes. Placed on top of hot cinders, it acts as a funnel.—Mrs M. O'Hagan, 108 Dorchester Avenue, Glasgow.

DRAUGHTS—To overcome a draught from hinged side of a door or casement window, open it wide and run a strip of adhesive tape about three inches wide from top to base to seal the gap. Paint to match.—F. W. Bell, 18 The Westlands, Chester Road, Sunderland.

COAL BAGS—Old paper bags can be partly filled with coal and placed in the coal bucket. They can be easily put on the fire when needed. This keeps the hearth clean, and makes no noise—especially helpful in sickroom.—Miss Eva Hobson, Hawthorn House, Birtley, County Durham.

PREVENTS DAMAGE—To prevent a fire-grate bottom from buckling and breaking, never allow ashes to pile up and come in contact with the bottom.—Wallace Scott, 21 Southesk Street, Brechin, wins a pair of towels.

COAL SAVER—To save coal, I place a piece of well-damped cardboard flat on a fairly low fire, then put well-damped dross on top. The dross cakes and burns like a solid piece of coal, and, used this way, it doesn't choke the fire.—Miss L. Ross, 21 Brucklay Street, Rosehearty.

CORKS—Old corks soaked in paraffin make excellent firelights. One cork placed among the sticks will set the fire going quickly.—Mrs G. Wood, 103 Green Road, Paisley.

KEEP DUST DOWN—By giving your fire a good clean out at night while the chimney is warm, the dust blows up the chimney. Left until morning, dust tends to blow out.—Mrs Johnston, 63 Port Dundas Road, Glasgow.

MATCHES—If a box of matches become damp and unusable, put a few grains of rice in the box to absorb the damp.—R. Plan, 267 Church Road, Sheldon, Birmingham.

CLEAN CORNERS—When dust and ashes collect in the corners of a tiled hearth and cannot be removed with a soft hearth brush, use a carpet brush. The stiff bristles soon dislodge all the particles.—Mrs T. Kennedy, 54 Hathaway Street, Glasgow.

HANDY GLOVE—Don't throw away an old drawstring sponge bag. Replace the string with elastic and use as a coal glove. It's waterproof, so dust doesn't penetrate to the hand.—Mrs S. A. Grant, 51A Duke Street, Huntly.

POKERS—Fix a rubber cycle handle grip on the poker handle. No fear then of broken hearth tiles.—Mrs R. Elsdon, 18 Palmerston Avenue, Walkergate, Newcastle.

COALS—Before taking in coals for the winter, spread a bag of coke on the cellar floor. When the coal is put on top of the dross it sticks to the coke which then burns like coal.—Mrs D. Smith, 16 Unwin Avenue, Bedfont, Feltham.

FIREGUARD FIXING—To overcome the difficulty of fixing a fireguard to a tiled fireplace, without damage to the tiles, use self -adhesive plastic towel hooks.—Mrs Shepherd, Birkhill, Dundee.

NO DUST—Slip your ash-pan inside an old carrier bag on a windy day. You'll get to the dustbin without being smothered in dust.—Mrs F. H. Butcher, Braehead, Shieldhill, Falkirk.

LIGHTER WORK—When fetching coal in the dark, a good tip is to tie a torch to the handle of your shovel. It leaves one hand free for lifting the coal.—Mrs E. Blake, 46 Seamore Street, Glasgow.

The "Priscilla Page" of September 6, 1959

Snippets

HERE are up-to-the-minute snippets for the needlewoman. One big job has priority. All these winter dresses and coats have to be shortened. The shorter line will be with us again this winter. Usually this sort of sewing's a pretty dreary job and one that's difficult to do expertly. One little droop and the whole job's a mess. But a new gadget makes it much simpler. It's a wooden rule, with a plastic container for powdered chalk. Adjust the rule to the required length. Stand against it, wearing the garment about to be shortened. Then turn round slowly pressing the bulb attached to the plastic container. Out puffs a line of white chalk, marking the hem for you. The gadget costs 19s. 1d.

Perhaps you've come across the latest version of pin cushions? Made in foam plastic, they fit round the wrist with a plastic band. The latest idea is to fit them round the sewing machine. You take out the pins as you sew—and, hey presto! No more pins on the floor. Cost 2s.

Now, what about those shop counters? They're draped with beautiful materials just begging to be sewn! The new printed worsteds are proving most popular. Feather-light, they're easy to manage. They're ideal for blouses and suits, and come in floral or paisley designs at around 18s. 11d. per yard, 36 inches wide. One practical and pretty idea is to make them up as colourful and cosy linings.

Jersey is still fashion's favourite. The 66-inch width is a boon to the home dressmaker, as you need very little for a dress and there's a minimum of sewing necessary. In a host of colours, it's 39s. 11d. a yard.

For sheer, exotic glamour, I saw in a Glasgow shop a roll of white duchess satin from the Continent which quite took my breath away. It's exquisitely embroidered with pink orchids and delicate green leaves. The price took my breath away, too! Eight guineas a yard! But an ambitious and very-sure-of-herself dressmaker could make a gown to equal the 70-guinea creations from Paris and absolutely stun her friends. And can you just imagine it as a bridal gown?

A trifle less expensive, but still in the luxury class, there's lovely Lurex brocade. One example had cabbage roses in red and pink twinkling with gold thread. It's 69s. 6d. a yard!

There are lots of "quickies", too, for a needlewoman who hasn't loads of time. Red car cushion covers took my fancy. They're printed with the design of an authentic vintage car to be embroidered in bright yellow. Not a great deal of sewing to do—and being in one colour they can be done quickly. Cost 6s. 11d.

I liked the contemporary table covers in rayon. They're white at the centre and edged with large squares in different colours. All you have to do is embroider a posy of flowers in white in the centre of each square. Simple—but really most effective. Prices are 12s. 11d. and 13s. 11d.

Chapter 11
Sewing For Experts

IN the early 1950s there weren't many clothes to choose from. Clothes rationing ended in 1949, but it took a long time, and a good few bob, for the ordinary man, woman and child to get back to the point where they had a full wardrobe.

What little they did have was passed down and re-used, so needed mending and altering on the way. This became especially important when teenagers were discovered in the middle of the decade—clothes had sometimes to be reinvented into another garment altogether.

These women knew what they were talking about. They were, after all, vastly experienced tailors working for the most critical employers—those they lived with.

PREVENTS EYESTRAIN—To prevent eyestrain when sewing or knitting, always work with a white cloth on your lap to throw the work into relief. Use light needles when knitting dark wool and dark needles for light wool.—Mrs. A. Bird, St Anne's, 101 Westcliff Park Drive, Southend-on-Sea, wins a pair of towels.

AN EASY JOB—When cutting flimsy dress material, I find that it makes the job much easier to lay newspaper under the material, pin the paper pattern securely in position, then cut both material and newspaper.—Mrs Walker, 260 Glebe Road, Merewether, 2N, N.S.W, Australia.

HANDY—Use a marble as a miniature darning "egg" when mending finger-tips of gloves.—Mrs H. Smith, 14 John Street, Ruabon, Wrexham.

NEW LOOK—I have a pretty, washable bedroom rug. The edges had become frayed, but the rest was in perfect condition. With a packing needle and fine, soft string I blanket-stitched the rug all along the edges. It has made a wonderful job, and the rug will now last a few more years.—Mrs A. Bird, 101 Westcliff Park Drive, Southend-on-Sea.

★ TOP TIP ★

ALL READY—When dyeing any article of clothing, drop a reel of white cotton into the dye. Then you have matching thread for repairs. — Miss A. A. Mitchell, 5 North Shore Street, Campbeltown, wins a pair of towels.

SAFETY MEASURE—After oiling the sewing machine, run a piece of blotting paper through as you would material. This prevents fabric being spotted by oil.—Mrs D. Thomson, 1 Tower Terrace, Kirkcaldy.

GOOD FINISH—When making chair-backs, machine round one inch from edge then fray out the material. This makes a real fringe and gives a professional-looking finish.—Mrs Rita S. Gooch, Belhaven, 53 Milton Crescent, Portobello.

ZIP FASTENER—If the puller on the zip of your frock is small and awkward to pull, make a dainty tassel with matching embroidery thread or wool to suit the garment. Attach it to the puller and you've no further difficulty.—Mrs C. Gray, 18 Lippiatt Road, Otahuhu, Auckland, New Zealand.

HIDDEN—Broken shoulder straps often tear away part of the garment. The ensuing darn or mend can be attractively disguised by the application of a simple embroidered or lace motif.—Mrs A. M. Connelly, 23 Invergyle Drive, Cardonald, Glasgow.

PLASTIC CURTAINS—When sewing plastic curtains, rub your machine's plate well with talcum powder. Also sprinkle some on teeth and foot of machine. This stops the plastic from sticking.—Mrs Tulloch, 25 Acacia Grove, South Shields, Co. Durham.

THICK MATERIALS—Before machining thick material such as Turkish towelling (after tacking hems), run through a mangle to reduce the bulk of the hems and make them easy to machine.—G. Hadden, 13 Neville Terrace, Priestgate, Peterborough.

STITCH IN TIME—Children's shoe laces sometimes don't last long. Do a few rows of machine stitching up and down and they last much longer.—Mrs R. Horsham, 289 Maryhill Road, Glasgow.

ZIP SAFE—When you make a dress, fix the zip so that it pulls down to close. This stops it from opening accidentally.—Miss C. Wood, 53 Roxburgh Street, Kelso.

FOR THE INVALID—When making a bed jacket for an invalid, be sure to add a pocket. Then that much-needed hankie won't get lost in the bedclothes.—Mrs Queenan, Kirkton, Hawick.

VELVET—When trimming with velvet, sew on a backing of canvas. The velvet will lie flat.—Mrs J. Young, c/o Busby, 34 Hopetoun Place, Townhead, Glasgow.

PINHOLDER—Wrap a band of flannel, about two inches wide, twice round the horizontal bar of your sewing machine and secure with a safety pin. This saves minutes when sewing as there is always somewhere to put a pin and somewhere to find one.—Mrs M. McRae, 2 Manor Place, Broughty Ferry.

ZIPS—When the zip of a skirt refuses to stay closed, insert a piece of looped elastic through the hole at top of zip. Then attach to button on skirt band. You should then have no trouble.—Miss C. T. Bell, 913 Dumbarton Road, Glasgow, wins a pair of towels.

NEEDLES—When sewing stiff material and the needle is difficult to pull through, run needle through a cake of soap. Do this frequently and the sewing is easy.—Mrs Attwell, c/o Cunningham, 67 Elderslie Street, Glasgow.

SMOOTH RUNNING—If your sewing machine isn't running well, remove the needle. Take out the screw that holds the footplate, remove it, and you'll be surprised at the amount of fluff collected there. Clean the shuttle grooves and under the whole of the plate with a penknife. This may be the cause of the machine running hard and not carrying the work.—Miss M. Penny, by Stirling.

A NEW IDEA FOR THE PIN-CUSHION—When making a pin-cushion, pack it with steel wool. It keeps your needles and pins always shining and free from rust.—Mrs C. Bowie, 154 New Row, Dunfermline, wins a pair of towels.

BUTTONHOLE REINFORCEMENT—Fine string makes an ideal buttonhole reinforcement. Simply place the string round buttonhole and stitch in the usual way. J. Thomson, 404 Dumbarton Road, Dalmuir, Glasgow.

SEWING—When cutting a paper pattern, use pinking scissors to cut out seams. After they've been stitched and pressed they require no further attention.—Mrs N. Young, 11 Windsor Terrace, Glasgow.

TACKING THREADS—Use a buttonhook instead of scissors to take out tacking threads, then there's no risk of cutting the material.—Mrs J. Nicol, Gordondale, Port Elphinstone, Inverurie.

NON-SLIP—Put a pillow slip over shelf of your machine when sewing slippery material and the material won't slip off.—Mrs J. Scott, 15 Fairhill Place, Meikle Earnock, Hamilton.

CREASE-FREE—A firm shoulder pad, attached point downwards to the centre of a dress hanger at the base of the hook, prevents creasing frock and blouse collars.—Miss E. Walsh, 130 Barlow Street, Preston.

HANDY—Pieces of fine sandpaper kept in an envelope in your mending basket are handy for needles that become rusty.—Miss N. Gall, 1 chapel Court, Justice Street, Aberdeen.

LASTING—Instead of sewing buttons on with ordinary thread, sew with fine shirring elastic. If there's any pull on the button, the elastic will "give".—Mrs J. Byrne, 111 Fulton Street, Anniesland, Glasgow.

★ TOP TIP ★

PERMANENT PLEATING—When making a permanently-pleated skirt I found it difficult to tack the band on to the skirt. So first I held them together with transparent adhesive tape then machined them. This proved a great success and I only had to pull the tape off afterwards.—Mrs Paterson, 25 Hermiston Road, Springboig, Glasgow, wins a pair of towels.

HANDY HOLDER—To keep your tape measure clean and uncracked, roll it round a used one-inch Elastoplast container.—Mrs G. McKay, 39A Fraser Place, Dysart.

SKIRTS—When making a dirndl skirt, a quick method is to use Rufflette tape for the band. Sew it on to the material and pull cord to size of waist required.—Mrs A. Wallace, 6 Clepington Street, Dundee.

NEEDLES—Wash steel knitting needles and crochet hooks in hot soapy water before new work. Metal pins which have been left are apt to snag the first row of new garments or lace work.—Miss Wilson, Recreation Ground, Fulwell Road, Sunderland.

FINGER PROTECTION—One or two coats of nail varnish, painted on the first finger of the left hand, protects the finger when sewing.—Mrs M. Brown, 167 Station Road, Lochgelly.

PATCHING—When patching the leg of a pair of trousers, slip a cork table mat under the hole, then pin on the patch. No fear of pinning in the other side of the leg.—Mrs J. I. Tait, 23 Burgh Road, Lerwick.

SMOOTH FINISH—When making a new skirt, machine all the seams to the top, including the seam where the zip is to be. Keeping the skirt inside out, tack the zip in position, face downwards, exactly in the middle of the seam. Back-stitch round the zip as close to the teeth as possible, turn skirt right side out, and unpick the seam to the end of the zip. This will give a perfectly smooth finish.—Mrs Wilkie, 46 Croft Crescent, Markinch, Fife.

PAPER PATTERNS—When cutting out paper patterns, instead of cutting notches inwards, cut a pointed piece outwards. It is easier to match when putting the garment together and does not weaken the seam allowance.—Mrs Jackson, 22 Park View, Ashington, Northumberland.

DRESS REPAIRS—Matching material to repair a dress can be taken from the shoulder pads. The pads can be recovered with any piece of odd material.—Mrs D. King, Northward, Newmachar.

TACKING THREADS—Tacking threads are easily taken out if a buttonhook is used instead of scissors. There's no risk of cutting the material.—Mrs A. Wilson, 13 Barclay Street, Glasgow.

PREVENTS FRAYING—When making buttonholes in loosely-woven material, paint a thin line of colourless nail varnish over the mark where the buttonhole is to be made. Allow to dry, then cut with a razor blade.—Miss A. Spence, 14 Ravenshall Road, Glasgow.

EMBROIDERY TIP—When doing embroidery, keep all the silks between the pages of a closed book, leaving the ends showing. The colours can easily be picked out as needed.—Mrs E. Huston, 127 Oban Road, Byker, Newcastle.

RUSTPROOF—Prevent needles from going rusty by keeping them in a small bottle with a drop or two of sewing-machine oil.—Mrs M. Lawson, 21 Craigentinny Avenue North, Edinburgh.

MAKES THE JOB EASY—Cloth-covered buttons are difficult to sew on to a garment. The job is made much easier if a small eye (from hook and eye) is first sewn on to the centre back of each button. This makes a shank to hold the thread firmly.—Mrs Selbie, Toll House, Kinnernie, Dunecht, Aberdeenshire.

KEEPS SKIRT NEAT—If the waistband of your skirt is too slack, slot a piece of elastic (a little narrower than band) through the band at back of skirt. Finish off neatly. This keeps your skirt in position.—Mrs T. Vasey, 34 The Ridgeway, South Shields.

WON'T FRAY—Cut into an old candle with your scissors before cutting material that frays easily. The wax from the scissors binds the edges.—A. M. Murray, 44 Shuna Street, Ruchill, Glasgow.

NO SHRINK—Cord, which is to be used for piping in cushions, loose covers, etc., should always be washed with hot soapy water before use. This prevents the seams puckering through the cord shrinking when the articles are first washed.—Mrs McLellan, 74 Darnley Street, Glasgow.

PATCHES—Before sewing leather patches on elbows or cuffs, take the cut-out piece of leather and run round the edge with an unthreaded needle in the sewing machine, using a large sized stitch. Make the line of punctures as close to the edge as possible without splitting the leather. These holes will space your hand stitches evenly and make it easier to sew. A much neater patch will result.—Mrs W. Stewart, Dunfermline Road, Crossgates, Fife.

★ TOP TIP ★

FOR BLOUSES—To prevent blouses and skirts gaping, tack a one-inch strip of plastic foam rubber Inside the waistband of the skirt. It adheres to the flimsiest material.—Mrs M. Jeffrey, 27 Moyne Road, Glasgow, wins a pair of towels.

EMBROIDERY—When doing embroidery, tack cellophane paper over finished parts. This keeps it clean, while effect and colours can be plainly seen during completion of work.—Mrs C. Smith, 3 Harlaw Terrace, Inverurie.

PERFECT FIT—Elastic thread knitted along with the wool into the ribbing of waist, legs and all round top will give a perfect fit to a knitted swim suit.—Mrs Runcie, 6 Seatown, Cullen.

CHILDREN'S HELP—When small children are learning to dress themselves sew a coloured cross on the inside front of all their garments. These help the bairns to put clothes on the right way round.—Miss S. Cooper, 29 Parksway, Pendlebury, Lancs.

TOWELS—When the edges of towels show signs of fraying, double crochet down each side, using a ball of silk. The towel looks neat, and the edges last until the towel wears out.—Miss E. Coleman, 28 Peveril Street, Ormeau Road, Belfast.

INVISIBLE—After repairing a three-cornered tear in a suit, coat, etc., take a needle and scratch the seam on the right side. This raises the pile and makes an invisible mend.—Mrs H. Bingham, 8 Logie Place, Aberdeen.

STRING CLOTHS—Before using a new string dishcloth, stitch all round the edges. This prevents the string giving way and adds considerably to the wear of the cloth.—Mrs Briggs, Hollybrae, Brigham, Coldstream, Berwickshire.

PILLOW FEATHERS—When changing pillow feathers into new ticking, rip cover of old pillow at one end, and sew new ticking tightly to it. Shake feathers from old pillow into new. Rip out stitches and sew new pillow in usual way. Not a feather escapes. —Mrs McGuire, 71 Dukes Road, Cambuslang, Glasgow.

TAFFETA—If your hat is trimmed with taffeta loops, and they need freshening up, stuff the folds with tissue paper and hold them in the steam from a kettle. The ribbon stiffens up and looks like new.—Miss A. Tindal, 24 Baldwin Avenue, Glasgow.

SHIRTS—To enlarge a shirt neck and collar, cut two Vs, one at either side in the shirt neck, and over sew with buttonhole stitch. Work in similar fashion to inside part of collar.—Mrs Miller, 18 Fordyce Street, Glasgow.

REPLACING BUTTON—If a button is torn off and leaves a hole, don't "cobble" it. Sew the button to a small square of material as nearly as possible matching the garment. Push the button through the hole from the back then fell the new material to the old behind the button.—Mrs MacKenzie, 21 Cooper Street, Bishopmill, Elgin.

STEAM IT—Before using a new skein or card of darning wool, hold it in steam from a boiling kettle, then let it dry. The wool doesn't shrink after use.—Miss M. B. Brown, 1039 Tollcross Road, Glasgow.

FOR LOOSE COVERS—Boil the piping cord before making loose covers or cushion covers. If left until the covers are washed, the cord may shrink and the covers will pucker.—Mrs J. C. Wilson, 29 Brownhill Road, Glasgow.

MITT LININGS—After knitting winter mitts for baby, line them with white lint. The little hands are kept nice and warm. —Mrs A. Macdonald, 4 Kinkell Terrace, St Andrews.

UMBRELLAS—When the cover of an umbrella parts company with a spoke, stitch down with elastic thread. This provides the necessary "give".—Mrs J. Muir, c/o 8 Grossart Street, Salsburgh.

TANGLE-FREE—When sewing with double thread, knot both ends separately. This prevents the threat of tangling.—Mrs Craig, 12 Shore Street, Sandhaven, Fraserburgh.

RUG-MAKING—I use my ironing table for rug-making. It takes up less space and gives good support as the work progresses. Keep different coloured wools in cellophane bags to keep clear and easy to get at.—J. Anderson, 81 Burns Street, Clydebank.

STRAIGHT SKIRTS—Fashionable straight skirts (particularly those made of soft tweeds and woollens) must be lined if you don't want them to seat. Best material is a strong sateen or cotton, and for a first-class job, you should cut it on the cross. Stitch it into the waistband and catch it with a few stitches at the side seams.—Mrs J. Brown, Sunderland.

DARNING—If you find a darning mushroom too broad for a toddler's socks, the old fashioned type of egg cup with stem and base makes a good substitute. It does not stretch the sock. —Mrs G. C. Fisken, Mayfield, Tibbermore, by Perth.

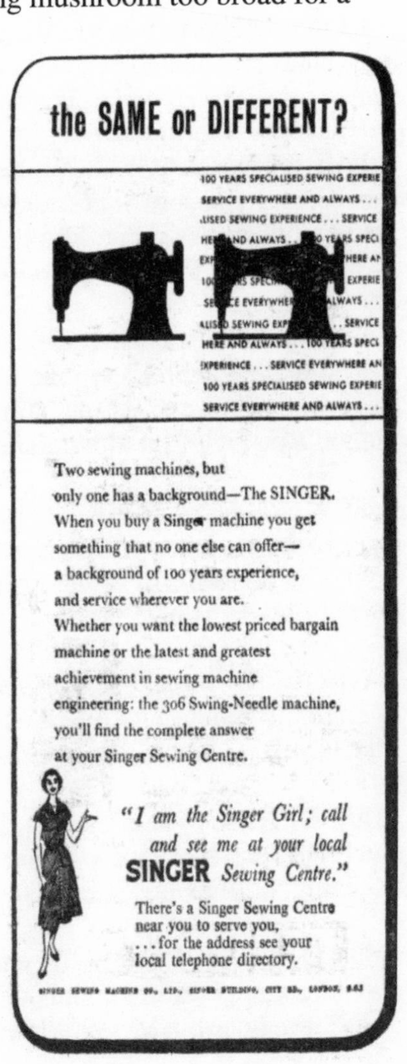

PERFECT MATCH—If you are planning to let out the seams of a dress, sew the new seams first then rip out the old ones. In this way the edges are sure to meet.—Mrs M. Thompson, 12 Davidson Street, Lancaster.

UNUSUAL PATCHES—When the knees of children's dungarees wear out, put on patches of contrasting colours, cut out in the shapes of rabbits, dogs, etc. Children love them.—Mrs A. Frew, 22 Back Rogerton Crescent, Auchinleck.

EASY TO FIND—A small cork, glued inside workbox or drawer, is an ideal stand for that thimble which so often gets lost.—Mrs N. McLellan, 74 Darnley Street, Glasgow.

STRONG POCKETS—When your husband is having a suit made, supply the tailor with a piece of cheap gloving leather for pocket linings. The pockets will outlive the suit.—J. Gray, 268 Saracen Street, Glasgow.

STRONG BUTTONS—To fix buttons on firmly, keep a piece of beeswax in your sewing box and run it along the thread. This strengthens the thread.—Miss E. Tappenden, 5 Nutt Street, London.

NO LOST BELTS—Some raincoats have no latches for belts. I solved this by cutting a bit off the hood tapes and making them into latches.—Mrs A. Fyfe, 39 Brandon Street, Dennistoun, Glasgow.

COAT LINING—When the lining of a coat is beginning to wear round the armholes, stitch on bias binding, taking care to catch both sides of the seams.—Mrs M. Martin, 6 Kinloan Crescent, Cupar.

KEEPS IN PLACE—Children's braces don't slip off their shoulders if you sew a short loop of tape to underside of one of the braces at the cross-point. Slip the other through the tape loop.—Mrs A. E. Shapland, 257 Turnpike Road, Pittsburg, Mass., USA.

SOCKS—I always darn my husband's Terylene and nylon socks with stranded embroidery silk. I find this lengthens their life, and I can usually get an exact matching shade.—Mrs J. Livingstone, 107 Station Road, Golcar, Huddersfield.

SEWING MACHINE—I keep my sewing machine on top of an ordinary tea trolley. This is excellent for easy moving to a good light. The bottom part of the trolley holds sewing materials etc. —Mrs H. Adamson, 53E Clyde Street, Helensburgh.

GLOVES—Mend chamois leather gloves with fine wool instead of cotton. Wool doesn't tear the leather so easily.—Mrs Jean McCulloch, 17 Mark Street, Galashiels.

EVEN HEM—To prevent a flared skirt drooping at the side, stitch in a length of tape when sewing up the side seams.—Miss G. B. Craig, 53 Benview Street, Glasgow.

DOES A GOOD JOB—If you've difficulty pressing sleeve and shoulder seams when making a garment, pad a rolling pin and use as a sleeve board.—Mrs A. McMaster, 28 Otago Street, Glasgow.

★ TOP TIP ★

HERE'S A TIP WHEN SEWING PLASTIC—When sewing plastic by machine or hand, take a piece of white chalk and make a thick line where you intend to stitch. This keeps the plastic from splitting.—Mrs Bushby, 23 Herbert Street, Harraby, Carlisle, wins a pair of towels.

RIBBING—When the ribbed wristband of a jumper or cardigan gets loose and baggy, tie a knot in the wristband and leave for a few days. On untying the knot the ribbing is tight again.—Nora J. Goodbody, 4 Clarendon Street, Cambridge.

DARNING—When you've a big hole in a sock to repair put a piece of fine net across the hole and tack in place all round. Darn through the netting in the ordinary way. This strengthens the darn and keeps heel or toe in shape.—Mrs W. Clements, 126 Coverington Road, Motherwell.

LIGHTWEIGHT BUTTONS—For thin materials most buttons are too heavy. For a silk housecoat I made I bought ordinary linen buttons and stem-stitched them with coloured sewing silks.—Mrs J. P. Roe, 28 Highholm Street, Port Glasgow.

REVERSED HANGERS—You will have no difficulty in keeping little gym tunics or pinafore dresses on an ordinary hanger if you reverse the hook and use the hanger upside down.—Mrs Henderson, 12 Nellfield Place, Aberdeen.

NON-TEAR ZIP—Lay a piece of stiff ribbon (one inch wide) flat behind a zip fastener. Stitch at both ends and down one side. This prevents underwear being caught in the teeth of the zip.—Mrs M. Mart, 36 Eskview Crescent, Musselburgh.

SNUG FIT—If you find your hat is loose after a haircut, take a strip of rubber foam and stitch it inside the band at back. The hat fits snugly.—Mrs A. Stewart, 4 Gauldry Avenue, Glasgow.

SOFTER KAPOK CUSHIONS—Remove dust bag from vacuum cleaner and in its place tie on a clean cushion cover. Spread the lumpy kapok on linoleum floor and run the machine over it. In a few minutes the kapok, beautifully milled, fills the cushion cover. Without a vacuum it must be fluffed by hand.—Mrs W. Whiting, 13 Friars Close, Hassocks, West Sussex.

APRONS—I make my own aprons. I sew the pocket on the wrong side, slantways. It's easy to slip my hand in. I never rip the pockets on knobs or have accidents catching them on projections.—Elizabeth Bowes, 10 Highfield View Road, Chesterfield.

QUICK TIDY—Home dressmakers know what a nuisance threads of cotton on the carpet can be. Try using a damp scrubbing brush over the carpet. It speedily and easily gathers up loose pieces of sewing thread.—Mrs D. MacIver, Victoria Terrace, Ardrishaig.

WARMER TEA—When making a tea cosy, put a sheet of aluminium foil between the outside and the lining. It keeps the teapot a lot warmer.—Mrs E. F. A. Wallace, 4 Alexander Drive, Edinburgh.

TO SEAL SEAMS—To stop edges fraying when dressmaking, use a plastic textile adhesive. Press out a light film of gum at edge of material. This doesn't stain material, nor is it affected by ironing. —Mrs B. Ferris, 29 Saughton Gardens, Edinburgh.

KEEP THIS IN MIND WHEN MENDING BEDSHEETS—To fix a big patch on a bed sheet, pin each corner of patch to the sheet, then run machine stitching right down the centre. Take out a corner pin at a time and run the sides down. By this method you get no crooked or loose patches.—Miss MacGregor, Sutherland Cottage, Keir Street, Dunblane, wins a pair of towels.

HANDY MEASURE—When sewing on several buttons which have to be evenly spaced, tack a tape measure in position first.—Mrs C. Proton, 410 Shieldhall Road, Glasgow.

BINDING—Stitching binding evenly to the edge of matting can be a tricky job. Ordinary pins are too short to fix the binding in position. But spring clothes pegs make for easier sewing.—Mrs Jean Gibson, 9 Church Lane, Denny.

CUSHIONS—When making a cushion, make the inner pad of thin plastic sheeting—the kind stocked by chain stores. Two 13-inch squares, stitched together, make the cushion. It can be stuffed with any old rags, yet the result is a lovely, smooth, squashy cushion.—Mrs M. John, 35 Coed-Saeson Crescent, Sketty, Swansea.

A USE FOR OLD COAT—My coat was silver grey. I took out the lining, measured evenly seven inches from bottom of coat and cut through this line. Then I inserted a seven-inch strip of dark red cord velvet. I cut off collar and lapels at turnover mark and put a two-inch binding of the velvet down the fronts and round the neck, two-inch strap on pockets and round bottom of sleeves. I bought a shilling cord girdle—and now have a cosy dressing gown.—Mrs C. Harkness, Kinmount Bungalow, Annan.

TROUSER POCKETS—If these are showing signs of wear, take a matching thread and closely buttonhole along the edge of pockets.—Mrs James Scott, 42 William Street, Tayport.

BATHROOM SET—When making towelling curtains for the bathroom, buy a little extra and make towel and bath mat to match. To make the bath mat, stitch the material by hand to a piece of foam rubber.—Mrs M. Caskie, 1 Akers Avenue, Locharbriggs, Dumfries.

IT'S A BOON ON A WINDY DAY—To help prevent your raincoat blowing about on windy days, sew a smooth piece of metal into the bottom corners of the front hem.—Mrs R. Donaldson, c/o Riddle, 22 Loganlea Drive, Edinburgh, wins a pair of towels.

★ TOP TIP ★

EXTRA COVERINGS—Now is the time to prepare extra bed coverings for winter. To increase the size of blankets that have shrunk, or to make single blankets big enough for double beds, sew to each side (and to the foot if necessary) a strip of flannelette or similar material. These can be tucked in, leaving the actual blanket for covering.—Mrs K. Leishman, 10 Wardlaw Place, Edinburgh, wins a pair of towels.

The Sunday Post

Morning Special

PRINTED AND PUBLISHED EVERY SUNDAY MORNING.

SUNDAY, SEPTEMBER 5, 1954. Radio and TV—Page 4 PRICE 2½d.

EVERY REASON FOR CONFIDENCE, SAYS SUPPLY MINISTER

COMET—GOOD NEWS!

LIKELY TO FLY AGAIN SOON

THERE is every reason for confidence that it will be possible to make the Comet safe.

Production may be resumed before very long.

This was stated yesterday by Mr Duncan Sandys, Minister of Supply.

He said—"Our technical investigations have yielded clear and positive results. These indicate that some strengthening of certain parts of the structure of the Comet is necessary.

"I am advised that introduction of these changes is entirely practicable, and should not involve any fundamental re-design of the aircraft.

"It is intended as soon as possible to modify a Comet in this way, and to test it out at Farnborough.

"We must reserve final opinion about future prospects until these further tests have been carried out, and the conclusions of the court of inquiry are known.

"But the extensive information already available gives every reason for confidence that it will be possible to make the Comet safe and satisfactory, and to resume production before very long."

Giant Jigsaw

The statement said that assembling technical evidence for the inquiry had inevitably been a lengthy business.

It involved, among other things, recovering the crashed aircraft from the bottom of the sea.

The investigations involved three main tasks:—

(1) Innumerable fragments of the wreckage—some large and others very small—had been pieced together like a giant jig-saw puzzle. Every scratch or dent on them had been closely scrutinised by experts.

(2) A carefully-planned programme of test flying had been carried out.

(3) A series of exhaustive tests had been made with a view to discovering any structural weakness.

18-Hour Day

Mr Sandys' announcement is the first official statement to be made about the results achieved by the scientists.

For months past, they have been working at high pressure—in some cases 18 hours a day—to establish the cause of the crashes which cost 99 lives.

These were at:—

Mr Duncan Sandys

Calcutta on May 2, 1953 (43 dead).

Elba on January 10, 1954, (35 dead).

Naples on April 8, 1954 (21 dead).

As a result of the accidents the Comets have been grounded for five months. Their airworthiness certificates were withdrawn after the third disaster.

Most of the work on Comet II and III jet airliners has been suspended while the scientists have been conducting their researches, so that any necessary modifications can be incorporated in the new planes.

Comets On Order

Orders for 63 new Comets, worth £30 million, had been received the time work on them was suspended.

A B.O.A.C. spokesman said yesterday the Corporation has 12 Comet IIs on order and 5 Comet IIIs, and an option on 5 more Comet IIIs.

"Our plans for the future include the use of Comets II and III on world-wide routes, together with the Bristol Britannia, another great British aircraft."

It Wasn't Meant To Be So Sore!

FREDDIE MILLS, 34-year-old former cruiser-weight boxing champion of the world, was knocked out last night on TV.

He was appearing in a programme from the National Radio Show at Earls Court.

With a comedy team known as the "Two Pirates," Freddie was clowning his way through a comedy boxing booth sketch.

Then someone picked up a stool and hit him over the head with it.

Freddie took his bow, staggered off and collapsed.

A B.B.C. spokesman said afterwards, "Mr Mills should have been hit with a property stool. Unfortunately a real stool was used.

"Mr Mills collapsed in a dazed condition in his dressing-room, but recovered later."

U.S. Officers Killed

TWO U.S. officers stationed on Quemoy Island were killed during the Chinese Communist shelling.

Shelling of the islands was resumed yesterday.

U.S. Defence Department experts held conferences yesterday to consider the significance of the Communist bombardment.

Chinese Nationalists thought the shelling a prelude to invasion.

Two 16-Year-Old Girls In The Runaway Queue At Gretna

THERE were four runaway girls at Gretna yesterday. Two of them are 16 years of age.

One of the runaways, 16-year-old Doreen Wilson, 6 Liverpool House, Holloway Road, London, made a plea to a reporter to ask her mother and father to forgive her and come to her wedding on Wednesday.

Doreen has not heard from home since she ran away nearly three weeks ago with 21-year-old Robert Scalley.

She said, "Robert's mother is coming to the wedding. More than anything else, I wish my mother and dad would forgive me and come, too."

There are nearly three weeks of waiting ahead for the other three girls—16-year-old Margaret Rice of Yelverton Cottage, Meavy Lane, Yelverton, Plymouth;

Sixteen-year-old Sylvia Dayus, paper bag maker, 26 Lichfield Road, Aston, Birmingham;

Seventeen-year-old Marlene Haddon, 187 Attleborough Road, Nuneaton, Warwickshire.

All fled to Gretna to be married because of their parents' objection to their weddings.

All three and their fiances will be at Doreen's wedding on Wednesday.

Police Ram Car

TWO young Glasgow policemen last night rammed a stolen car after chasing it for four miles.

The chase went on through side streets in the South Side of the city.

It began shortly before seven o'clock, when the patrol-car crew recognised a stone-coloured Daimler as a car reported stolen in Carlisle.

Soon after the chase began, the pursued car collided with another car.

Without losing speed, it raced on to Shawlands Cross. There, the patrol car cornered it and rammed it.

Three men jumped out and ran off. Later, three men were arrested after a struggle.

Elizabeth Comes By Helicab

Woman Alleges Player Struck Boy

Today's Weather

Chapter 12
Hems

HEMLINES, whether the skirt was flared or pencil, stayed fairly constant throughout the 1950s, dramatic shortening didn't happen until the Sixties swept in.

But if hems didn't rise or fall very much, they were certainly thought about.

And then there were the hems on clothes of ever-growing children which were to be lengthened (or shortened) depending on which child was to be handed the garment next.

There was a lot of hemming to be done.

EASY HEMMING—Before turning up hem of a circular skirt, run a row of machine stitching all round, then hem in the usual way. Then there's no puckering.—Mrs W. Stewart, 51 Cairndhuna Terrace, Wick.

READY TO HAND—Always carry a roll of transparent, sticky tape in your bag. Then, if you are unfortunate enough to catch your heel in the hem of your skirt, the tape makes a quick, effective repair.—Mrs McKay, 712 Ferry Road, Edinburgh.

LADY GOLFERS—In windy weather pin the back and front hems of your skirt together with a large safety pin. This keeps the skirt from blowing about.—Robert King, 23 Baker Street, Shawlands, Glasgow.

HANDY GUIDE—An 18-inch ruler, stuck vertically into a lump of plasticine, is invaluable when turning up the hem of a garment.—Miss M. Walsh, 130 Barlow Street, Preston.

CHILDREN'S DRESSES—Turn children's summer dresses to the wrong side when hanging out to dry. This fades the hem. So when the dresses are let down, there is no difference in colour.—Mrs M. Dow, 162 High Street, Laurencekirk.

★ TOP TIP ★

HEMS DOWN—Before putting away children's winter clothes for summer storage, let down all hems. Next winter, when you measure and re-hem them, there'll be no creases where the old hems were.—Mrs M. Gellatly, 58 Church Street, Dundee, wins a pair of towels.

HEMS—When measuring hems of frocks, etc., instead of leaving ugly pin marks on the material, hold in position with flat spring in curl clips.—Mrs A. Sillers, Flemington Manse, Cambuslang.

INVISIBLE STITCHING—Use a blanket stitch when hemming a nylon dress. The thread is carried from stitch to stitch behind the hem and is invisible from the right side.—Mrs M. McGovern, 7 Hornbeam Drive, Parkhall, Dalmuir.

SKIRT HEMS—Always sew up skirt hems with several short threads instead of one long one. A heel, caught in a hem, then brings down only a short length. Running and permanent repairs are also made easier.—Mrs S. Smith, Parknook, Arbuthnott, Laurencekirk.

STRAIGHT HEMS—If you have no-one to help get the hem of a dress even, put the dress on a coat hanger. Next hang over it a finished dress the length you want. It is then a simple matter to pin the hem of the unfinished dress in line with the finished one.—Miss K. Douglas, 32 Cumlodden Drive, Glasgow.

SKIRT HEMS—When adjusting the hem of a skirt, turn the skirt inside out and slip it over an ironing board. In this way the material lies flat and the upper part is out of the way, making the work easier.—Mrs M. R., Dumbarton.

DRESSES—Little girls' dresses with the hem let down, are often short in the bodice. Avoid this by cutting bodice a little longer than the pattern and making a tuck at the waist seam, which can be let down as required.—Mrs S. B. Guy, 37 Burnhead Road, Larbert.

NO HEMMING—When making a blouse, if the bottom is "pinked" instead of hemmed, no ridge shows when worn under a thin skirt.—Mrs M. Mars, 37 Thorncliffe Gardens, Glasgow.

PERFECT FINISH—To get a perfect finish when letting down the hems of children's clothes, mix four cups hot water with two tablespoons white vinegar and a tablespoon of borax. Cover the old hems with a cloth wrung out of this mixture. Press until the steam rises then hang out to dry and brush with a soft brush.—A. Edgar, 48 Pennywell Road, Edinburgh.

COATS—When letting down the hems of girls' coats, cover the mark of the original hemline with several rows of machine stitching. It looks as though the coat had been bought that way.—Mrs M. Reid, 13 Hazel Drive, Dundee.

A NEAT JOB—When shortening children's coat sleeves take a tuck in the lining of the sleeve only. It makes a neater job and saves double thickness material at cuff.—Mrs T. Redfern, 49 Kirk Road, Wishaw.

SKIRT HEM—When adjusting the hem of a skirt, turn the skirt inside-out and slip it over an ironing board. In this way the material lies flat and the upper part is out of the way, making the job easier.—Mrs M. McCormick, 136 Levern Crescent, Barrhead.

PLASTIC—When hemming plastic material, to save perforating with pins use spring pegs to hold the hem in place while machining. The hem can also be adjusted for width much more quickly.—Mrs Hawthorne, 97 Riversdale Road, Romford.

SKIRT LENGTH—I have overcome the difficulty of putting up a straight hem by the simple method of measuring the required length on the kitchen table and marking with two chalked lines. Hold the waistband at one mark on the table and pin up the hem so that the edge falls on the other chalked line. Hems are speedily and neatly put up in this way.—Miss Elizabeth K. Allan, 151 Caledonian Avenue, Bellshill.

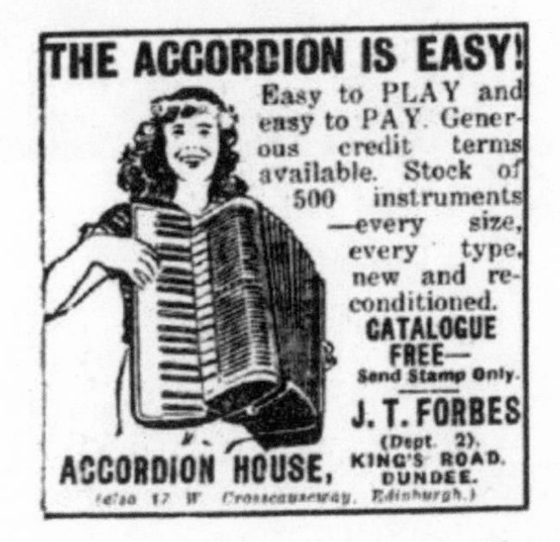

THE SUNDAY POST, JANUARY 9, 1955

The Sunday Post

Morning Special

PRINTED AND PUBLISHED EVERY SUNDAY MORNING.

No. 2576. [REGISTERED AT THE GENERAL POST OFFICE AS A NEWSPAPER.] SUNDAY, JANUARY 9, 1955. Radio and TV—Page 4 PRICE 2½d.

PRINCESS ALEXANDRA THROWN FROM HORSE

But Continues With Hunt

PRINCESS ALEXANDRA was thrown from her horse while hunting in Northamptonshire yesterday.

The Princess, who had attended the Pytchley Hunt Ball at Holdenby House, near Northampton, was hunting from Guilsborough.

The hunt had been in progress for about an hour when the Princess was thrown while taking a jump.

She fell into the mud, but pluckily insisted on going on.

A hunt follower told a reporter last night:

"The Princess was on a bay hunter and was jumping a brook in open field.

"The horse apparently slipped and she was thrown.

"She went into the mud, but she remounted and carried on the hunt."

Princess Alexandra travelled to Northamptonshire on Friday for the hunt ball.

After dancing until 3.30 a.m., she attended the hunt meet seven hours later.

She is spending the week-end at Cottesbrooke Hall, near Northampton.

Her mount for the hunt was lent to her for the day.

At Cottesbrooke Hall,

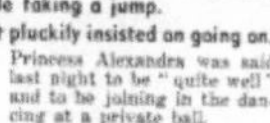

Princess Alexandra was said last night to be "quite well" and to be joining in the dancing at a private ball.

Minister Killed

THE Rev. C. M. Lee, Glatton Grange, Hunts, secretary of the Fitzwilliam Hunt, was killed yesterday. His horse shied and he was thrown heavily on his head.

Mr Lee's 12-year-old son was out with the Hunt at the time but did not see the accident.

Both Mr and Mrs Lee were keen riders to hounds. Mrs Lee is a well-known exhibitor at horse shows and gymkhanas.

Mr Lee had been Hunt secretary for two years.

All meets have been cancelled until after his funeral.

PRINCESS ALEXANDRA

Man Crushed By Truck

A DALMUIR man, Andrew Bridges, jun., aged about 30, was killed instantly when he was crushed between a cleansing truck and a wall, at Clydebank yesterday.

£4000 Of Tea Just Vanishes!

FOURTEEN days before Christmas a London firm of tea wholesalers arranged to send 319 cartons of tea, worth £4000, from their Bethnal Green depot to Glasgow.

A man arrived at the depot with a lorry. He said that he had come from a lorry hire firm to take the tea North.

The cartons were loaded. The lorry started on its journey.

The wholesalers learned yesterday that neither the lorry nor the tea arrived at Glasgow.

Police have added another case to their files of lorries which have never reached their destination.

Factory Blaze At Prestwick Airport

FIREMEN rushed to Prestwick Airport when fire broke out in the main production building of Scottish Aviation, Ltd., yesterday.

About 3000 square feet of the roof were destroyed.

The fire began when four workmen were working on the roof.

A stretch of guttering 200 feet long and full of tar suddenly became a mass of flames.

Firemen found a wall of flame that threatened to burn down the whole building and its valuable contents—including aircraft worth tens of thousands of pounds.

But brigades from Kilmarnock and Ayr and the airport did a splendid job. They had the outbreak out in less than half an hour.

A [illegible] of debris which fell into the interior of the building—the largest at the airport—narrowly missed [illegible] York aircraft parked there. [illegible] damage was done by water.

The building, which is on the north side [illegible] the airport, is used for construction and conversion of aircraft.

It was originally the Palace of Engineering at the 1938 Exhibition at Bellahouston Park, Glasgow.

Afterwards it was dismantled and rebuilt at Prestwick.

Several additions have since been made to it.

Dundee Garage Fire

FIRE broke out in the Baffin Street premises occupied by Midland Motors (Dundee), Ltd., and Thomas C. Stocks, joiner, last night.

Mr John Milne, 32 Springhill, was washing his car which he garages there, and the fact that he was there prevented what might have been a serious outbreak.

He smelt smoke, and sent for a director of the firm, Mr Kenneth Hogg.

When Mr Hogg arrived flames were licking through into the garage office from the joiner's shop above.

The two men tackled the blaze with extinguishers until the arrival of the fire brigade, who extinguished the fire.

Today's Weather

RATHER cold. Sleet or rain in places. Bright periods.

To Paris For 4d!

IN an Army "initiative test," 32 men of a unit at Woolwich were each given a shilling at the barracks last Wednesday. They were told: "Get as far as you can on that!"

Two of the men (Gunners J. Ross and Geo. Patchett) decided to try to cross the Channel.

Not only did they manage that. They got as far as Paris and back—and still had 4d each left of their shilling!

They arrived back at barracks yesterday, but refused to tell how they had managed the trip as "it might embarrass a number of people who helped us."

Both brought back a document bearing the official stamp of the British Military Attache in Paris.

The bridal group at the wedding of the Hon. Caroline Barrie to Captain Neil Baillie-Hamilton. (See Page 2.)

Duchess's Suitcase Stolen

POLICE in Edinburgh are searching for a suitcase belonging to the Duchess of Hamilton which was stolen from a car.

The case contains correspondence and files.

Edinburgh C.I.D. stated the car was parked during the course of the evening in Heriot Road, Canonmills [illegible] Bank, and Waverley Station.

The case is made of leather and about three feet long. The name Clydesdale is stamped along the top.

Police say that the papers in the case are of "extreme importance" to Her Grace, but are of no value to any other person.

A pair of fur lined boots was also stolen from the car.

£100 STOLEN FROM HOTEL

WHILE guests were sipping coffee and reading in the lounge of Learmonth Hotel in Edinburgh's West End, thieves broke a lock of the hotel office and made off with cash totalling about £100.

Chapter 13
Bide Safe

HEALTH And Safety legislation is a new phenomenon. In the 1950s it was left to the individual to keep themself safe.

There were two weapons to help with this. The first was a good dose of common sense, the second was to read The Sunday Post's Pass It On column.

In truth, not everything in this chapter would be advisable in today's world. In fact, you should be very wary of some of these "safety" tips.

THE VERY THING FOR BROKEN GLASS—I broke a very fine crystal glass, which shattered into minute fragments. It was impossible to lift them all with a damp cloth, so I took a bar of household soap and went over all the area. Even the tiniest piece adhered to the soap. I scraped the glass off the soap and destroyed it.—Mrs Scott, Benholm, Johnshaven, wins a pair of towels.

PLAY SAFE—If your child has a teddy bear, remove its glass eyes and sew on coloured eyes with bright wool. This prevents the glass eyes being accidentally swallowed.—Mrs G. French, Sen., 13 Longay Place, Milton, Glasgow.

EASY TO FIX—If your ears are pierced, and you find it difficult to fix in your earrings, touch each ear with any kind of oil, and the rings slip in easily.—E. Morrison, 232 Easter Road, Leith.

HANDY BOX—Put a candle, matches and fuse wire in a tin and place beside fuse box. They're ready to hand if you've a "blackout".—J. Clarke, 245 Meadowpark Street, Dennistoun, Glasgow.

NO SCALDED FINGERS—Crochet a loose string bag (with handles) large enough to hold a pudding basin. When making steamed puddings, you can then lift the basin from the boiling water without scalding the fingers.—Mrs M. Grant, Bank Street, Freuchie.

FOR SAFETY—When packing tumblers, store them in threes with a piece of tissue paper wrapped round the middle one. This prevents them sticking together.—Mrs I. Burns, 106 Burns Road, Greenock.

NO DAMAGE—Don't lift off a hot saucepan which has been accidentally placed on an oilcloth-covered table. Instead, remove the hot food from it, fill with cold water, and leave for ten minutes. It then lifts off without doing any damage.—Mrs H. Cummings, 79 Woodburn Drive, Dalkeith.

HAND COMFORT—While preparing vegetables or rinsing out clothes in cold water, I keep a basin of hot water on the draining board, and frequently plunge my hands into the comforting warmth. This winter my hands are smoother and softer than they have ever been.—Mrs Agnes B. Wotherspoon, 33 Cordale Road, Renton.

SAFETY MEASURE—If you have a precious ornamental jar, it's worthwhile to half-fill it with sand or similar weighty substance to prevent it being knocked over.—Mrs Stewart, Mill House, Gatehouse-of-Fleet, Castle Douglas.

★ TOP TIP ★

PROTECTS THOSE FINGERS—To prevent bruised fingers when hammering in nails, use an old comb to hold nails in place. Wedge the nail between the comb's teeth and you can hammer away in perfect safety.—Mrs Cassidy, 73 Blackwell Road, Carlisle, wins a pair of towels.

NO BLISTERS—I wrap a wet rag round the handle of my carpet beater before I start. My hands don't blister.—Miss N. Mills, 76 Ronald Street, Coatbridge.

LITTLE INVALID—If a child has to have meals in bed, it's a good idea to serve them in a small drawer. It saves time and trouble if anything is upset.—Mrs L. Paul, 9 The Parade, Harrogate.

NO MORE BURNS—When browning meat in a pressure cooker, before putting the lid on turn the meat over with a toasting fork instead of an ordinary fork. Then there's no hot fat splashes.—Mrs S. Fletcher, 7 Bolton Street, Barrow-in-Furness.

★ TOP TIP ★

MAKE THE STEP LADDER SAFER—Make your household steps safe by painting the steps, and, while paint is still wet, sprinkle with sand. This gives a rough surface which helps to prevent slipping.—Mrs Wilcox, 30 Jasmine Terrace, Aberdeen, wins a pair of towels.

PREVENTS COLDS—To help to prevent head colds, after shampooing the hair make the last rinse one of cold water.—Mrs I. Davidson, 66 Fintry Drive, Dundee.

TIMELY HINT—Mothers of very young babies should keep a small towel or piece of absorbent cloth always handy to place over the left shoulder before picking up baby. This easy precaution protects the dress shoulder.—Mrs H. Smith, 14 John Street, Ruabon, Denbighshire.

FIRE PRECAUTION—Many fire casualties could be prevented if a strong rope, knotted every two feet, were kept in one or more upstairs rooms. Make it long enough to reach to the ground. The rope could probably be attached to a strong wall fixture.—Mrs D. M. Bruce, Deansland, Auchterarder.

EASILY MOVED—To move a hair mattress out of a room when spring cleaning, roll it up, tie ends firmly, then put it on the tea trolley lengthwise. It can be wheeled anywhere without stress.—Mrs J. Millar, 178 West Princes Street, Glasgow.

TAKE CARE—When putting hair-combings in the fire, make sure they burn. Otherwise they stick to the chimney and gather large deposits of soot.—J. Royan, 166 Butterbiggins Road, Glasgow.

PAINT REMOVER—My small son got paint on his lips and near his mouth. I put a small amount of almond oil on a cloth and wiped gently. The paint came off easily, and the oil isn't so foul-tasting as paraffin.—Mrs L. Irvine, Woodend Cottages, Hillhouse, Troon.

THE **Policy** OF THE PEARL

is to make sure your insurance cover *really* meets your needs—to provide the right kind of benefit at the right time. Whether you live near John o' Groats or Land's End, whether you want to secure an income for retirement or fire insurance protection on your property, your local Pearl representative is ready to give you practical help. You are never at a loss with the Pearl.

REST ASSURED—BE PEARL ASSURED

Pearl
ASSURANCE COMPANY
LIMITED

CHIEF OFFICES: HIGH HOLBORN, LONDON, W.C.1

WINDOW SAFETY—We've steel-framed windows which open outwards. To prevent our young child from falling out, we screwed rubber door stoppers into the window ledges outside. This allows windows to be opened only a certain distance. The rubber doesn't damage the window frames.—Mrs C. Halcrow, 4 Winburne Crescent, Hamilton.

NO DAMAGE DONE—When carrying nail scissors in your handbag, always put a small cork on the points. This prevents damage to bag and contents.—Mrs Belton, 25 Ashcroft Gardens, Peterborough.

NO MISTY OUTLOOK—To prevent steam settling on your spectacles when working at the stove, rub a little dry soap on them, and polish until clean.—Mrs Mabs Jarrod, 16 Eskdale Street, Glasgow.

★ TOP TIP ★

TINNED FOODS, A WARNING—Tinned foods are generally quite safe. But is your tin-opener? Food-poisoning often arises because the spike of the opener hasn't been cleaned since it was last used, and germs from it get into the food when it punctures the can.—Mrs R. Watson, Partick, wins a pair of towels.

NON-TEAR ZIP—A piece of stiff ribbon, one-inch wide, laid flat behind a zip fastener, stitched at both ends and down one side, prevents underwear being caught in the teeth of the zip.—Mrs R. Macfarlane, Westray House, Bedford Place, Alloa.

NAIL HOLDER—Try using a buttonhook to hold nails in place while hammering them in. This prevents bruised fingers.—Miss H. Riddoch, Parknook, Arbuthnott, Laurencekirk.

SAFETY MOVE—Place a face cloth in the hand basin when cleaning dentures. This prevents breakage if they happen to slip from your hand.—Mrs S. J. Allan, 146 Burghead Drive, Glasgow.

IT'S SAFER TO DO THIS AT THE KIDDIES' PARTY—When giving a children's party, sew tapes on corners of tablecloth and tie to the table legs. This prevents accidents through children pulling the cloth.—Mrs M. Thomson, Garage Flat, Cripland Court, Lindfield, near Haywards, Sussex, wins a pair of towels.

SAFETY TIP—Put a damp cloth under a tin of meat, fruit, etc., before opening it. This keeps the tin from slipping, and so prevents accidents.—Mrs S. Anders, 8 Cumbrae Road, Saltcoats.

HANDY—If a piece of steel wool sticks into your hand, try a magnet to draw it out.—Miss Helen Walsh, 158 Craigbank Street, Larkhall.

LIVING ALONE—A good idea for those who live alone is to hang a whistle at the head of the bed. Assistance can be summoned at any time of day or night. It gives confidence to old people.—Mrs May Gosling, Rose Villa, 188 Grovehill Road, Beverley, Yorks.

NEW COMBS—When you buy a new comb and find the points of the teeth are sharp, draw them along the striking side of a matchbox two or three times. This takes off the sharpness.—Mrs A. Wilson, 13 Barclay Street, Glasgow.

INVALID COMFORT—When an invalid wishes to sit up in bed, always place a pillow under the knees. This prevents the patient slipping down, and greatly adds to his comfort.—Mrs E. Ritchie, 2 Brooklands Avenue, Sidcup, Kent.

SAFETY FIRST—When using a razor blade for household purposes, cover one edge with adhesive tape. This makes the blade easier to handle and there is less risk of cut fingers.—Mrs J. Macdougall, Columba Road, Edinburgh.

SOOT DESTROYER—If a strong solution of salt and water is thrown over the coals periodically, less soot will collect in the flues and chimney. The fire, too, will burn clear and bright.—Mrs Johnston, 63 Port Dundas Road, Glasgow.

SAFETY MEASURE—When putting scissors back into the workbox, press the closed points into a cork. This prevents accidents to the fingers.—Mrs M. Kyle. 3 Avon Street, Hamilton.

SAFE—Sew a small zip fastener to inside breast pocket of your husband's jacket. His wallet cannot fall out when he takes his jacket off.—Mrs E. Mackenzie, 103 Retford Road, Harold Hill, Romford, Essex.

HANDY OPENER—When opening a tin of sardines slip a clothes peg over the handle of the key. You get more leverage, and no hurt hands.—Mrs Parker, 6 Bowman Flat, Larkhall.

★ TOP TIP ★

A SIMPLE WAY TO FIND THAT SPLINTER—If you find it difficult to locate a splinter in the finger, touch the spot right away with iodine. The splinter turns dark, and is then seen clearly.—Mrs McLellan, 74 Darnley Street, Glasgow, wins a pair of towels.

SCALDS AND BURNS—Dissolve a small packet of Epsom salts in a breakfast cup of hot water. Put in a bottle and keep near the cooker. When fat spurts out or boiling water scalds, instantly apply the salt solution.—Mrs F. W. Bell, 18 Westlands, Sunderland.

★ TOP TIP ★

PREVENT EYESTRAIN WHEN WATCHING TV—When watching TV programmes for a long while in a dark room try wearing sunglasses of a fairly light tint. They prevent eye-strain.—Mrs R. A. Blake, 20 Clarence Place, Lower Weston, Bath, wins a pair of towels.

EGG WHITE DID IT—I burned my finger with hot fat while cooking the breakfast. It was stinging like mad. As there were some empty egg shells lying, I dipped my finger in one. The white of egg that was left in the shell sealed the burn and I had no more trouble with it.—Mrs D. Mitchell, 6 Edinburgh Road, Selhurst, London.

FIRST-AID—I always keep a bowl of sour milk in my kitchenette, as I find it invaluable for burns and scalds. Place affected part in the sour milk, it immediately soothes and avoids blistering.—Mrs M. Wood, 24 Featherstone Street, Roker, Sunderland.

STEP SAFETY—Nail or screw a piece of wood to the side of household steps and extending about two and a half feet above top step. This gives a hold when standing on the top step and helps to prevent accidents by slipping.—P. Dobson, 35 Braemar Place, Aberdeen, wins a pair of towels.

SAVE THE HANDS—I put rubber cycle handles on the handles of my pots. This saves my hands from the heat.—Mrs G. J. Currie, 4 Knox Place, Aberdeen.

USEFUL—Always include a blue bag in the picnic basket. If stung by a wasp, apply bag immediately.—Mrs J. Dishington, Muirfield, Gullane.

NON-SLIP—Wear a rubber thimble when scrubbing small potatoes. This prevents them slipping from your fingers.—Miss Williams, c/o Clubb, Roseneath, Lower Road, Summerhill, near Wrexham.

THORNS—To remove thorns from the fingers, castor oil is simple and effective. Wash the part thoroughly and apply a pad of lint saturated with castor oil, and bandage. Twelve hours is generally long enough to bring out deeply embedded thorns.—Mrs Reid, 20 Lindsay Drive, Glasgow.

NO BURNT FINGERS—The aluminium handles of saucepan lids often become too hot to lift. Attach a spring clothes peg to the handle and you're able to see how the contents of the pan are doing without fear of scorched fingers.—Mrs Gibb, c/o Wilton Bank, Knoxland Square, Dumbarton.

FOR A POULTICE—I had to apply a poultice recently and found I had no oil silk. I used a piece of Polythene which did as well, as it kept the poultice nice and moist.—Mrs M. Craig, 8 Hatfield Drive, Glasgow, wins a pair of towels.

SAVES BURNS—When replacing a hot burned-out bulb, slip the cardboard container from the new bulb over the old one before unscrewing from the socket. It's simple and safe.—Mrs J. Macfarlane, 129 Paisley Road West, Glasgow.

PLAY SAFE—When using caustic soda for cleaning, keep a bowl of salt water handy. Should the soda come in contact with hands or eyes the salt water prevents burns.—Mrs J. A. Fletcher, c/o Mrs Garvie, 1 London Street, Edinburgh.

SAFETY TIP—When you empty an electric kettle, leave the lid only half on. This lets you know the kettle is empty and requires to be filled before switching on. It saves the price of a new element.—Mrs A. Jenkins, 24 St Thomas Crescent, Arbroath.

DARK STAIRS—If you use a dark stairway, paint a broad white band down one side and, by contrast, you see the glimmer to the bottom step.—W. Slater, 12B Scotland Street Lane, Edinburgh.

★ TOP TIP ★

FOR KNEELING JOBS—When doing kneeling jobs, instead of carrying a kneeling pad around, place a piece of foam rubber under your stockings at the knee. It protects the knees and gives a wonderful cushion effect.—Mrs Robin S. McCreadie, 3 Hamilton Drive, Largs, wins a pair of towels.

CURE—People who suffer from headache after bathing should try stuffing their ears with lambswool before going into the sea. It contains a natural oil which is waterproof, so that water can't penetrate into the ears.—Mrs Fulton, 3 Barnes Street, Barrhead, Glasgow.

KEEPS HOT—If an invalid fancies a boiled egg, wrap it in aluminium foil as soon as it's cooked. It reaches the patient as hot as when first taken from the pan.—Miss E. Aitken, 146 Tettenhall Road, Wolverhampton.

SAVES THE FINGERS—To save scalding fingers while dishing a "clootie" dumpling, I find that putting it in a large sieve or colander is the simplest way. After untying it, I put a plate on top and then turn it over.—Mrs Sturrock, 10 Abbotsford Place, Dundee.

SAVES ACCIDENTS—To close windows without getting up on a chair, unscrew the shaft of your carpet sweeper and use as a window pole. The rubber cap on the shaft helps to safeguard the glass against breakage.—Mrs J. Davidson, 11 Victoria Road, Grangemouth.

COMFY GRIP—To give a permanent cushion grip on heavy holiday cases, cut a short length of foam rubber sheet about one inch wide and wind it round the handle of case. Fix with rubber solution.—Mrs N. Malcolm, 25 Croftburn Drive, Glasgow, wins a pair of towels.

USEFUL TOPS—Don't discard children's white socks that are beyond darning. Boil first, cut off the ribbed tops, and keep them in the medicine chest. They are excellent for holding in place dressings on grazed knees and elbows.—Mrs Rolston, 20 Upper Canning Street, Belfast.

FOR THE SICK—As a small gift to a sick friend, give her a stick of frozen cologne. It cools a hot forehead, but doesn't spill on the bedclothes.—Mrs Helen Smith, 18 Bank Street, Glasgow.

FOR COMFORT—For ladies who are allergic to metal clasps on necklaces, etc., fix an earring pad with a little glue behind the clasp and so avoid discomfort.—E. I. Michael, 3 Morain Avenue, Drumchapel, Glasgow.

FROSTY WEATHER PRECAUTION—During frosty weather, add half a teacup of methylated spirits to the water before washing the doorstep. The doorstep dries quickly and doesn't become icy or slippery.—A. Murray, 44 Shuna Street, Ruchill, Glasgow.

HANDY ALARM—For those living alone I suggest a push bell where it's easy to get at. It should ring above the outside door, and be placed high up where no one could get near it.—A. Fleming, West End Park Street, Glasgow.

BED SAVER—Insert a cork mat between bed lamp and headboard of bed. This saves the wood from becoming marked by heat from the lamp.—Miss Wilson, 109 Ashdown Road, Farringdon, Sunderland.

TALCUM—When applying talcum powder, use a foam rubber sponge as used for cake make-up. You will find it most economical, as the talc clings to the sponge instead of settling on floors, etc.—M. M. Rushford, 53 Malden Road, London.

ICY ROADS—If you wear leather-soled shoes, and the roads become icy and difficult to walk on, try criss-crossing the soles with adhesive tapes. It helps to keep you from slipping.—A. G. Thomson, 52 White Street, Glasgow, wins a pair of towels.

SMOOTH HANDLES—Before using a new shopping or picnic basket, wind Sellotape round the handles. This protects gloves, and a wipe with a damp cloth keeps the handles clean.—Mrs L. M. Ansley, 52 Radford Road, Exeter.

The Sunday Post

Morning Special

PRINTED AND PUBLISHED EVERY SUNDAY MORNING.

No. 2592. SUNDAY, MAY 1, 1955. Radio and TV—Page 4 PRICE 2½d.

Locomen To Carry On Work On Tribunal's Offer

RAIL STRIKE OFF

Billy Graham addressing the huge crowd at Hampden.

Hampden Scenes That Will Never Be Forgotten

THERE were unforgettable scenes at Hampden Park last night when Billy Graham held the farewell service of his crusade.

And what a moving farewell it was!

Greatest Battle

"Through Eternity"

Immediate Discussions To Be Held On "Differentials"

THE rail strike has been called off.

This news was given last night after negotiations had gone on all day.

There were only about 30 hours to go to the deadline when the settlement was announced.

For 3 hours and 5 minutes, leaders of the Associated Society of Locomotive Engineers and Firemen and British Transport Commission chiefs had been talking.

Then, just after 5.30 p.m. Sir Brian Robertson, the chairman of the Commission, came out and said—"I am glad to tell you that agreement has been reached."

The agreement means that the A.S.L.E.F. men will continue at work on the terms laid down by the Railway Staff National Tribunal last month.

They have been persuaded to do this by an assurance from the Commission that both sides will enter into immediate discussion of the question of "differentials."

MEETING TOMORROW

The first meeting is to take place tomorrow at three o'clock between the B.T.C. and A.S.L.E.F.

At later meetings, N.U.R. representatives will be brought in.

The Commission also agreed that neither of the recent awards of the Railway Staff National Tribunal would be regarded as establishing principles which will preclude free and immediate discussion of any proposals which might be submitted.

Before leaving for his Hampstead H.Q. to supervise the despatch of "carry on work" telegrams to 440 branches, Mr Hallworth, the society's secretary, said—"Don't talk of our withdrawing our strike notices. At the moment all we are doing is instructing our men to continue working."

N.U.R. COMMENT

Mr James Campbell, general secretary of the N.U.R., declared—"We have been assured by the British Transport Commission that this preliminary meeting will have no reference to any claim or submission made by A.S.L.E.F., and will be a purely informal meeting to be followed by formal discussions with all parties concerned.

"It is quite clear from the settlement, that action by individual unions must fail in their objective if that objective is beneficial to a section of the staff without regard to all other sections."

● The award of the Railway Staff National Tribunal rejected the claim by A.S.L.E.F. for an all-round increase of 8s a week, which would have meant rises of from 1s 6d to 8s 6d above the Commission's offer.

Indignation At Students' Parties Reports

Strike Cost 2000 Tons A Day

Today's Weather

Chapter 14
Still Useful

A GOOD idea is a good idea, whether the lightbulb moment was 60 years ago or 60 seconds ago. Some of the details might have changed and some of the problems that these tips can address now might be different from the problems they were originally devised for. But they are still useful.

Nowadays, tips are known as "life hacks" and several websites are dedicated to this sort of thing.

But whether these "hacks" will still be of use in half a century is debatable.

BATHROOM SCALES—To protect all working parts of bathroom scales from steam, keep them in a transparent polythene bag. They can be easily seen without having to remove from the bag.—Mrs R. Malcolm, 11 Southlands Road, Auchterarder.

SOCKS—It's better to fold men's socks rather than roll them when putting away. Rolling stretches the tops and causes them to slip down when worn.—Mrs H. Miller, 41 Benview Street, Ruchill, Glasgow.

EASY FITTING—Immerse the bottom ends of decorative candles in hot water for a few minutes before putting into candlesticks. They are easy to mould into position.—Mrs Robertson, Moffat Mills, Airdrie.

WARDROBE TIDY—A small plastic clothes peg clipped to each end of a coat-hanger allows sleeveless dresses to be hung up without slipping.—Miss A. Yuill, 64 Mackie Avenue, Port Glasgow.

SILVER—A small piece of camphor kept in the display cabinet helps to keep silver from tarnishing.—O. Reid, 10 South Street, Greenock.

CLEANER POTS—If a nob of butter is put in the pot before making the breakfast porridge, the pot is much easier to clean later as the butter prevents, the porridge from sticking to the pot.—Mrs M. Johnson, 39 Dalnair Street, Glasgow.

CREPE SOCKS—When washing children's crepe nylon socks, pull them over the hands like gloves and rub gently. The dirt and stains come out easily and the socks keep their shape.—Mrs Elizabeth Burse, 13 Dalveen Way, Fernhill, Rutherglen.

CLOTHES BRUSH—When travelling I always carry a foam sponge which makes an excellent clothes brush and can be washed easily.—J. Thomson, 404 Dumbarton Road, Dalmuir, Glasgow.

DECK CHAIRS—When putting deck chairs away for the winter, put them into large plastic bags. This keeps them clean and free from dust until required again. A large wardrobe-size bag fits a standard deck chair very neatly.—Mrs E. V. McLelland, 292 Knightswood Road, Glasgow.

FIRM JOB—Always keep a piece of beeswax in your sewing basket. Before sewing on buttons, rub, the thread with the beeswax. It will be much stronger, the buttons will be firmer and will stay on much longer.—Miss Edna M. Finlay, 120 Templemore Street, Belfast.

DIRTY HANDS—Try a little olive oil with a sprinkling of sugar. Rub the hands as if washing them. This removes the dirt and leaves the hands clean and soft.—R. Smythe, 14 Glenmachan Street, Donegal Road, Belfast.

ICE CUBES—If you have a fridge and like to keep ice cubes for drinks, they look very decorative with tinned cherries or other fruit popped into each cube before freezing. Adds flavour, too. —Mrs J. McWhirter, 6 Mayfield Road, Saltcoats.

CUCUMBER—To keep cucumber fresh, immerse in dish of cold water until required for salad.—Mrs R. W. Wilson, 33 Heugh Street, Falkirk.

Campbell's Soups are back in Britain!

These world-famous soups return to your grocer's shelves for the first time since the war

From today you can enjoy soups that are world-famous for their luxury of flavour! *Campbell's Soups are back in Britain!*

Campbell's Soups. America's favourite soups. Canada's favourite soups. Soups that are *still remembered here from the days before the war*—they taste *that* good!

The extra richness of flavour that makes people like our soups so much is the result of a motto we have at Campbell's: "To make the best, begin with the best—then cook with extra care."

And that's just what we do. *Only the finest ingredients; only the most skilled preparation and patient cooking.* You can taste the difference immediately!

* CONDENSED—AMERICA'S FAVOURITES, CANADA'S TOO!

There'll be four favourite kinds of Campbell's Soups to begin with: *Cream of Chicken Soup, Tomato Soup, Cream of Mushroom Soup, Vegetable Soup (made with Beef Stock).* (And many more delicious kinds to come.)

BURN TINS—On emptying tins containing meat, fish, etc., I immediately burn the tins clean in the fire before placing in bin. A simple idea, but it does much to prevent any unpleasant smell and flies.—Mrs Randall, Tomich, Beauly.

RE-HEATING—To re-heat a pie, take a sheet of greaseproof paper and dip in cold water. Drip off surplus water, then wrap the pie in the paper, parcel fashion. Heat in a moderate oven. This prevents pastry from becoming hard and dried up.—J. D. Bain, 75 Malcolm Road, Culter.

DAMP CUPBOARD—If you've a damp kitchen cupboard, line shelves with blotting-paper instead of shelf paper. Blotting-paper absorbs moisture and leaves the atmosphere of the cupboard dry.—Mrs A. Christie, 14 Foster Road, Kingsway, Dundee.

GOOD RINSE—Add a little lemon juice to rinsing water after shampooing the hair. This removes all traces of soap, and leaves the hair soft and fluffy.—Mrs Helen Smith, 6 Allan Park, Stirling.

FOR PIANOS—A bag of camphor hung inside a piano absorbs damp and prevents moths from attacking the felt on hammers and dampers.—Miss I. C. Mackay, Arch House, Lairg.

KEEPS NAILS OK—If your nails, like mine, soften when using a home perm, give them a good coat of nail varnish.—Mrs E. McLean, 36 Ailsa Place, Dundee.

LABELS—If you require a stick-on label and haven't one handy, cut a piece of plain white paper to size and affix it to the parcel with transparent sticky tape.—Mrs Levy, 621 Gallowgate, Glasgow.

UMBRELLAS—You can freshen up your silk umbrella by brushing it with a solution of ammonia and water. Don't open an umbrella to dry it, as the moisture causes the ribs to warp. Dry upside down so that the water can drip from the tops of the ribs and not at the ferrule, where the strain is greatest, as this rots the silk.—Mrs Henderson, Glasgow.

★ TOP TIP ★

IT FRESHENS THE ROOM IN SMOGGY WEATHER—To freshen the air in bedrooms during smoggy weather, place a teaspoonful of eau-de-cologne in a coal shovel and set fire to it. Move the shovel about the room. A fragrant and refreshing scent remains.—Mrs R. Alderson, 29 Hylton Street, North Shields, Northumberland, wins a pair of towels.

DATES—Keep a little flour in the jar with dates. Shake well. This keeps them from getting sticky.—Mrs A. Mitchell, 59 Cairngorm Crescent, Kincorth, Aberdeen.

NON-SLIP—When wrapping a gift in a circular box, the ribbon doesn't slip if first taped to the bottom of the box.—Miss W. Martin, 34 Balgarvie Crescent, Cupar.

SELF-CLOSING BOX—If you have a box of matches which is slack, put an elastic band round the box lengthwise. This allows the box to be pushed open and causes it to close after the match has been taken out.—J. Cowan, 1 Glasgow Road, Milngavie.

SOLDERING—When doing a very small soldering job, stick the pieces that are to be soldered in a lump of modelling clay. It holds them in position. If clay isn't available, use a raw potato cut so that it stands upright.—D. Lumsden, Cumbrae Lighthouse, Millport.

CLEAN BIN—I keep a thick pad of blotting paper stuck inside my dustbin lid with adhesive tape. Well soaked with strong disinfectant, this prevents any unpleasant smell in warm weather and also keeps flies at bay.—Mrs E. Palmer, 101 Westcliff Park Drive, Westcliff-on-Sea.

FOR YOUR TEA CADDY—To give tea that "China" flavour, keep a piece of dried orange peel in the caddy.—Mrs R. Richmond, 161 Corsock Street, Alexandria Park, Glasgow.

The Sunday Post — Morning Special

PRINTED AND PUBLISHED EVERY SUNDAY MORNING.

No. 2595. | SUNDAY, MAY 22, 1955. | Radio and TV—Page 4 | PRICE 2½d.

Two Different Decisions At Yesterday's Meetings:—

DOCK STRIKE IS ON —RAIL PEACE BID

Ships May Take Cargoes Back To America

THIS is a momentous week for Britain.

It brings a General Election—and the threat of two major strikes.

AT THE DOCKS, the strike called for tomorrow is still on.

The strike has been called for 8 a.m. tomorrow by the National Amalgamated Stevedores and Dockers, which has members in London, Hull, Liverpool and Manchester.

The Executive Committee and port delegates of the N.A.S.D. left their H.Q. yesterday afternoon and went to their homes.

Unless there is outside intervention, which is considered improbable, no further steps are likely before tomorrow morning, when the strike is due to start.

Mr Newman, assistant secretary of the N.A.S.D., summed up the situation when he told reporters yesterday—"The strike is on."

ON THE RAILWAYS, two new moves were decided at yesterday's meetings in an effort to avert the strike called for midnight next Saturday—

1—Tomorrow British Transport Commission chiefs will meet the Minister of Labour.

2—On Tuesday, representatives of the Associated Society of Locomotive Engineers and Firemen will go to the Ministry.

● A letter from the British Transport Commission urged the Associated Society of Locomotive Engineers and Firemen to "carefully reconsider the whole matter."

The A.S.L.E.F. Executive met at their London H.Q. yesterday for over two hours.

They will assemble again tomorrow afternoon.

There will also be meetings of T.U.C. chiefs and of the Executive of the National Union of Railwaymen.

● The Minister of Labour yesterday saw the Prime Minister, Sir Anthony Eden, at No. 10 Downing Street.

● It is felt among shipping quarters on Merseyside that the effect of the dock strike would be widespread. Complete gangs would be unable to work because some of their number are N.A.S.D. members.

During the week-end, two Cunarders are due to arrive at Liverpool—the Parthia from New York with 5047 tons of general cargo, and the Franconia from Quebec, with 152 tons.

A Cunard official said—"If the worst comes to the worst it is likely the ships will cross the Atlantic with their cargoes undischarged."

90,000 At Billy Graham Finale

NINETY THOUSAND people crowded into Wembley Stadium for Billy Graham's final meeting last night.

... took the "decision for Christ." ... the meeting, Dr Graham, ... to people who had attended ... taken the decision for Christ." ... "In one week we have had ... as many as we had in six weeks in the United States.

"I seriously doubt if, in the annals of evangelism, there has been anything like it in history."

Tied Bootlace Round Boy's Neck

A 10-YEAR-OLD boy was yesterday found unconscious on a bank at ... Colliery, Harthill, with a bootlace tied tightly round his neck. ...

The injured boy was taken to the ... and the doctor was summoned from Harthill.

The boy was treated for face injuries ... and taken home.

Two Ladies—In Men's 220!

TWO rain-coated old ladies, complete with umbrellas, found themselves involved in the 220 yards sprint at the Caledonian Games at the White City, London, yesterday.

As the six runners swept into the first bend, the two women, chatting quite unconcernedly, decided to cross the track.

Then they noticed the runners bearing down on them. They realised their peril, and beat a hasty retreat back on to the grass.

But they were not quite quick enough. The inside man, W. Henderson of Scotland, had to run off the track and out of the race.

Today's Weather

BRIGHT periods and occasional rain or showers. Rather cool.

Princess's New Hair-Do

PRINCESS MARGARET'S new hair style was much admired at Windsor yesterday.

The hair is brushed straight down from crown to nape and back from the ears.

It has a boyish and casual effect.

The new style has yet to be named.

On left is picture of the Queen at Windsor. She wore an outfit of grey and white ribbed wool, with an off-white circular hat.

Wae's Me For The Walker Cup!

BRITAIN nearly suffered a grand slam in the Walker Cup at St Andrews.

Two players saved them from a total eclipse—David Blair and young Ian Caldwell.

U.S.A. won all four foursomes on Friday and six singles yesterday, giving them a 10-2 runaway win.

Both the British victories finished on the last green.

Caldwell beat D. Morey after a tense fight-back finish by the American.

J. W. Conrad made Major Blair fight it out to the last putt, after being dormie 2 down.

"Big Bill Campbell," the American captain, said at the presentation afterwards—"Events have now confirmed what I originally thought—that my side was the best ever to leave America for a Walker Cup match."

Alec Hill, the British captain, said—"Britain have been beaten by a team of complete golfers."

(See page 23.)

DARK CLOTHES—When brushing dark clothes, sprinkle methylated spirits on the brush. It removes all specks.—Mrs J. Low, 9 Whytehouse Avenue, Kirkcaldy.

FLOWER HOLDERS—I don't throw away empty coconut shells. I saw them in half, bore a small hole on each side near the top, and attach a chain. I then have two hanging baskets for my house plants. —Mrs Brisbin, 1127 North East Walnut Street, Roseburg, Oregon, USA.

NEW TOWELS—Before using new hand or tea-towels, soak them for 24 hours in salt water. This strengthens the fibres and the towels will not leave fluff on the face or glasses.—Mrs A. Miller, 189 Childwall Road, Liverpool.

DRIPPING PIPES—Pipes along the kitchenette wall are apt to drip through condensation. Wrap them with carpet binding and there'll be no more drips.—Mrs Munro, 41 Cumming Park Circle, Aberdeen.

FOR THE "LEFTIES"—If you're left-handed and don't have a suitable potato peeler, hold an ordinary peeler in your left hand and use with a downward motion.—Mrs A. N. McNair, 2 Holmston Road, Ayr.

WALL PLAQUE—An old plate, thickly covered with foreign stamps and varnished over, makes an unusual and attractive wall plaque. Two packets of assorted stamps, plus one or two from your own letters, give ample variety and colour.—Louie Smith, 9 Acklam Avenue, Grangetown, Sunderland.

DOORBELL TRICK—If you've a patient in the house who must be kept quiet, pull the finger of an old glove over the hammer of the doorbell.—Mrs D. McDougall, Braeside, Scarsdale Avenue, Allestree, Derby, wins a pair of towels.

The "Priscilla Page" of August 30, 1959

Snippets

I'VE just had some red-hot news about the newest types of knitting wools we'll all want to try in the coming months. Mohair will still be the most popular—and the newest in this range is brushed mohair. It's made of 50% mohair, 30% nylon, and 20% lambswool. Sounds luscious, doesn't it?

When knitted, it has an unevenness of texture which is ideal for new designs of lacy blouses and evening jumpers. There are 15 shades to choose from, and it will sell at 3s. 3d. a half-ounce ball.

A romantic-looking evening stole I saw was knitted in another new yarn. A mohair and wool mixture, this is something quite special. It gives the garment an airy-fairy lightness, but an oh-so-costly look!

There's also a lovely Orlon yarn which costs only 2s. 3d. an ounce. This knits up beautifully and gives a real luxury look at a budget price. Of course, the thing that makes Orlon such a winner is that it washes like a dream. What it doesn't like is being allowed to get really dirty. Like stockings, it's best to treat Orlon to almost a daily dip.

Did you know you can now knit in Terylene? This is 100 per cent. Terylene made from a continuous filament, which means the knitted garment cannot fluff ever. It washes excellently without harm to the fabric, shape or colour. It will be on sale this autumn in half-ounce balls, 1s. 10d.

Another newcower to the wool counters is "Curlane". Remember the poodle-type wool we used last winter? Well, this is very similar, but is a much finer version and is ideal for making suits, cardigans and jumpers. Costs 1s. 9d. an ounce.

There's a big exhibition in London this week, when many firms will be showing their latest models. And I've heard whispers some wonderful things will be seen. The policy of big firms seems to be, "If it's made in wool or synthetic yarn, you can knit it yourself." I won't be surprised if I find I can now knit a nightdress or a kilt! There also seems to be a trend towards stocking stitch. Most women find they can cope comfortably with stocking stitch while watching television, but "fiddly" patterns where concentration's necessary are impossible.

Watching a friend of mine do sleeves for her little boy's sweater the other night gave me a tip. Doing the hard-worked elbows, she strengthened the knitting by working a matching 3-ply strand along with the double-knit wool she was using. For added wear and tear that's certainly Something I'll remember.

In one shop I had a real find. A new cold-water shampoo for knitwear. Suitable for all the synthetic yarns and all types of woollens, including angora and blankets, this little sachet solves the problem of shrinking and felting. The well-known knitwear firm who recommend its use are convinced that using too-hot water is the commonest fault in washing woollens.

Chapter 16 Knitting, The Necessary Hobby

KNITTING was as natural, and almost as common, as breathing. The family needed clothes, after all. Every woman could do it so well that they could chat, listen to the wireless and dispense good advice, with needles clicking all the while.

And the work wasn't done when the knitting was over. When elbows or heels became worn, they were darned.

Sunday Post readers were experts in both disciplines and, as ever, found a few novel uses for their skills along the way.

Very few knitting tips earned "tip of the week" status, probably because the 1950s sub-editors choosing top tips were predominantly male and didn't fully appreciate clever knitting.

SOCKS—When knitting socks for our fighting lads, knit a few odd sized pieces to patch heels, etc. And remember to leave a long length of wool and enclose a darning needle.—Mrs M. Smith, 13 Seaton Road, Aberdeen.

EXTRA STRENGTH—When I finish knitting pullovers, gloves, etc., for children, I double crochet all round the double knitting wool to strengthen edges of welt, cuffs and collar. It saves broken loops.—Mrs C. Laurence, Greenden Cottages, Farnell, Brechin.

SUBSTITUTE—Get a card of fuse wire (5 or 10 amp). With two No. 10 knitting needles, cast on 20 stitches and knit a square. Knit another square the same size with odd pieces of string. Join the two squares together. The result is a pad for purposes where steel wool was used before.—M. Stephen, Doonieshill, Nigg, Aberdeenshire.

TANGLE-FREE—When knitting and putting spare stitches on to a safety pin, first slip a tiny button on the pin. Then the wool doesn't tangle round the hinge.—Mrs Queenan, 1 Edina Place, Hawick.

NEEDLES—If the point of your celluloid knitting needle snaps, use a nail file to shape a new one.—Mrs T. Haggerty, 24 Otago Lane, Hillhead, Glasgow.

EXTRA STRENGTH—When knitting the sleeves of cardigans, knit for eight inches then join in a second ball of wool. Knit with the two balls for four inches then continue in single wool. This "double" elbow is undetectable and does not wear out.—M. M. Finlay, 54 Otago Street, Glasgow.

CLEAN WORK—When knitting, I have found it useful to pin to my dress or skirt a fairly large polythene bag to keep the wool clean. The wool runs freely, and no pulling required.—Margaret Roger, 14 St Mungo Road, Inverness.

DARNING—Always use a short thread when darning. A long thread pulled back and forth across a tear or hole in a garment is liable to pull and stretch the darn out of shape.—Miss MacGregor, Sutherland Cottage, Keir Street, Dunblane.

POLO NECKS—When knitting pullovers with polo necks, cast off with double wool and a larger-size knitting needle. This makes the neck much stronger, and it stretches easily.—Mrs I. J. Kean, 2 Somertrees Avenue, Grove Park, London.

FOR KNITTERS—I knit a lot and find the underpart of my sleeves wear thin with the friction of the needles. I now slip an old glove finger over the head of each needle. As well as saving my cardigans, it is much more comfortable.—Mrs J. Ewan, 3 Camphill Avenue, Langside, Glasgow.

NYLONS—When darning nylons, the ordinary mending silk is too thick, so pull a thread from an old silk or rayon stocking and repair with this. The result is an invisible mend which is very durable.—Miss Violet McCallum, Campbeltown.

SIEVE REPAIR—To mend holes in a sieve, use fine waxed string or fine catgut and a large darning needle. Finish off ends neatly.—R. Harris, 8 Denholm Drive, Giffnock.

ODD WOOL—To prevent odd balls of wool becoming entangled, wind firmly, thread the end in darning needle, and push through to opposite side of ball. Leave a short tail for pulling back again when wool is required.—Mrs J. Noble, 2 Academy Road, Fraserburgh.

NEATER DARN—When you've a three-cornered tear to mend, dampen edges of tear and the threads go into their natural position. Then you get a neater darn.—Mrs M. R. Anglesey, Tui, R.D.2 Wakefield, Nelson, New Zealand.

FRESH OUTLOOK—When knitting a dark jumper for a schoolgirl, knit a few collars in pastel shades. These are easily stitched on, giving the jumper a fresh appearance without constant washing.—Miss S. McArthur, 24 Baldwin Avenue, Knightswood, Glasgow.

NO CLOGGING—To clean a pepper pot lid, there's nothing like drawing a darning needle, with white thread, through the holes.—Miss R. Lock, 84 Watermoor Road, Cirencester.

HANDY—Use a marble as a miniature darning "egg" when mending finger-tips of gloves.—Mrs Harriet Smith, 14 John Street, Ruabon, Wrexham.

TIDY SOCKS—When knitting children's knee-length socks, after knitting the turn-over I do a row of holes. When the socks are finished I thread elastic through the holes. This keeps the socks much tidier.—Mrs D. Murray, 1 Hill Crescent, Aged Miners' Homes, Dawdon, County Durham.

DARNING—When darning woollen socks, I find that a wooden spoon fits the heel and toe best. It makes the task easier, and there's no bulge left.—Mrs T. J. Gill, 82 City Road, Beeston, Notts.

★ TOP TIP ★

MAKE THE BAIRNS' JERSEYS LAST LONGER—When knitting jumpers for my three children, I always make back and front exactly alike and fasten them on both shoulders. This makes them reversible and distributes wear over main parts as well as sleeves where elbows are rubbed.—A. Thompson, Thornton Park, Berwick-on-Tweed, wins a pair of towels.

UNSIGHTLY CUFFS—Instead of darning badly-worn cardigan cuffs (children's particularly) replace complete cuffs with jerkin elastic. This gives an effective and lasting finish to the garment. —Mrs M. T. L. Graham, 59 Marchfield Avenue, Paisley.

DARNING—When you've a big hole in a sock to repair put a piece of fine net across the hole and tack in place all round. Darn through the netting in ordinary way. This strengthens the darn and keeps heel or toe in shape.—Mrs W. Clements, 126 Coverington Road, Motherwell.

DIFFERENT—Knit tops of boys' stockings in a different colour for each boy. Then there's no excuse for picking wrong ones.—Miss C. Murdoch, 42 Kyle Street, Ayr.

SOCKS—I always darn my husband's Terylene and nylon socks with stranded embroidery silk. I find this lengthens their life, and I can usually get an exact matching shade.—Mrs J. Livingstone, 107 Station Road, Golcar, Huddersfield.

KNITTING—I found while knitting that the needles sometimes caught into any garment I was wearing. So I bought two rubber corks to pass the needles through. This saves any wear and tear.—Mrs R. Alexander, 117 Sunderland Street, Kirkcaldy.

NEW USE FOR A CAST-OFF—I successfully lengthened a woollen dress by opening the waist seam and inserting the ribbed welt of a cast-off jumper. A bought jumper does the job much better than a hand-knitted one.—Mrs D. Cameron, Brucefield Road, Rosemount, Blairgowrie.

STEAM IT—Before using a new skein or card of darning wool, hold it in steam from a boiling kettle, then let it dry. The wool doesn't shrink after use.—Miss M. B. Brown, 1039 Tollcross Road, Glasgow.

LONGER LIFE—Socks will last much longer if toes and heels are reinforced by darning before wearing.—Mrs J. Wales, 92 Cardross Street, Glasgow.

THIN TOWELS—When towels show signs of thinning, darn with candlewick cotton. This thickens with washing and makes the towels last longer.—Miss B. Fraser, Port Elphinstone, Inverurie.

TEARS—If you make a clean tear in a tablecloth or sheet, don't repair by hand. Run a few rows of machine-stitching across one way and then the other to cover the tear completely. This will be almost invisible after laundering. Coloured materials can be darned in the same way, using thread to match.—Miss H. Black, 27 Cleghorn Street, Dundee.

WON'T SLIP OUT—Babies' mitts and bootees have ribbons which slip out when washed. Instead, use a cord made of wool. Knit two small squares and fill them with balls of cotton-wool and attach to ends of cords. These don't slip out, and stand washing better than pom-poms.—Mrs M. Reid, 13 Deeside Gardens, Aberdeen.

PERFECT FIT—Elastic thread knitted along with the wool into the ribbing of waist, legs and all round top will give a perfect fit to a knitted swim suit.—Mrs Runcie, 6 Seatown, Cullen.

FOR KNITTERS—When knitting a cardigan or jumper for a narrow-shouldered person, change to smaller needles at half-way up the arm-holes. —Christine Brown, 9 Arthur View Terrace, Danderhall, Dalkeith.

LONG WEAR—If you wear rubber boots or Wellingtons, wear undersocks knitted from industrial sewing cotton. They'll lengthen the life of socks or stockings by many months. The cotton is a blue twine, sold by string merchants. Use two-ply and knit in the usual way.—Mrs E. Grant, 41 High Buckholmside, Galashiels.

MITT LININGS—After knitting winter mitts for baby, line them with white lint. The little hands are kept nice and warm.—Mrs A. Macdonald, 4 Kinkell Terrace, St Andrews.

CASTING OFF—When casting off top of sleeves of knitted garments, take two stitches together at beginning and end. This rounds off the corners and makes a neater finish.—Mrs Eadie, 33 Eskview Crescent, Musselburgh.

KNITTING—When knitting children's garments, knit the welt last by picking up the stitches along bottoms of the garment and sleeves. The cast off line on the welt is easily unpicked to lengthen the garment when outgrown.—Mrs E. Dixon, 33 Dene Crescent, Wallsend-on-Tyne.

NEAT JOB—When knitting strapping separately for the fronts of a cardigan, knit about nine inches then start sewing it on. Keep the edges stretched. Knit a few inches more and sew again. Keep on until the strapping is the correct length. A neat job results, and the work isn't so tedious.—Mrs Tasker, 14 Percival Street, Kirkcaldy.

NEEDLES—Always wash steel knitting needles and crochet hooks in hot soapy water before starting new work. Metal pins which have been left are apt to snag the first row of new garments or lace work.—Miss Wilson, Recreation Ground, Fulwell Road, Sunderland.

HANDY TABLE—I bought a knitting machine and did not have a table for it. I found using my ironing board was ideal.—Mrs E. Carberry, 324 Cragpark Drive, Glasgow.

KNITTING MACHINE—My knitting machine works much better if kept in a warm room in this damp weather. I put the wool in the airing cupboard a day before knitting it.—Mrs A. Smith, 16 Unwin Avenue, Bedfont, Feltham.

FOR KIDDIES—The new "jelly-bag" cap for kiddies can be made from sleeves of an old jumper. Make the ribbed border to fit the head, draw up other end neatly, and finish off with large tassel.—C. Reid, Conicavel, Darnaway, Forres.

KNITTED CUFFS—When my boy's lumber jacket sleeves got short, I knitted cuffs and sewed them on after removing cuff bands.—Mrs W. Findlay, 13 Strathmore Avenue, Arbroath.

FOR KNITTERS—When knitting a Fairisle pattern, copy the chart on to a sheet of graph paper, using coloured pencils to match the wool you are using. You will find it much easier to follow than black and white.—Miss Emily Master, 41 Parkhouse Road, Ardrossan.

FOR RIGHT SIZE—When I want to buy buttons for a new knitted cardigan, I search my button box for one that fits the buttonholes and take it to the shop along with a piece of wool for colour. That way I don't have to carry the garment with me.—Mrs F. Rennet, 126B Rannoch Road, Letham, Perth.

KNITTING PINS—When coloured steel knitting pins have become rough at the points with constant use due to the coating wearing off, apply two coats of colourless nail varnish. The wool doesn't catch and you work much quicker.—Mrs E. Corr, 130 Greenock Road, Largs.

WON'T TANGLE—When using a ball of crochet cotton, push a hat-pin through the centre and impale it in the padded arm of a chair or other arm surface. The ball then spins round and the cotton doesn't tangle or roll away.—Mrs J. T. Tait, 23 Burgh Road, Lerwick.

SOCKS—When knitting socks, knit one round with a different shade of wool just about halfway between heel and toe. This coloured line is then simple to cut and pull out, halving the foot in two when the time comes to re-toe the socks.—Mrs D. S. Murray, 207 Broadway, Horsforth, near Leeds.

FINGER PROTECTION—When a finger becomes sore with continual knitting, try wearing a finger-stall cut from an old kid glove. I find it a great help and it even makes me knit faster.—D. Linn, 45 Dunstable Road, Flitwick, Bedfordshire.

WOOL-WINDING—When winding wool in a ball which isn't to be used immediately, use a mothball for a core. The wool can be stored indefinitely in safety.—Miss M. Rizza, 14 Balmore Terrace, Aberdeen.

WOOL CONTAINER—Empty oatcake drums, with a small hole pierced in the top, make good holders to keep wool clean while knitting.—Mrs G. Young, 402 Main Street, Rutherglen.

The Sunday Post

Morning Special

PRINTED AND PUBLISHED EVERY SUNDAY MORNING.

No. 2608. [illegible] SUNDAY, AUGUST 21, 1955. Radio and TV—Page 4. PRICE 2½d.

Memorable Scenes At Royal Sale Of Work

Queen Sells Biscuits—Is Told "Keep The Change"

THE Queen sold tins of biscuits at 1s 6d to 15s.

The Duke of Edinburgh, grouse at 25s a brace.

Prince Charles and Princess Anne sold postcards.

Princess Margaret sold children's mugs at 5s each.

All to help a church sale of work at Abergeldie Castle, near Balmoral, yesterday.

The sale was organised by the Queen Mother, and was to raise funds for the building of a vestry at Crathie Church.

Thousands poured into Deeside. They queued up four deep long before the gates opened.

When one customer wanted to buy a tin of sweets the Duke of Edinburgh told him—"There's no price on it. Will you give me a couple of bob for it?"

The man smilingly agreed, handed over two half-crowns, and told the Duke to accept the change as a donation.

The Queen was also asked to "Keep the change!"

Miss Muriel Anderson, 412 Great Western Road, Aberdeen, bought a pin cushion from the Queen.

A tall girl, she stretched over the heads of people in front waving a pound note.

The Queen leaned forward and smilingly asked what she would like.

"Anything," said Miss Anderson. The Queen looked around before selecting a pin cushion.

Handing it to Miss Anderson, she said—"Just a moment and I'll get your change."

Miss Anderson replied—"Keep the change," and Her Majesty nodded smilingly to her.

Gales Of Laughter

The Queen and Princess Margaret joined their mother in the biggest of the marquees and were more than two hours busily serving the public.

The Duke, inside another marquee, provoked gales of laughter from crowds of womenfolk purchasing vegetables, biscuits and other provisions.

When one woman asked for the biggest tin of biscuits on the stall, the Duke lifted it in both hands and asked her with a laugh—"Have you a barrow to wheel it away?"

Prize Draw

The admission charge was 1s, with a similar charge for car parking.

Earlier in the day, the Queen, the Duke and other members of the Royal Family helped in the preparations.

While the Queen arranged articles on the Queen Mother's stall, the Duke was busy erecting a notice advertising a "grand prize draw" with tickets at 1s each.

Prince Charles ran from stall to stall inspecting the articles for sale.

6d A Guess

Royal gifts on the stalls, or offered as competition prizes, included a huge cake.

The public were to guess the weight at 6d a guess.

On the Queen Mother's stall, apart from grouse and salmon from the Royal estates, there were joints of venison at 25s each, sweets, vegetables and fruit.

All the week the Queen Mother had been supervising arrangements for the sale, and early yesterday was at work among the marquees and tents.

Among prizes given by the Royal Family for draws were:—

A clock.

A crocodile handbag.

A china teaset.

An 18-inch doll in a pink dress, which can walk, sleep and say "Mamma."

Other prizes included three bottles of whisky, a set of silver tea knives and a dog-basket packed with foodstuffs.

There were vegetables for sale at 2s 6d a basket, and large tins of [illegible] at £4 [illegible] each.

Princess Anne caused a laugh at her mother's stall when she spotted a handsome casket of chocolates lying unsold on a table.

(CONTINUED ON PAGE 2.)

Princess Margaret Falls As She Leaves Sale

PRINCESS MARGARET stumbled and fell full length in the grass as she was leaving the sale at Abergeldie Castle yesterday.

The crowds gasped as they saw her fall.

She had caught her foot in a hole in the long grass and lost her balance.

The Hon. Dominic Elliot, who had escorted the Princess during the afternoon, and another man, who was accompanying her, helped the Princess to her feet.

The Princess stood for a few seconds before continuing her walk to the car.

As she began to move off, she seemed to be limping slightly.

She said to Mr Elliot, "I think I have sprained my ankle."

She was able, however, to take the wheel of the green [illegible] car for the drive back to Balmoral.

The resident physician at Balmoral, Dr G. P. Middleton, was summoned to examine the Princess's ankle.

Dr Middleton was able to assure her no serious damage had been done, and that the pain would disappear after a night's rest.

The Hon. Dominic Elliot is the youngest son of the Earl and Countess of Minto, and is among the guests at Balmoral Castle this week-end.

THE QUEEN BEHIND THE COUNTER.

£40,000 BANK RAID

C.I.D. PROBE IN PERTHSHIRE

LAST night, two Glasgow detectives were in Perthshire, continuing their investigations into the Glasgow bank robbery in which £40,000 was stolen from a van.

With Superintendent Robert Colquhoun, acting head of Glasgow C.I.D., the two Detective Inspectors—James McAulay and Robert Kerr—went by fast car to Perth after receiving an urgent message.

They spent several hours in conference with Perthshire Police.

Then Superintendent Colquhoun returned to Glasgow. He left his two senior detectives in Perthshire to continue their work.

The bank robbery — Glasgow's biggest [illegible] on July 19.

[illegible] ambushed a bullion van outside the [illegible] Street branch of the British Linen Bank. They kidnapped a messenger and drove off with the van.

When Superintendent Colquhoun arrived back in Glasgow late yesterday, he had a conference at H.Q. with Chief Constable Malcolm McCulloch.

A Sunday Post reporter was told: "There may be developments later."

Peterhead Boy Drowned

WILLIAM WILSON, [illegible]-year-old son of Mr and Mrs James Wilson, [illegible] Road, Peterhead, was victim of a drowning tragedy at Peterhead yesterday.

He was playing among the rocks at [illegible] when he fell into a pool.

He was seen floating on the water.

When the alarm was raised, his father went into the water but could not reach the boy.

The boy was eventually brought ashore and artificial respiration was applied, but without success.

Crowds Mob Captain Townsend

SPECIAL police had to be called in yesterday to deal with traffic jams at the small Ostend race track.

The crowds had come to see Group-Captain Peter Townsend ride in the international gentlemen's course event.

About one in five in the crowd sweltering in the bright sunshine seemed to be a British tourist intent on catching a glimpse of the 41-year-old Battle of Britain pilot.

People crushed to the fence around the paddock when the Group Captain strolled into view in a light grey suit, smiling and chatting with track officials.

He soon changed into maroon cap and riding silks of grey circles on a silver background and was helped into the saddle of his horse [illegible].

After the race started, the Group Captain was in a bad position, lying fourth.

As the horses neared the finish and passed the grandstand, shouts of "Come on, Townsend," rose from the crowd.

And the Group Captain won the race.

The judges confirmed the result after studying photographs.

The event, the Prix de Cyrano, carried a first prize of 28,000 Belgian francs (about £200).

At the finish the crowd broke through the fences and ran towards Group Captain Townsend shouting, "You've won!"

[illegible] towards the exit, he was [illegible] by cheering spectators and had to be helped to his car by policemen.

The Group Captain is on local leave as Air Attaché in Brussels until the end of the month.

He does not intend to return to Britain until September 3, when he is due to fly to London for the Farnborough Air Show.

He may stay on until September 12 when he is due to attend the annual British Air Attachés' conference, or return to Brussels in the interval.

Today's Weather

SUNNY and warm, but some cloud and rain in places.

Chapter 17
The Man O' The Hoose

EVERY man was expected to be able to work with his hands.
As ever, the focus was on ingenuity and saving money. There are also insights into life at the time. You'd grow your own veg, of course, and take a zealot's pride in how well you could turn your hand to every trade. You'd also have a ready supply of alum, size and paraffin wax.
Interestingly, the majority of these tips were sent in by women. The men were the ones expected to do the tasks, but they may not have been the gaffers who handed out the jobs.

ASK HUBBY—Here's a way many husbands can help their wives. If there's a back door to your house get him to build a waist-high shelf next to it. Then, when you come home with your arms loaded with groceries you put the bundles on the shelf and have your hands free to open the door.—Mrs Mitchell, Partick, Glasgow.

WHY YOU SHOULD NEVER PAINT A LADDER—Paint hides weak, split wood and makes rungs slippery. Preserve with linseed oil instead.—Mrs A. Baird, St Anne's, 101 Westcliff Park Drive, Westcliff-on-Sea, wins a pair of towels.

TAP WASHERS—Use only moderate pressure when turning off water taps. Loose pressure allows water to drip and loosens the washer; and if you screw too hard it wears the washer.—Mrs H. Blundell, 142 Dean Swift Road, Ballymun, Dublin.

STEPS—If you're painting steps, do every other one and you can still use the remainder. When dry, paint the rest. The dry steps may then be walked on.—Mrs M. Watt, 178 Bank Street, Coatbridge.

THE VERY THING FOR THE VACUUM—To prevent the flex coming adrift at the plug end of electrical equipment in daily use, vacuum cleaner, iron, etc., attach a strong cord to take the strain of pulling. I've benefited by this since my husband applied the idea to all my electrical equipment.—Mrs A. Summers, 15 Cardell Drive, Paisley, wins a pair of towels.

HANDY SPIRIT LEVEL—A handy substitute for a spirit level is a flat bottle, such as a medicine bottle. Fill it with water and cork tightly, but leave enough air inside to form a bubble.—Andrew C. Lode, William Street, Tayport.

DON'T LET THE ROT SET IN—Constant wetting of the draining board causes an unpleasant form of rot. To make board waterproof, let it become perfectly dry, then rub well with paraffin wax. Heat with warm iron so that wax melts and sinks into the grain. A few treatments do the trick. Repeat periodically. Hard woods benefit most.—Mrs H. Elliott, Kidds House, Allenheads, Hexham, wins a pair of towels.

MEN ONLY—After shaving, place your razor (complete) in a screw-top jar containing surgical spirit. It's ready for use at all times, clean and sterilised.—David Muir, 6 Hunthill Road, High Blantyre.

CLEARS FROST—If you have to leave your car outside overnight and find the windows frosted in the morning, sprinkle a dry duster with table salt, and rub the windows. They clear in a moment.—Mrs W. Anderson, 16 Harvey Street, Carlisle.

★ TOP TIP ★

NO NEED TO HAVE SHOOGLY PICTURES ON THE WALL—If a screw has worn a hole too big to hold it, fill the hole with steel wool, as much as you can pack in. Put the screw back in and it will hold indefinitely.—Mrs E. F. Elworthy, 6 Elm Road, Rutherglen, Glasgow, wins a pair of towels.

NO MARKS—A strip of adhesive tape pasted over the head of a hammer prevents marks when driving in upholstery tacks. It also stops the hammer slipping off round-headed tacks.—Miss I. Morris, 5 Harriet Street, Kirkcaldy.

FOR MEN—An elastic band round your lighter will prevent it slipping out of your pocket.—T. Green, Millview, Shieldhill, Lochmaben.

RUSTY LOCK—Instead of oiling a rusty lock, oil the key and turn several times.—Mrs M. Macintyre, 67 Seamore Street, Glasgow.

FOR STUBBORN CAPS—To remove difficult screw-on caps such as those on sauce bottles, twist a rubber band round the cap. Then the cap can be loosened quite easily by hand.—James Murphy, 9 Gameshill View, Stewarton.

DRAWING PINS—A large cork kept in the tool box is useful for keeping odd drawing pins.—Mrs M. Cassell, 96 New City Road, Glasgow.

FROSTING—When my bathroom windows need re-frosting. I paint on a mixture of Epsom Salts dissolved in warm beer. The beer evaporates as it dries and leaves a frosted effect.—Mrs M. McDonald, Dundee.

★ TOP TIP ★

SEVEN THINGS WE SHOULD NEVER DO IN THE HOUSE—Don't have long flexes for electrical equipment. They may become unsafe, especially if at all frayed. Don't roll up flexes tight, this kinks the wires and breaks them. Don't leave flexes under carpets or lino or through doors or windows. Don't pull out a plug by flex, pull out plug itself. Don't fill kettle or pour from it when it's switched on. Don't plug a vacuum or other appliance into lamp-holders. Never touch any gadgets that are switched on while hands are wet.—Electrician, Glasgow, wins a pair of towels.

BROOM HANDLES—To prevent a handle working loose, paint the end of the handle and inside of the socket. Put the end of the handle inside the socket. Allow to dry. The handle will remain firmly fixed.—Mrs Thrussel, 2 Brunswick Place, Edinburgh.

VACUUM CLEANER—When the flexible tube of the vacuum cleaner becomes leaky through use, don't discard it. Buy an inside tube for a bicycle tyre, put it across the air valve, and pull rubber tube over flexible tube. Cut the length to suit, and seal the ends with adhesive tape. A first-class service can still be had for years. —James Y. Davidson, 5 Sycamore Place, Dundee.

NAILS—When driving a nail into a plaster wall, put a piece of cellulose tape across the spot to be nailed. No loose bits of plaster fall out of the wall.—Mrs F. Orchard, 97 The Crescent, Walsall.

WOODWORM—Mix one gallon paraffin with one gallon creosote. Coat the affected part with the mixture and leave for a day and then give another coat. It dries into the wood and clears out the woodworm.—R. Storey, 18 Sandridge, Newbiggin-by-Sea.

MAK SICCAR—Now that spring is round the corner, it is wise to sprinkle the drains and back yard with carbolic. This keeps down pests and insects when the warmer weather comes.—Mrs Appleton, 19 Ellengowan Drive, Dundee.

RUST—Stubborn rust is removed by rubbing with a piece of emery paper soaked in paraffin. Very obstinate patches should be wrapped in paraffin-soaked rags and left for a day or two.—Mrs Blacklaws, 42 Cameron Street, Stonehaven.

TOOL-HOLDER—Two or three small holes drilled through the topmost step of household steps make handy parking for screwdriver, gimlet, etc., when working at high-up jobs such as curtain rails.—James Martin, 20 Bearford Drive, Glasgow.

SQUEEZE BOTTLES—Empty polythene squeeze bottles are handy when plastering. They can be filled with water and used to dampen cracks before filling. The water comes out with such force that it washes away dust and loose plaster.—Mrs D. Bowen, 17 Victoria Place, Brechin.

STONE STEPS—I live upstairs with stone steps leading up. We tried several things to stick rubber mats down, but nothing was successful until I tried paint. They now stick down well, and have been in use for a year.—Mrs J. H. Campbell, Kildonan View, Drummore, near Stranraer.

OIL CANS—The squeeze-type bottles of washing-up liquid make handy oil cans when empty. Simply remove bung, rinse well, fill with oil and replace bung.—George E. Fulcher, 10 Queen Street, Thornley, Durham.

★ TOP TIP ★

CHOKED SINK—Having a choked sink and not having an orthodox plunger to clear it, I found a polythene basin effective. I filled the sink well up, immersed the basin over the outlet, gave several strong pushes on the flexible basin bottom. The sink cleared in record time. John Wallace, 20 Brucefield Terrace, Lochgelly, wins a pair of towels.

FUSES—Householders should renew electric fuses before the dark nights set in. It is better to do the job now than have to search around with matches or candle when the lights "go" suddenly. —Mr P. Devlin, 127 Harnall Lane West, Coventry.

ELECTRIC PLUGS—There is always a danger of slackening electric wall fittings through time if the plugs are stiff to insert. Vaseline or any lubricant applied to prongs of plugs helps to prevent this.—Mrs D. M. McGregor, Holborn View, Thurso.

EASY TO SEE—If you've an electric point in a dark corner paint round the edge of the pin holes with white paint. This makes it much easier to insert plug.—Mrs M. Gilmour, 21 Eliot's Park, Peebles.

FISHING GUIDE—Wind from the north, fish rise short. Wind from the east, fish bite the least. Wind from the south, fish take it in the mouth. Wind from the west, fish bite best.—Mrs Julia Pike, Elmbank, Bonhill, Alexandria.

GOOD GUIDE—If a car reflector is nailed or stuck in the centre of your garage wall it saves time and annoyance when backing the car in late at night.—Alberta Walker, 26 Woodside Crescent, Halifax.

RAZOR BLADES—A child's money box, painted to match the bathroom, makes a handy container for old razor blades. It takes a long time to fill, and dangerous old blades are easily disposed of.—Mrs J. S. Symington, 11 Windyedge Crescent, Glasgow.

HANDY PIN—When removing hard cotton wool from your cigarette lighter, you can prevent the wick pulling out if you place a pin through the exposed end.—F. W. Bell, 18 Westlands, Sunderland.

NO SCRATCHES—Fix lady's small rubber heels on the bottom of fireside chair legs. This prevents scratches and other marks on lino.—Mrs P. Hilton, 38 High Street, Old Basford, Nottingham.

★ TOP TIP ★

PREVENTS MARKS—Glue a piece of plastic foam on to the back of the enamel-type bathroom cabinet before screwing to wall. This prevents the wall being marked and also absorbs moisture.—Miss Wilson, 109 Ashdown Road, Farringdon, Sunderland, wins a pair of towels.

LOOSE KNOBS—Drawer knobs that repeatedly work loose are made firm by slipping a rubber band round the head of the bolt on the inside, then fasten tightly. The rubber acts as a lock washer.—James Marshall, 190 Bellfield Street, Glasgow.

SQUEAKY HINGES—It is rather a nuisance in these days of light painted doors when hinges become squeaky. To avoid any stain which might appear with oil, etc., rub the hinges with the rind cut from bacon before cooking. I've tried it, with perfect results.—Mrs D. Hughes, 10A Mottram Close, Northwood, Kirkby, near Liverpool.

SPLINTER FREE—Every now and then I go over the clothes-horse with glass paper and rub-down any small splinters there may be. One small splinter can cause a lot of damage to nylons, etc.—Mrs Freeman, 291 Chesterfield Road, Dronfield, Sheffield.

STOPS OVERFLOW—When cistern or outlet pipe leaks or overflows, tie up the regulating ball inside the cistern to keep it in a high position. This prevents water entering till plumber arrives.—J. Turner, c/o 2 Clifford Road, Southport.

FOR WATER TANKS—Every few years it's a good thing to paint the inside of your attic water supply tank. Drain off water, dry thoroughly, then paint with anti-corrosive paint. Allow to dry before refilling tank. This adds life to the tank.—Mrs Robertson, Dundee.

STEEL WOOL—To protect hands when using steel wool, grip it in a clamp-type paper clip. Fold wad of wool once and insert ends between jaws of the clip.—Mrs M. Alberti, 24 Longay Street, Glasgow.

HINGES—Hold hinges in position with cellulose tape while screw holes are marked out, drilled and screws secured.—W. Morgan, 40 Clare Street, Manselton, Swansea.

CYCLES—When laying up a cycle for the winter, stand it upside down with the handlebars and seat resting on a mat or board. This preserves the tyres.—Mrs Sievewright, 6 Castle Street, Turriff.

FIRM JOB—When putting new webbing under chairs, first soak it overnight. Nail on while still damp and it dries taut and firm.—Mrs Birchall, 6 Primrose Terrace, Mill Hill, Blackburn.

FOR THE HANDYMAN—Handiest gadget for the handyman is 20 feet of wire with a bulb at one end and a plug at the other. For jobs in awkward places you always have a light just where it is wanted.—Mrs B. C. Thomson, 30 Murray Terrace, Carnwathe Lanark.

Meridian

—man and boy!

Only Meridian make 'Double Lock' the perfect fabric for sensitive skins

DOUBLE LOCK	Lightwt. 34"-38"	Heavywt. 34"-38"
Singlet	7/-	9/3
Trunks	7/-	10/3
Jockey Shorts	7/-	-
Vests (button front half sleeve)	10/3	13/-
Vests (closed front half sleeve)	9/6	11/9
Pants (long)	12/6	15/3
Trunks (button front)	9/11	11/3

Larger sizes extra

Boys: Singlet and Jockey shorts from 4/- Trunks from 4/6 Vests from 6/-

MERIDIAN LIMITED · NOTTINGHAM

THE SUNDAY POST, JANUARY 8, 1956.

The Sunday Post

Morning Special

PRINTED AND PUBLISHED EVERY SUNDAY MORNING.

No. 2628 | REGISTERED AT THE GENERAL POST OFFICE AS A NEWSPAPER | SUNDAY, JANUARY 8, 1956. | Radio and TV—Page 4. | PRICE 3d

Lucky Black Cat!

The wedding took place yesterday at St Mary's Church, Ealing, of 21-year-old actress Miss Helen Lennox, and producer Bryan Blackburn.

U.S. Has "Unbelievably Powerful Weapon"

WORLD'S GREATEST EXPLOSIONS SOON

THE United States will probably explode two hydrogen bombs in a new series of tests in the Pacific early this year, and cause the greatest explosions the world has ever known.

This was announced in Washington yesterday.

The biggest blast will come from a bomb dropped from the air.

In 1952 and in 1954 the U.S. exploded hydrogen bombs in the Eniwetok Islands.

They were so big they had to be housed in sheds, and were far too large to be carried by an aircraft.

But the U.S. has now developed an almost unbelievably powerful weapon, small enough to be delivered by modern atom-bombers, said Congressional sources yesterday.

A Soviet test last November was reported to have been between one to five megatons.*

There were reports that the United States planned to detonate an even bigger bomb—perhaps in the order of 20 megatons—immediately after the 1954 blast.

But this plan was shelved temporarily, some sources said, because of the widespread radio-active fall-out from the earlier explosion, which produced protests from abroad.

Japanese fishermen in boats operating outside the officially proclaimed danger area were exposed to radiation.

New explosions will be in the Eniwetok testing area in the Pacific.

Under present plans, more than one island site will be used in order to conduct a quick series of tests.

New Trigger

There has been a big school of thought in Washington that the adverse impact on world opinion would outweigh any gains.

But since the Soviet explosion, most authorities have come round to the view that the U.S. would have to conduct further tests to make sure that the knowledge acquired by Soviet scientists was also available in Washington.

Yesterday's reports caused no immediate stir in many embassies.

There has been talk in scientific quarters in U.S. that a recent U.S. "breakthrough" has led to the development of a new-type hydrogen weapon which does not require an atomic bomb as a trigger.

Hitherto the millions of degrees heat generated by the explosion of an atomic bomb core has been necessary.

It causes the fusion process of light hydrogen elements, which gives the hydrogen weapon its awesome power.

Cutting out the atomic bomb core would mean that the size of the weapon could be considerably decreased.

** A megaton is the explosive equivalent of 1,000,000 tons of T.N.T.*

EDEN TO RESIGN RUMOUR DENIED

A SURPRISING rumour gained currency last night that Sir Anthony Eden intends to resign the Premiership in a few months' time, and that he will then be succeeded as Prime Minister by Mr R. A. Butler.

This was categorically denied when I made inquiries at 10 Downing Street, writes a political correspondent.

A Downing Street spokesman said, "This story is false and without any foundation whatever."

Friends of the Prime Minister say that he has been in noticeably vigorous health.

This, indeed, was demonstrated to some extent by the fact that he presided on successive days over Cabinet meetings that lasted two hours and twenty minutes and three hours respectively.

In addition, he has been extremely busy with a series of Ministerial consultations on departmental issues.

Sir Anthony is spending the week-end at Chequers.

Another Cabinet meeting is expected this week. He has an important public speech and a party political broadcast to make before he leaves with Mr Selwyn Lloyd, Foreign Secretary, on January 25 for the Washington talks with President Eisenhower.

The German newspaper "Die Welt's" London correspondent wrote yesterday — "The British Prime Minister is facing the most dangerous crisis of his political career.

"In diplomatic quarters there are increasingly strong rumours that his resignation is to be reckoned with in the coming summer."

ARMED GUARD AT DUNDEE GIRL'S WEDDING

A DUNDEE girl was married in Cyprus yesterday—and there was an armed guard at her wedding.

She is 22-year-old Patricia Jane Halley, a secretary at the political office, Middle East Armed Forces, based on Nicosia.

[illegible]

Dies In Vapour Bath

MR JACK [illegible], aged 61, of [illegible], Edgware, Middlesex, collapsed and died last night while taking a vapour bath at [illegible] Baths.

Blizzard Hits North

HEAVY snow fell last night in Aberdeen and many parts of the North-East.

In Aberdeen conditions were particularly bad between 7 p.m. and 8 p.m.

Blinding snow showers cut down visibility in the streets.

As windscreens became blocked up, traffic had to proceed with great caution.

The melting snow on the road surfaces made conditions trying.

A telephone round-up last night showed that snow was general in the area from Stonehaven to Braemar and to Elgin and Fraserburgh.

Huntly had severe snow showers and was one of the areas worst affected.

Detectives Search Near Murder Tee

POLICE investigations yesterday switched back from Blantyre to East Kilbride, as the hunt for the murderer of 17-year-old Ann Kerr[illegible] entered its fifth day.

[illegible]

Today's Weather

RATHER cold, with frost at night. Bright periods. Scattered showers of snow or rain.

Chapter 18
Those Sensible Women

THE sensible housewife, full of good advice and unstoppably going to give it, was a familiar creature in the 1950s. They had sensible hair-dos, wore sensible skirts and strode forth purposefully in sensible shoes. They'd keep you right, whether you wanted to be kept right or not.

Their common-sense approach to life and the tasks it held was achieved with rolled-up sleeves, hard graft and a sharp word for any who didn't live up to their high standards.

They were the bane of shirkers, lazybones, good-for-nothings and small boys who looked like they might grow up to be a member of one of those evil categories.

Sometimes it wasn't just what they said, it was the way they said it.

It has been claimed that they did not take kindly when it was pointed out they may be wrong, although there are very few examples of them ever actually being wrong and no examples at all of them admitting they were wrong.

In the few quiet moments they got from keeping the world on the right track, they penned grammatically perfect letters, in neat handwriting, to The Sunday Post. They had strength of character and knew, from the tips of their fingers to the depths of their soul, that all problems could be solved with honest-to-goodness sense and hard work.

It's a pity there aren't more of them in the world today.

QUICK WAY—To open a packet of water or other biscuits, take a sharp knife and cut smartly down centre. There are no casualties and no waste of time.—Mary Thomson, 42 Carlton Place, Aberdeen.

FOR STAINS—To remove beetroot stains from a tablecloth, place a saucer of cold water underneath the stain with a piece of bread on top. The moistened bread absorbs the stain. The cloth can then be washed in the usual way.—Miss Ritchie, 13 Bolivar Terrace, Glasgow.

CARPETS—When washing carpets I stand my pail containing water on a tray. It is easily moved across the carpet, leaving no mark. There is room on the tray for extra cloths, brush, etc.—Mrs J. Crawford, 11 Wynyard Square, Sunderland.

HANDY CUTTER—I made a handy soap cutter from a length of fuse wire with a small brass curtain ring attached to each end.—Mrs Ellen Craig, 27 South Sperrin, Knock, Belfast.

PAINT REMOVER—My little girl got red paint down one side of her cardigan. I rubbed butter well into the paint, then rinsed it in lukewarm water. The mark disappeared.—Mrs G. Wilson, 8 Baden Street, Chester-le-Street.

SAVES THE HANDS—Slip a rubber bicycle handlebar grip over the end of your bamboo carpet beater. You get a much better grip and the beater is far more comfortable to use.—Mrs J. Macleod, 26 Kenneth Street, Stornoway.

SINK OVERFLOW—To clean the overflow in the sink, purchase a plastic extension for the tap. Fit it on, then turn on the water and bend the extension until the water is running into the opening. This can be done several times a day.—Mrs I. Watt, 29 Easter Drylaw Avenue, Edinburgh.

NON-SLIP STRAPS—To the inside of heel straps of sandals or sling-back shoes, fix an elastic band with rubber solution. This prevents straps slipping.—E. Crombie, 38 Gadloch Street, Glasgow.

DOUBLE PURPOSE—A small nailbrush, carried in the handbag, makes a handy travelling clothes brush.—Miss A. Yuill, 64 Mackie Avenue, Port Glasgow.

HANDY HOLDER—Buy a plastic plant pot holder to match your kitchen colour. Put screws five inches apart and hang it near the sink. It holds pot scrubbers and small things required daily.—Mrs Violet Drover, Murtle Den Cottage, Milltimber, Aberdeen.

CURDS—Having failed to make curds with essence of rennet, I discovered they don't set when made with pasteurised milk.—Mrs W. Nicholson, 2 Caerlaverock Road, Prestwick.

KEYS—If you have a several similar keys on a ring, paint the top of the one most used with bright nail varnish. This saves delay. It's easier seen and feels smoother than the others in the dark.—Mrs B. Morton 46 Winchester Walk, Wideopen, Northumberland.

★ TOP TIP ★

EASY CLEANING—To clean behind a wardrobe or other piece of furniture too heavy to move, put a dust sheet over the top at the back and pull it from side to side, working to the bottom. Dust and fluff comes down with the sheet and is easily gathered up. I found this a wonderful help at spring-cleaning time.—Mrs G. D. Tilley, Fernbank, 195 Maxwellton Avenue, East Kilbride, wins a pair of towels.

CLEAN BOOKS—Save your polythene potato bags. Wash them and slip them over your books. It keeps them clean and dust free.—Mrs A. Macnamara, 1 Ferry Road Avenue, Edinburgh.

EMERGENCY CONTAINERS—If you run short of containers for your fridge (and also want to get the utmost use from the space in a small one), use jam jars as holders for odds and ends of food.—Mrs Shaw, 11 Ruthven Avenue, Giffnock.

SOAP HELPS—To make a lamp shade simpler to unscrew, smear a small quantity of soap round the inner thread of the round Bakelite holder. When fitting a new lamp shade it will unscrew very easily.—Mrs E. Prentice, 110 Hamilton Road, Glasgow.

PYJAMA CORD—Use a crepe bandage. It boils, stretches to any length and wears for ages.—Mrs H. Caney, 218 Glasgow Street, Ardrossan.

HANDY JACKET—Make a plain jacket of terry towelling and wear it under your rubber-lined mackintosh. It absorbs moisture which collects and keeps the rubber from perishing. If a gay and colourful towelling is used, the jacket could serve as a beach coat for a seaside holiday.—Mrs J. Brown, 64 Grange Estate, Church Crookham, Near Aldershot.

ORNAMENTS—When placing fine glass ornaments on a glass-topped table or display cabinet shelf, place them on plasticine. This prevents the most delicate ornaments from being broken should the cabinet or table be disturbed.—Mary Gallagher, 27 Cumberland Place, Old Monkland, Coatbridge.

DRY SALT—After filling salt shakers, seal carton with sticky tape to keep out moisture.—I. P. Smith, Parkneuk, Arbuthnott, Fordoun.

KEEPS STEADY—Instead of filling miniature arrangement containers with water, fill them with damp sand. The flowers stay fresh longer and the risk of upset is lessened by the weight of the sand.—Mrs Ingram, The Smithy, Manbeen, by Elgin.

SOAP-SAVER—I place my soap on a piece of one-inch-deep plastic foam cut to fit my soap dish. This allows the soap to dry off, and I find it lasts much longer.—Mrs Morrison, 34 Granville Road, Bradford.

BASKETS—By varnishing your new shopping basket with clear varnish, it lasts much longer and keeps its bright new look. —Mrs C. Stevenson, 302 Linthaugh Road, Glasgow.

IN PLACE OF CORKS—Fingers cut from worn out rubber gloves make good replacements for lost corks of bottles. The finger fits firmly over the mouth of the bottle.—Mrs Olive Tait, 23 Burgh Road, Lerwick.

BADGES—Before sewing on a blazer badge, blanket stitch round the edges to stop fraying. It is then easily taken off to fix on to another garment.—Mrs M. Spence, Gasworks House, Duns.

NON-SCRATCH VASES—Stick circles of adhesive plastic material to the bottoms of unglazed pottery vases. This prevents them scratching polished surfaces.—Mrs J. McGowan, 17 South Street, Greenock.

NO SMELL—After using forks for fish or any oily food, it is sometimes difficult to get rid of the smell and taste. Simply push forks into some soil, the nearest potted plant will do, and the smell or taste disappears.—Mrs J. Hide, 20 Mill View Close, Westham, Pevensey, Sussex, wins a pair of towels.

MARSHMALLOWS—If marshmallows have become hard, put them in a polythene bag and dip into hot water.—Miss R. Shepherd, Kalokeri, Silverknowes Road South, Edinburgh.

ROUGH EDGES—When buying a cheap straw message bag sometimes the inside edge is very rough. Bind round with Rufflette tape. Also sew a zip pocket on either side for purse, keys, etc.—Miss Helen Gray, 7 Columshill Place, Rothesay.

HAND LOTION—For good economical hand lotion put a dessertspoonful of very finely sieved oatmeal into a jar, add the same quantity glycerine, lemon juice and methylated spirits and half a teaspoonful of almond essence. Leave overnight and shake before using.—Mrs M. Jeffrey, 27 Moyne Road, Glasgow.

UMBRELLAS—To keep an umbrella in good condition on damp days, rub all the ribs and handle with a good wax polish. It keeps steel parts from rusting and makes it easy to open and shut. Do this from time to time.—Mrs W. Littlejohn, 15 Hebburn Crescent, Arbroath.

CAMOUFLAGE—When giving tablets to children, I have found that a good idea is to halve a glacé cherry and put the crushed tablet inside. The other half should then be replaced. As most children love glacé cherries, they don't make any fuss.—Mrs J. Bates, Meikle Ussie, Conon.

CUTLERY DRAWER—Cut foam rubber the size of the divisions in your cutlery drawer and lay in the bottom. This stays put and is easily taken out and washed.—R. Black, 135 East Main Street, Broxburn.

TIE A KNOT—When lacing boots or shoes, invariably we finish with one lace longer than the other. To prevent this, tie a knot in the centre of the lace. No matter how hard you pull, you'll find both ends even.—Mrs D. Feeney, 30 Sandaig Road, Barlanark, Glasgow.

★ TOP TIP ★

VASELINE—I found the stud fasteners of my plastic coat were difficult to fasten. I applied Vaseline to both sides of studs, and have had no further trouble.—Miss Ina Mckay, Holburn View, Thurso, wins a pair of towels.

ANTI-FREEZE—Put a teaspoonful of glycerine in the toilet cistern overnight. It helps to prevent the water freezing.—Mrs M. White, 38 St Magdalen's Road, Perth.

STICKY JOB—Dip your kitchen scissors in hot water before cutting up sticky things, such as dates, marshmallows, etc.—Mrs R. Pattinson, 7 Chertsey Mount, Carlisle.

FOR INVALIDS—For invalids or children in bed, use a tray cloth cut out of plastic foam rubber. If anything is spilled, it's quickly absorbed and the cloth easily cleaned. It also prevents plates, etc., from slipping about.—Miss Murdoch, c/o MacKay, 117 Dalry Road, Edinburgh.

PRACTICAL HINT—If you do not have a rotary beater, tie two forks back-to-back. This makes an excellent whisk.—Mrs M. Denton, 33 West Avenue, Balkwell, North Shields.

TIME SAVERS—Put all dusters and cleaning materials in a paper carrier bag when starting the morning cleaning. Carry from room to room as you clean and dust.—Mrs J. McKenzie, 17 Dalkeith Avenue, Bilton, Rugby.

HANDBAG CLEANER—A few drops of eau-de-cologne, used on cotton wool to clean the lining of your hand-bag, removes powder or grease marks and leaves the bag beautifully fresh.—G. Morris. 5 Harriet Street, Kirkcaldy.

HANDY—I keep a stock of stamped envelopes and postcards. Then, if anyone has to write a letter in a hurry, there is no need to worry about a closed Post Office or empty stamp machines.—Miss M. A. McIntosh, 34 Montague Street, Glasgow.

★ TOP TIP ★

HAT SECRET—Instead of marring the beauty of your new hat by using a hatpin, sew a small comb, teeth upwards, inside the hat in the band at the front. The comb keeps the hat securely in place.—Mrs C. Stevenson, 302 Linthaugh Road, Glasgow, wins a pair of towels.

CHALK—Keep a stick of white chalk, as used for school blackboards, in the box with your trinkets. It prevents tarnishing.—Miss M. B. Brown, 1039 Tollcross Road, Tollcross, Glasgow.

USEFUL STAND—I have found a three-tier cake stand most useful in a sickroom. Placed at the bedside, it has held a table lamp on top tier, and medicines, books and other small items on the others. It is quickly and easily lifted aside for cleaning and tidying up.—Nurse P. Cunningham, 3 Garway Road, Westbourne Grove, London.

MORE SPACE—When baking, if you find your kitchen table is a bit small, pull out the drawer and lay a tray across it.—Mrs G. Robertson, 18 Keystone Avenue, Milngavie, by Glasgow.

CORKS—If a cork breaks off in the neck of a bottle, push a fine steel crochet hook gently through. You'll draw it out easily.—M. Wollaston, 8 Tame Street, Palfrey, Walsall.

TEACUPS—To prevent teacups from becoming stained, always pour the milk in first.—Mrs J. Graham, 42 Wilson Avenue, Falkirk.

ANT TRAP—I've found this ant trap very effective. Pour water used for cooking peas into a bowl and place overnight where ants are most evident.—B. Fox, 6 Averill Street, Hammersmith, London.

LESS NOISE—To keep brushes from banging every time the brush cupboard door is opened, glue a piece of thick felt or foam rubber to the inside of the door.—Mrs J. Shanks, 64 Preston Crescent, Linlithgow.

GOOD BEATER—A length of rubber hose-pipe makes an excellent carpet beater. It's not hard on the carpet.—G. Suttie, 44 Back Dykes Terrace, Falkland.

NEW SAUCEPANS—Before using new saucepans or frying pans, first boil a few potato peelings for ten minutes. This prevents any tendency for food to stick.—Mrs A. Haig, 79 Cheviot Road, Kirkcaldy.

CYCLES—To remove rust from the rims of bicycle wheels, put a piece of paper between the brake blocks and the rim. Apply brakes, turn pedals, and rims will be quite clean.—Mrs C. Douglas, 53 Clouston Street, Glasgow.

WELL STUCK—I always found those rubber suction cup gadgets kept falling down, and had to be replaced every few days. I rubbed the part which fastens to the wall with castor oil. Now they are clamped firmly as if stuck on with glue.—Mrs A. Duffy, 17 Dalcross Street, Glasgow.

GAS COOKERS—Many a gas cooker would be improved if, once or twice a week, the burners were removed, turned upside down, and gently tapped to remove particles of food or dust. The apertures should be cleaned by running a pipe cleaner through them and the whole kept clean by frequent rubbing and scouring with hot suds.—Miss A. W. Caw, 19 Falcon Gardens, Edinburgh, wins a pair of towels.

SAFE POSITION—To protect a fragile object when packing it up for the post, cut a slit in one end of a plastic foam sponge and slip the article inside. It travels safely and its cheaper than using cardboard for packing.—A. W. Wilkie, Park Lane, Aberdour.

BOTTLE TOPS—Bakelite and plastic bottle tops are often hard to unscrew at the first opening. Apply a cloth soaked in hot water to the top for a few minutes and they will unscrew without strain.—Mrs M. Fleming, 1 Smith Avenue, Inverness.

THE SUNDAY POST, JUNE 24, 1956

The Sunday Post

PRINTED AND PUBLISHED EVERY SUNDAY MORNING.

No. 2652 | REGISTERED AT THE GENERAL POST OFFICE AS A NEWSPAPER | SUNDAY, JUNE 24, 1956. | Radio and TV—Page 4. | PRICE 3d

It's To Be The Greatest Trade War In History

EDEN WARNS THE NATION

"Unless We Work Harder—"

"WE are witnessing the start of a trade rivalry, the like of which we have never known."

This stern warning to the nation about its position in the world markets was given yesterday by Sir Anthony Eden.

"Please stand back from your daily life for a moment and consider with me what is actually happening around us.

"Events are taking place in the world today which are very much more serious than the question of who shall bore holes in what, or how to keep up with the Joneses'.

"In the last war we could picture the dangers only too vividly. They were close and real.

"The contrasting dangers of today make less impact on the mind, but believe me, they, too, are very real.

"The loss of our export markets could do to our country what the U-boats twice failed to do.

"The 1960's and 1970's are rich in the promise of the nuclear age.

"But I must say to our people today—unless we work harder, unless we look on these years of the 50's as decisive for good or ill, then we shall never enjoy that promise.

"It will fall to others.

"I do not believe that British people will be so short-sighted as to throw away this splendid chance.

Spending Cuts

"Over the years the value of money has fallen.

"What we are doing now is to use all the resources at our command to check that fall.

"It is quite true that we had a Budget surplus last year.

"It is equally true we are budgeting for an even larger surplus this year, and that we are making every effort to add to this by further economies in Government expenditure.

"We intend to announce the first instalment of these next week.

Tax Cuts When—

"You may say it would have been possible for us to have given some of that surplus away in the form of further tax reductions.

"If we had, either to the middle classes or to anyone else, at a time when our reserves are still so slender, we should have weakened the pound. That would have hit those on fixed incomes most of all.

"Once we have established our reserves at a level we consider safe, and are really paying our way, then we shall be able to reduce taxation again.

"The less we spend on ourselves, and the more we can divert to exports, the sooner shall we build up our reserves to the safety mark.

"That is why we appeal for savings in a variety of forms.

"We all know the old phrase 'Save for a rainy day.' I would rather say—'Save for a sunny day.'"

MISS EVELYN BRUCE, well-known fashion model, and Mr John Mackinlay Boyd, after their wedding in the University Chapel, Glasgow, yesterday. (See Page 3.)

Women Weep At Marion's Wedding

THE bridal carriage drew up outside Portobello Old Parish Church. Out stepped the bride, pale and nervous.

And hundreds of women wept as [illegible]-year-old Marion Watson was helped into her wheelchair and pushed down the church aisle to meet her bridegroom.

For Marion lost her legs in a motor cycle smash three and a half years ago.

That day she was out on a spin with Mr George Davie, [illegible] Park Terrace, Edinburgh. It ended in a smash.

Marion was taken to Bangour Hospital and remained there for [illegible] months. She had [illegible] grafting operations.

Then she went to Leeds to learn how to walk on artificial legs.

All through the long crisis, George was by her side. They became engaged. And they planned their wedding.

YESTERDAY Marion intended walking up the aisle, but it was too much for her.

But she smiled all day — even though many women in the church were weeping openly. One had to be assisted from the balcony.

After the service, the groom wheeled his bride to a small table in front of the organ.

Rev. [illegible] had brought it in to save Marion the trouble of going to the vestry to sign the marriage certificate.

As they signed, a friend sang—"I'll Walk with God."

Then George wheeled his young wife out to the taxi and helped to lift her into the back seat.

And they set off with the good wishes of hundreds ringing in their ears.

Lightning Hits Dundee Power Cable

THUNDERSTORMS in Perthshire, Fife, Angus and along Tayside last night came at the end of a day of sweltering heat. They caused havoc in the Fintry area of Dundee.

[illegible]

FIRE SWEEPS HOSPITAL

SIXTY Army patients, including 18 in bed, were evacuated when fire broke out in a block of Army buildings at Shorncliffe, near Folkestone, last night.

One section of the block was used as a hospital, and the other by the garrison Army education centre.

[illegible]

CYPRUS POTATOES CHEAPEST SINCE WAR

HUNDREDS of tons of Cyprus potatoes are pouring into Scotland this week-end.

They're selling cheaper than at any time since before the war.

And because of the cheapness of the Cyprus potatoes, Ayrshire merchants have stopped hundreds of workers digging their crops meantime.

They can't get the price they want for the Ayrshires.

Army curfews in Cyprus are given as the reason for the cheapness of the foreign potatoes.

The Cyprus boats were held up for several days. Finally, they all managed to get away—together. And they arrived together, to make a potato glut.

Ike Out Of Hospital In A Week

PRESIDENT EISENHOWER'S doctors told him yesterday he would be discharged from hospital in about a week, "if his recovery continues as it has to date."

Yesterday afternoon's medical bulletin said that wire sutures used during the operation on Mr Eisenhower were cut yesterday and will be removed within 24 hours.

Harding Flies Back

FIELD MARSHAL SIR JOHN HARDING, Governor of Cyprus, arrived in Nicosia by air yesterday from London, after talks with Sir Anthony Eden.

His departure from London was kept secret until his R.A.F. plane was well on its way.

Sir John said: "I was given an ample opportunity to explain my view to responsible Ministers and we were in agreement on all points."

He had no doubt that the British Government would be making a statement in due course.

Terrorists yesterday threw two bombs at a party of British servicemen at [illegible] village. There were no injuries. Two men were later arrested.

Today's Weather

RATHER cloudy, with a little rain or drizzle in places. Bright periods.

Chapter 19
Carpets And Linoleum

WALL-TO-WALL carpets are a relatively recent luxury. In the 1950s, a carpet was in the centre of the room (sometimes this was only a "good" room), while the outer areas were varnished floorboards or were covered by cold, shiny linoleum.

If you got new lino, you laid it yourself—then you wrote to The Sunday Post about it.

CARPET DENTS—To remove marks left on a carpet by heavy furniture, lay a damp cloth over the spot and place a hot iron on top. The steam restores the pile. When thoroughly dry, brush the pile gently with a stiff brush.—Mrs E. J. Tocher, 43 Watermill Road, Fraserburgh.

LINO TILES—When laying tiles, I found a paint roller quick and efficient for applying the adhesive. The roller is easily cleaned with hot water.—J. Abel, 20 Begg Avenue, Glenfuir, Falkirk.

LINOLEUM—When cutting linoleum, heat the blade of the knife. It will cut through without tearing.—Mrs Ireland, Ruthwell Station, Dumfries.

NO SCRATCHES—Fix lady's small rubber heels on the bottom of fireside chair legs. This prevents scratches and other marks on lino.—Mrs P. Hilton, 38 High Street, Old Basford, Nottingham.

CARPET SAVER—Before lifting a carpet for cleaning, put a safety pin in one corner. Then, when relaying, that corner can be put to the other side of the room, and so change the tread.—Miss A. Campbell, 18 King's Park Avenue, Glasgow.

★ TOP TIP ★

IF THE NEW LINO WON'T LIE FLAT—I had trouble with a new lino square which would not lie flat after coming off the roll. I filled several hot water bottles, laid them along the troublesome edge, and covered them over with an old travelling rug. By the time the bottles were cold the lino lay lovely and flat on the floor.—Mrs W. Culbert, 10 Perth Road, Stanley, wins a pair of towels.

LINOLEUM—An easy way to replace worn linoleum is to buy two or three linoleum tiles each week. The small sum of money expended is never missed, and the tiles are easily stored until required.—Mrs K. Leishman, 10 Wardlaw Road, Edinburgh.

LINO—When removing, always roll linoleum with the pattern outside. This keeps it from turning up at the sides when re-laid.—Miss H. McDonald, Lundie Lodge, Brechin.

CHAIR CASTORS—To keep chair castors from marking and tearing the linoleum, I run a strip or two of adhesive tape round the castor. It's been a great success.—Mrs M. Keir, Perth Road, Coupar Angus.

SAVES THE LINO—Metal wringer stands sometimes score the linoleum. To avoid this, get four rubber door stops the size nearest to diameter of stand leg, and insert them in the bottom of the legs.—Mrs Mary Smith, 27 Ibrox Street, Glasgow.

QUICK CLEANER—Steel wool dipped in water and rubbed on soap takes boot polish off linoleum where scrubbing won't.—Mrs M. A. McLachlan, 3 Linnet Road, Greenock.

A TIP FOR LAYING LINO—When laying linoleum on an uneven stone floor, fill up the uneven parts with clean, fine sawdust, so making an even surface. This prevents hollows underneath the lino, and enables it to wear much longer.—Edward Clark, 20 Upper Canning Street, Belfast, wins a pair of towels.

KEEP RUG FROM CREEPING—To prevent a rug creeping towards the hearth, sew flat, lead weights, three inches apart, between two lengths of upholsterer's binding. Stitch one side of binding to edge of rug, and slip the loose end under the carpet.—K. D. Watt, 18 Ruthrieston Circle, Aberdeen, wins a pair of towels.

CARPETS—A quick and easy method to remove grease spots from carpets is to cover them with a paste of baking soda and warm water. Rub in lightly, leave to dry, then brush off.—Mrs D. Gardiner, 40 Cromarty Gardens, Clarkston.

MARKS DISAPPEAR—For bad marks and stains on chairs and carpets use a nylon pot scrubber and soapy water. This moves the most stubborn marks and doesn't injure fibre or pile. Rub afterwards with clean dry cloth and leave to dry.—Mrs M. Anderson, 80 Cornhill Drive, Aberdeen.

UNDER CARPET—I put a large bundle of old newspapers to good use by fixing them, twelve sheets at a time, together with gummed paper, and laying them under my carpet. They make a lovely underpad, and help keep moths at bay.—Mrs I. Gillespie, 10 Glebe Street, East Kilbride.

LINO—A little linseed oil rubbed well into lino gives an excellent polish, and doesn't leave the surface slippery.—Mrs H. Smith, 14 John Street, Ruabon, near Wrexham.

FOR DIRTY LINO—Fill the foot of an old woollen sock with black soap, tie firmly, rub over the lino instead of scrubbing. It lifts the dirt like magic.—C. Cree, 138 Brassey Street, Glasgow.

TRY THIS IF YOU CAN'T TACK THE LINO DOWN—When laying lino where it can't be tacked down, give it time to "tread out," then rub a strip of transparent Cellophane tape down the joins. The lino is kept flat and dust doesn't get underneath.—Miss G. Mullard, 10 Prospect Place, Ashton, Preston, wins a pair of towels.

LINO WISDOM—Before laying lino, let it stand in a warm room for 24 hours. This will prevent it from cracking or peeling.—Miss A. Wilson, O.F.O. Grounds, Fulwell Road, Sunderland.

LINO TILES—To those bothered with lino tiles becoming loose on a dry cement floor, lift the loose tiles, scrape and clean, also clean cement floor. Apply a fairly strong solution of waterglass to cement floor. Allow to dry, then replace tiles as before.—W. Hepburn, Potterton, Whitecairns.

A FLYING START IN LIFE

for a boy like you

The next group of boys to start their R.A.F. Apprentice training at an "air public school" will shortly be chosen. They will be chosen for one reason only . . . the Selection Board considers they are the right material for the backbone of the Air Force as skilled tradesmen. Many have a future as highly skilled instructors, as technical and flying officers; some, perhaps as high ranking leaders and administrators.

What a chance for a boy like you! Talk it over with your parents. Then send the coupon for information about the "flying start" that may lead you to a great future.

★ **POST BEFORE SEPT. 26 TO BE IN TIME**

TO: AIR MINISTRY, Dept. G.P.40, VICTORY HOUSE, KINGSWAY, LONDON, W.C.2.

I am between 15 and 17½. Please send (without obligation) details of R.A.F. Apprenticeships.

NAME ____________________

ADDRESS ____________________

GOOD VARNISH—Tip a quarter pound of orange shellac into a bottle, add half pint of methylated spirits and leave to dissolve, shaking frequently. This makes a durable varnish for kitchen or bathroom floors to save constant washing. It gives a high gloss, is non-slippy and marks are easily washed off.—Miss Anne M. G. Phillip, 1 Stafford Street, Barrow-in-Furness.

★ TOP TIP ★

A CARPET MADE NEW FOR 4s—I had a faded pink, Indian carpet. I bought eight sixpenny crimson dyes and went over it twice. I now have a new carpet at a cost of just four shillings.—Mrs Agnes Caldow, 52 Larchfield Avenue, Glasgow, wins a pair of towels.

RUBBER LINO—To revive black rubber floor covering, wash first, then, when dry, brush on black shoe polish. Leave for half an hour. Brush off in the ordinary way and give a good final rub with a duster.—M. Dewar, 6 Henry Bell Place, Helensburgh.

CLEAN FLOORS—To clean and polish floors in one operation, apply the floor polish on a piece of steel wool.—Mrs A. Den, 3 Brunton Quadrant, Glenrothes.

CARPET CLEANING—When shampooing a carpet, instead of using a brush cut a loofah in half and use the broad end. You get a good lather without wetting the carpet too much. Finish with a rough, dry cloth and the carpet looks like new.—A. Fletcher, 17 Millgate Avenue, Tannochside, Uddingston.

NO CREASES—When laying linoleum or applying adhesive material to flat surfaces try using a rolling pin to smooth out any air pockets and seal well.—Miss R. Parkhill, 74 Bushmills Road, Coleraine, N. Ireland.

UNDERFELT—A good substitute for underfelt for a carpet runner is to use a roll of corrugated paper the required length and an inch narrower. This gives a soft, springy tread, and can be replaced at little expense when necessary. It is best laid with the corrugated side to the floor.—Mrs Helen B. Wallace, West Norton Place, 27 Heron's Lane, Lochee, Dundee.

THE SUNDAY POST, SEPTEMBER 2, 1956

The Sunday Post

Morning Special

PRINTED AND PUBLISHED EVERY SUNDAY MORNING.

No. 2662. [REGISTERED AT THE GENERAL POST OFFICE AS A NEWSPAPER.] SUNDAY, SEPTEMBER 2, 1956. Radio and TV—Page 4. PRICE 3d.

Russians And British Train Together — "No Bad Feeling"

NINA IS STILL IN LONDON

Says Soviet

THREE of the Russian girl athletes seen running in the rain at Hurlingham yesterday.

POLICE were still unable last night to trace Nina Ponomareva, the 27-year-old Russian discus thrower charged with shoplifting.

But the Soviet newspaper "Pravda" said yesterday: "Nina is still in London."

And the Russian athletic team is expected to leave for home by air today or tomorrow.

The Russian athletes withdrew from their match with a British team in protest against the charge against Nina.

There was no aircraft available for the team yesterday.

After an unhappy morning in their West End hotel, the team donned track suits and went by coach to Hurlingham to continue their Olympic training programme.

Diane Leather, the British half-miler, said that most of the British athletes there were invited by the Russians to train with them, to show that no bad feeling existed between the teams.

The British contingent included, in addition to Diane Leather, Thelma Hopkins (high and long jump), Monica Podmore (javelin), Maya Giri (discus), Derek Johnson (half-mile), John Young (sprinter), Ken Box (long jump) and javelin throwers Malcolm Harradine, Clive Loveland and Peter Cullen.

Bitterly Disappointed At Cancellation

"This shows clearly that Russian and British athletes will have their friendship drawn even closer," said Pavel Potatkin, deputy manager of the Russian team.

But despite the atmosphere of friendly rivalry as the athletes went through their usual training routine, it was obvious that many of the Russians were bitterly disappointed at the turn of events which caused the cancellation of the match.

(CONTINUED ON PAGE TWO.)

This Was Not THE Nina

CUSTOMERS and assistants in the Southampton branch of C. & A. Modes watched Mrs Annie Sibley, Clarence Street, Southampton, shop for a hat yesterday.

For on her back was a card bearing the name "Nina" in large, black letters.

Mrs Sibley tried on hats for ten minutes, then paid 32s 11d for one.

Her explanation, "My husband and I were talking about the Russian girl and the hats over breakfast.

"I wanted a new hat to go with my new costume.

"My husband bet me the price of the hat that I wouldn't go into the shop with 'Nina' marked on my back."

Strikers Got £18 Pay This Week-End —£13 Next Week

YESTERDAY thousands of families in the riverside streets of Govan, Greenock and Clydebank were preparing for a long strike.

They were families of the 5550 men on strike from the shipyards and the 2000 men laid off because of the strike.

Many expect it will be at least six weeks before work begins again.

The strikers drew an average of £18 wages this week-end.

Next week they will collect about £13 "lying time," plus 30s strike pay.

Then they go on to 40s strike pay.

Tomorrow it is expected other sections of the industry will be affected.

The platers' assistants have been laid off.

As the yards "run down," other trades will run out of work. In a fortnight the yards will be at a standstill.

The Clyde District Committee of the Confederation of Shipbuilding and Engineering Unions is holding an emergency meeting tomorrow.

Wedding Guests Fight Fire With Champagne

A MARQUEE on the lawn of a Bradford house, being used for a wedding reception, burst into flames yesterday.

Wedding guests in top hats and tails fought the blaze with bottles of champagne.

Nine guests were taken to hospital.

The wedding, with six bridesmaids in period dresses, took place at St Luke's Church, less than 200 yards from the reception marquee.

Then the guests assembled in the marquee.

Speeches were made congratulating the young couple.

The alarm was given by a woman guest, who saw flames rising from behind a gas-heater, while a toast to the parents was being proposed.

More than 180 guests scrambled to safety under the flaps of the marquee, which was quickly burned to a pile of ashes.

The giant three-tier wedding cake was an unrecognisable mess.

Silver cutlery was damaged.

The bridegroom was Mr Frank Brown and his bride Miss Shirley Patricia Armitage.

The bride's father is chairman of H. Armitage & Co. (Rockmill), Ltd., bleachers and finishers.

The bridegroom's father, Mr Frank Brown, is a director of H. E. & F. J. Brown, Ltd., wholesale clothing manufacturers, of Bramley, Leeds.

The young couple later left on their honeymoon.

Malta Wants Welfare State Benefits

FAR-REACHING proposals for the integration of Malta with Britain, and the introduction of British Welfare State benefits to Malta, are expected to be made by Malta's Prime Minister, Mr Dom Mintoff, in London this week.

Mr Mintoff arrived in London last night.

1000 M.P.H. Planes For Farnborough

THE Fairey Delta 2, holder of the world air speed record of 1132 miles per hour, will break the sound barrier in level flight at the Farnborough air display which opens tomorrow.

Two models of this research aircraft will take part and will make a level supersonic run at 30,000 feet or above, to minimise the sonic bang.

It is intended to make this run at more than 1000 miles per hour, or considerably faster than anything previously seen at Farnborough.

Hunters and Swifts will fly fitted with the Fairey "Fireflash" guided missile, the first British air-to-air missile to destroy a target aeroplane, which has been ordered by the R.A.F.

The total of 6500 visitors expected from overseas is a record and includes delegations hundreds strong from the U.S.A., France and the Netherlands, as well as two small Russian delegations.

MYSTERY CLOUD AT DUNDEE POWER STATION

WORKMEN dug a hole with the ground smouldering below them [illegible] in Dundee last night.

[illegible]

Last night more workmen were called in. Eventually they dug a crater six yards long and six feet deep.

They found the ground was composed almost entirely of shale, which was burning. The workmen were affected by the fumes.

They could only stay in the crater for short spells.

The red hot shale burned their boots.

It was found the cables were safe. After isolating them with wooden boards, the firemen flooded the rest of the hole to keep the heat down.

Today's Weather

MAINLY dry, but showers at times in some areas. Rather warmer.

BRITAIN'S Diane Leather (left) and Thelma Hopkins chat with two of the Russian team on the steps of their London hotel yesterday.

Chapter 20
Repairs

"MAKE do and mend" was the title of a widely-distributed pamphlet, issued in 1943, to help households survive the war years and austerity that followed.

Readers of The Sunday Post took the advice to heart, carried on in that vein—and came up with their own solutions.

A CURE FOR THAT RUST ON THE BASIN—Enamel wash-hand basins sometimes wear around the plug hole, then begin to rust. Remove as much of the rust as possible, apply china cement liberally, and allow to dry for 24 hours. Result is a smooth, hard finish which even boiling water won't remove.—Mrs J. C. Meade, Sussex House, Kingussie, wins a pair of towels.

REPAIRS—To repair frayed binding at the heels of children's gym shoes and to prevent the back seam splitting, use iron-on adhesive tape. Cut a 1-inch wide strip and fold it over back of the shoe. Toe of the iron can be run round the inside. It makes a neat, firm job.—Mrs A. G. Lyall, Springbank, Tweed Road, Galashiels.

PLASTER WALL—When repairing a plaster wall, dampen the cracks before patching. Do this with a child's water pistol. The water penetrates right into the crack and there is less mess than by any other method.—Mrs E. Mann, 115 Sunnyside Road, Aberdeen.

STRONG REPAIR—My polythene washing-up bowl was burned, causing a hole in the bottom. My grandson lit a candle and heated all round the hole then pressed until the hole was completely sealed. Now I use it daily with no leakage.—Mrs M. J. Muir, 16 West Annandale Street, Edinburgh.

NYLON GLOVES—When repairing nylon stretch gloves, darn with shirring elastic in a matching colour and preserve the stretching quality of the article.—Miss E. Anderson, 2 Agnew Terrace, Edinburgh.

UPHOLSTERY REPAIR—If the piping cord at the arms of chairs or settees, has become frayed and bare, oversew very closely with six strands of matching embroidery cotton. The result is an almost invisible repair.—Mrs E. McKail, Waverley, High Street, Grantown-on-Spey.

DRIPPING CISTERN—If you have a porous cistern, tie up the ball and run the water off. Dry out thoroughly. Give the inside (but not the fittings) two coats of rubber paint, and the cistern is as good as new for only 2s.—Charles Crawford, 3 Lothian Road, Ayr.

STRONG MEND—Common alum, melted in an old iron spoon over a fire, is a strong cement for mending glass, fancy china and ornaments. It's safe to wash them in hot water without fear of their coming apart.—Mrs D. Hardie, 6 Backmarch Crescent, Rosyth.

A SIMPLE CURE FOR A LEAKY KETTLE—Our aluminium kettle started to leak where the spout joins the body. I painted two coats of aluminium paint round the seam, working it well in. Now the kettle is as good as new.—D. C. Rillie, 74 Bandeath Road, Fallin, Stirling, wins a pair of towels.

LINO REPAIR—To repair a hole in lino, fill with plastic wood, leave until hard, then smooth with sandpaper.—Mrs M. Blance, 84 Braewick Road, Lerwick.

★ TOP TIP ★

STRONG REPAIR—The other day the chain attached to my sink broke just at the plug. I took the split ring off a key label and joined the two together, making a neat strong join.— Mrs M. Maxwell, Glenlee, Drummore. Stranraer, wins a pair of towels.

WOOL REPAIR—When repairing knitted woollens I weave my darning stitches across the work as usual, then embroider in chain stitch down the darning threads until the hole is filled in. This makes a less-noticeable repair and, if done in the same colour wool, looks like the original knitting.—Mrs E. Blaikie, St Lawrence, 166 Lanark Road West, Currie.

FIRM REPAIR—A split in the bottom of a drawer can be strengthened by glueing a piece of strong canvas to the underside.—Mrs F. W. Bell, 18 Westlands, Sunderland.

NEW LOOK—If your chair covers have shrunk, cut the cover straight up the centre from front to back and insert a band of contrasting material just wide enough to allow cover to slip on easily. If the frill is short, add a hem of the contrasting material. —Mrs Russell, 1 Lilybank Avenue, Cambuslang.

CISTERNS—Modernise an old iron cistern by removing old paint and covering with one of the new adhesive materials to match the bathroom colour scheme. —Mrs Dorothy Symon, 17 Link Road, Cumnock.

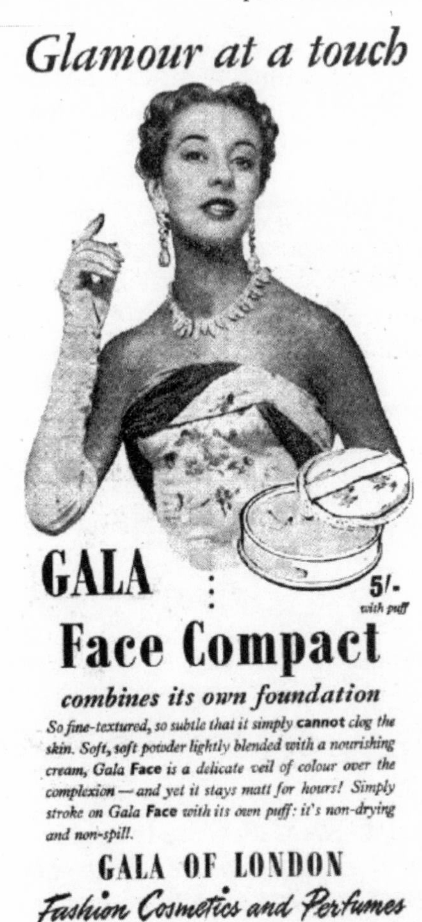

LEAKY VASE—To repair a leaking porcelain vase, place it in a warm place to heat through. Melt a little paraffin wax, pour into the case, and turn round so that the inside is well coated.—Mrs J. L. Macdonald, 203 Avonspark Street, Balornock, Glasgow.

FOR FLOORS—A varnished floor at a door, where the polish is a bit worn, takes on a new appearance with dark tan shoe polish brushed in and rubbed up with a soft duster.—Mrs R. Jamieson, 37 Calder Street, Lochwinnoch.

CHAIRS—When re-covering dining-room chairs, and the padding has gone lumpy, cut a piece of foam rubber and use in place of padding. It makes a neater job with no unsightly bumps and is a nice soft seat.—Mrs Janet Gates, 5 Mitchell Street, Craigmillar, Edinburgh.

REPAIRING NET CURTAINS—Tack tissue paper over the hole. Slacken the tension of your sewing machine and cover the paper with fairly loose rows of stitching. Work as you would a darn. This forms a strong mesh. When the paper is torn away the mend is almost invisible.—Mrs A. Duffy, 32 Mansion House Drive, Carmyle, Glasgow, wins a pair of towels.

MATTRESS MEND—I mended a small rent which appeared in one of my interior spring mattresses with a piece of adhesive plaster. It made a perfect job.—Mrs M. I. Allan, 11 Hill Street, Inverness.

NO SNAGS—Use transparent sticky tape to cover rough edges of chairs which are liable to snag nylons. It does the trick.—Mrs M. Stephen, 83 Corthan Crescent, Kincorth, Aberdeen.

IT'S THE VERY THING FOR MENDING SHEETS—When repairing a sheet, put a piece of paper over the hole, stitch back and forward then across on the sewing machine. The paper dissolves on washing, leaving a perfect darn.—Miss W. Whiting, Milton House, Keymer, Hassocks, Sussex, wins a pair of towels.

EVEN WEAR—For my living-room I bought two smaller, identical carpets instead of one large one. I can change them round, and so share out the wear and tear.—Mrs W. Menzies, 3 Carrochan Crescent, Balloch.

PLASTIC REPAIR—My plastic mac tore at the buttons. To repair, I removed the buttons, opened out the belt and machine stitched it down the front, then stitched the buttons on again. This is practically invisible, and made my mac like new.—Mrs E. Kirkland, 8 Millfield Gardens, Hexham.

NEAT REPAIR—I have just mended a hole in the upper of my suede boot with a waterproof first-aid dressing. I fixed the circle inside the boot over the hole and it is very successful.—Miss C. Reid, Conicavel Post Office, Darnaway, Forres, wins a pair of towels.

SQUEAKY DOORS—A squeaky door annoyed me, especially at night time, till I rubbed the hinges and jamming edges with boric powder. This acted both as a lubricant and silencer.—Mrs Mary Gray, 25 Mount Road, Montrose.

SKIRT HEMS—When sewing up hems of extra-wide skirts, make a knot stitch at short intervals all the way round. Should a heel catch in the hem, only a short portion will drop. Makes for quicker and easier repair.—Miss M. Birnie, 17 High Street, Sandhaven, by Fraserburgh.

WAG AT THE WA'—If your clock requires oiling or is perhaps losing time, soak a small piece of cotton wool in machine oil and rub the chain several times. This helps to lubricate the interior and at the same time keeps the chain clean and in good order.—G. Park, 8 Eskdale Place, Langholm.

SUNDAY POST, NOVEMBER 4, 1956

The Sunday Post

Morning Special

PRINTED AND PUBLISHED EVERY SUNDAY MORNING.

No. 2671. [REGISTERED AT THE GENERAL POST OFFICE AS A NEWSPAPER] SUNDAY, NOVEMBER 4, 1956. Radio and TV—Page 4. PRICE 3d.

British-French Operations To Go On

TROOP LANDINGS ARE BELIEVED IMMINENT

Emergency U.N. Session

BRITISH and French amphibious landings at each end of the Suez Canal are expected soon.

Replying to the United Nations resolution calling for an immediate cease-fire, the Allies said their operations must be "urgently pursued to prevent a renewal of hostilities, and to open a way for a settlement."

But military action will be willingly stopped if the United Nations will put in a force to keep the peace between Egypt and Israel.

A statement giving these conditions was made by Sir Anthony Eden to a special session of the House of Commons yesterday. (See Page 2.)

The United Nations General Assembly met last night in emergency session to consider Britain's statement.

FIRST WAVES

Meantime, Anglo-French forces were marshalled in growing strength last night for early amphibious landings at either end of the Suez Canal, after a four-day pulverising of Egyptian military targets by combined air forces.

Military experts calculated that the first waves of Anglo-French occupying forces could be ashore by tomorrow, if necessary, after the massive convoys taking tanks, guns and troops had reached their assembly points in the Eastern Mediterranean.

"NAVAL ATTACK"

A communique issued by the [illegible] of the Egyptian Armed Forces last night claimed that British and French naval units attacked Suez harbour yesterday.

The communique claimed that several British ships were sunk or [illegible] in the battle, Beirut radio reported.

The communique said that British landing craft tried to land their troops at Suez harbour.

WARNING—

[illegible], "Voice of Britain" [illegible] Cyprus warned Egyptians to keep away from Nile harbours [illegible] Rashid, in the vicinity of Alexandria, at Damanhour and at Benha.

An Air Ministry communique, issued in London yesterday, said—

"The emphasis of the Allied air attacks has been switched from airfields to the Egyptian Army, particularly against its armour, during the past 24 hours.

"The destruction of tanks and other military material has been considerable."

A British communique said—

1—The Allied air offensive, kept up since Wednesday night, has brought about the virtual destruction of the Egyptian Air Force as a fighting force.

2—This conclusion is inescapable, since British and French pilots, searching the length and breadth of the country, have failed to find any but the most flimsy evidence that Egypt any longer has anything approaching an effective Air Force.

TO BLOCK CANAL

H.Q. Allied Forces said last night the Egyptians made a further attempt yesterday to block the Suez Canal.

The supports of El Firdan Bridge, spanning the Canal south of Port Said, had been demolished, depositing the structure in the Canal.

A British spokesman said altogether six ships were now sunk along the Suez Canal—four at the mouth near Port Said and two near Lake Timsah.

ISRAELIS REACH CANAL

A Tel Aviv spokesman said last night Israeli patrols had "almost certainly" already reached the banks of the Suez Canal.

"Oil Stations Blown Up"

AN Iraq Petroleum Company spokesman said last night he [illegible] unconfirmed reports that [illegible] of the company's pumping stations in Syria had been blown up. He added that no oil had gone through to the Tripoli and Banias terminals of the pipelines from Iraq since [illegible] night.

The Iraq Petroleum Company yesterday suspended the pumping of oil through Syria, a company statement announced.

[illegible]

Today's Weather

OCCASIONAL rain. Normal temperature.

JET fighter pilots scramble at an airfield in Cyprus. They are doing strafing runs over Egypt.

Father And Daughter Found Shot Dead At Aberdeen

LAST night Aberdeen City Police were piecing together the evidence to explain a double tragedy that occurred yesterday afternoon at the sea beach.

Two people lost their lives—a father and his young daughter.

Their badly injured bodies were discovered about 3.30 p.m., lying on the grass beside a motor car which had been parked off the promenade, near the Cors Bridge, about half a mile from the Bridge of Don.

The nearest house is a salmon fisher's bothy, which is unoccupied.

Beside the bodies was a shotgun, which bore evidence of having been recently discharged.

The car, a light green saloon, was visible from the promenade, although it had been drawn up in a recess formed by a collection of wartime anti-invasion blocks.

The tragic discovery was made by two schoolboys who had been playing on the links.

They at once ran to the promenade and stopped the first man they met.

He was an ex-police officer and he immediately notified the police, who arrived with an ambulance and cordoned off the area.

The police believe that the child died first and the man shortly afterwards. A note is believed to have been left in the car.

At a late hour they were identified as Alexander Sutherland (47), [illegible] Cottage, [illegible], Dyce, Aberdeenshire, and his daughter Carolyne, aged six.

Sutherland was married, with four other children, the eldest a son of 22 and three other daughters, aged 21, 19 and 16.

He was employed on farm work for five years in the Fordoun district of Kincardineshire.

"We Must Go On," Says Eden

THE Prime Minister, in a broadcast to the nation from No. 10 Downing Street last night, said—

"I believe before long it will become apparent to everyone that we acted rightly and wisely.

"Our friends are coming, as Australia and New Zealand have already done, and I believe that Canada and the United States will soon come, to see that we acted with courage and speed to deal with a situation which just could not wait.

"All my life I have been a man of peace, working for peace, striving for peace, negotiating for peace . . .

"I am still the same, with the same devotion to peace.

"But I am utterly convinced that the action we have taken is right."

It seemed that Israel had succeeded in securing the bases in Sinai and Gaza, at which the Egyptian commandos were trained for their attacks on Israel.

Once the British and French forces had occupied positions on the Canal, H.M. Government would ensure that Israel forces would withdraw.

Out of this could come not only peace in the Middle East but a strengthened United Nations, one with power to act as well as to talk.

"If the United Nations will take over this police action we shall welcome it.

"Indeed, we have proposed that course to them.

"Until the United Nations are there ready to take over, we and France must be ready to go on with the job until the job is done."

Chapter 21
For The Bairns

A HOUSEWIFE'S first job was to make a comfortable home for her family. That meant looking after the bairns properly.

But children tend to grow, to wear out their clothes and to want to eat some things, and not eat others. They were given hand-me-downs, and when they didn't like taking their medicine a way had to be found to make that easier.

As anyone who grew up in the 1950s will confirm, many of the things inflicted upon them weren't easy to bear. In fact, modern young people might find it difficult to believe what their parents and grandparents were put through.

But though cod liver oil wasn't very tasty, and wearing their cousin's old woolly jumper was hardly high fashion, most who lived through it would probably agree that growing up in the 1950s was fantastic. As they all say – those were the days.

RIGHT OR LEFT?—Children learning to put on their shoes often get them on the wrong feet. Mark arrows inside each shoe on the insoles and explain they must always point to each other.—Mrs M. Whittaker, 38 St Martin's Road, South Shore, Blackpool.

FOR THE KIDDIES—Children's long corduroy trousers can be made to last another season by the addition of three-inch ribbed anklets knitted in matching double-knitting wool. They look smart and are much warmer.—Mrs A. R. McQueen, 9 Burnbrae Gardens, Falkirk, wins a pair of towels.

PLAY PIT—If you want to make a sandpit for a child, get an old tractor tyre, lay it flat, and fill the centre with sand.—Mrs Margaret Roy, Little Kerse Farm, Polmont.

COT-SEAT—A child's old cot can be made into a useful and attractive piece of furniture. Remove one side, shorten the legs, and give the cot a coat of bright paint. Cover the mattress with Cretonne, make cushions to match. Result—a seat for the bedroom or garden.—Miss L. Ross, 21 Brucklay Street, Rosehearty, Fraserburgh.

KEEPS BABY SAFE—If a metal key ring is fitted to each arm of baby's high chair, he can then be hooked in by his pram harness and anchored safely. He can be left to play in his high chair with no danger of falling out.—Mrs Jane Hickie, 3 Queen Street, Alva.

RAIN HOODS—The hoods of little girls' raincoats are inclined to blow off in windy weather. Prevent this by threading elastic through the front. The hood then fits snugly to the head and doesn't catch in the wind.—Mrs A. Gunn, Millhouse, Weisdale, Shetland.

CHILDREN'S SOCKS—To save socks being stained from sandals, cut a sole the size of the sandal from self-adhesive material. Insert in the sandal and press down.—Mrs H. L. Male, 4 Campbell Street, Greenock.

ELECTRIC BLANKET—When your electric blanket is past repairing, take all the wires out, wash the blanket, then quilt it with chintz or satin. I have just finished one and it makes a nice winter cover for my grandchild's cot.—Mrs Eliza Forest, 6 Grahamsdyke Road, Bonnybridge.

KNEE PROTECTORS—I find that by sewing a patch on each knee of a tiny tot's dungarees and padding with nylon foam sponge, it prevents sore knees after many a fall.—Mrs McCreadie, 4 Hyslop Crescent, Colconell, Girvan.

★ TOP TIP ★

FOR DRYING—Use children's balloons for drying woollen caps and bonnets. Blow up the balloons to the required size and cover with the damp article.—Mrs E. Blake, 46 Seamore Street, Glasgow, wins a pair of towels.

FAIRY PARASOLS—A treat for the kiddies' party can be made as follows: Coat the outside of ice cream cones with thin water icing and roll lightly in hundreds and thousands. Leave to dry. Make a jelly and, when cool and on the verge of setting, fill the cones and insert half a drinking straw.—L. Hook, 2 Oakwood Villas, Alnwick.

PRAM HANDLE—For a shoddy pram handle, bind white plastic embossed cycle handlebar tape neatly round the old rubber.—Mrs R. Kinghorn, 90 Iona Street, Leith, Edinburgh.

HIGH CHAIR—To prevent baby from sliding down in his chair, line the back and seat with foam rubber.—Mrs M. Caskie, 2 Akers Avenue, Locharbriggs.

PILLOWS—To prevent small children losing their pillows during the night, put the pillows into double bolster cases. The long ends can then be tucked firmly under the mattress.—Mrs E. Kitley, 12 Ashfield Road, Andover.

COLLARS—Little boys' shirt collars have a habit of curling up at the peak. To avoid this and have a neat collar, sew the smallest size snap fastener at peak and corresponding one on to shirt.—Mrs Marion Murray, 91 Curling Crescent, Glasgow.

SPACE SAVER—In children's wardrobes place an extra rod half-way down. Small tots can then keep their own clothes tidy and reach them easily. Clothes not in everyday use can be hung on the upper rod.—I. Smith, Parkneuk, Arbuthnott.

SCHOOL JOTTERS—Jotters have an annoying way of turning up at the corners. To prevent this, cut off the bottom two corners of an envelope, and slip the jotter corners into these "pockets".—Mrs M. Abbot, 160 Culrain Street, Glasgow.

TOY BOX—Paint a wooden box a bright colour and put rubber wheels on it. Let the children use it. They enjoy wheeling it about to pick up scattered toys.—N. J. Hill, 122 Younger Street, Alloa.

HANDY FOR MOTHER—Attach a towel rack to the back of baby's meal-time chair. Keep bib, wash cloth, and towel on it handy for ready use.—Mrs Wallace M. Brisbin, Brockway, Oregon, USA.

RATTLE—Unscrew the top from a Bakelite darning mushroom, put inside half a dozen small buttons and you'll have a good rattle for a child.—Mrs H. Clegg, 72 Spittalfield Road, Inverkeithing, Fife.

JIG-SAW JUMBLE—When the children receive a jig-saw as a present mark each piece on the back with initials of title. When odd pieces of puzzle are found on the carpet, they're easily restored to the proper box.—Mrs McClure, 29 Broomvals Drive, Newton Mearns.

STUFFED TOYS—When children have outgrown cuddly toys, remove the stuffing and make them into glove puppets.—Mrs M. M. Kilbride, 57 Whitburn Street, Glasgow.

COT BLANKETS—When buying cot blankets, get two of the same colour. As baby outgrows the small size, it's the easiest thing to make a large one by stitching the two together.—R. Adam, 129 Langlands Road, Govan.

SNAPSHOTS—To get a natural snapshot of baby, put a piece of cellulose tape in his hand. That keeps him interested. I know, I've twins!—B. Ladnit, 24 Laurel Avenue, Dalmuir West, near Glasgow.

BALLOONS—Balloons for parties can be inflated with safety and ease by using a cigarette holder in the mouthpiece.—Mrs Henderson, 261 Ayr Road, Newton Mearns.

NO TEARS—Children don't like a big towel put over their heads when having their hair dried. Use a mitten made from an old towel instead.—Mrs Pirie, 76 Chapel Street, Aberdeen.

TOYS—To make plastic toys safe for young children, rub off the ragged bits with a nail file. It is quick and easy to do and prevents cuts and scratches.—Mrs A. Sanderson, 24 Carnwath Road, Braehead, Lanark.

FUN FOR BABY—When baby is old enough to lie and kick, keep him in brightly coloured bootees. He gets a great deal of fun watching his feet, and the exercise strengthens his legs.—Mrs J. Ewan, 3 Camphill Avenue, Langside, Glasgow.

EASY TO HANDLE—Instead of using tape or ribbon on children's feeders, try a piece of narrow white elastic. It slips easily over the head and does not become knotted.—Mrs A. Macgregor, 17 Yorkhill Street, Glasgow.

PRAM AND COT COVERS—Use layers of cheese-cloth instead of cotton wool for padding when making pram and cot covers for baby. They can then be washed without losing their plumpness.—Miss L. Ross, 21 Bruckley Street, Rosehearty.

FOR AN EGG CUP—Serve a boiled egg to a young child in a doll's tea-cup instead of an ordinary egg cup. The child can then hold the handle and is not so likely to burn his fingers.—Mrs Murdoch, 7 Ogilvie Terrace, Edinburgh.

TIDY SOCKS—Toddlers' socks tend to sag and slip, then bunch under the heel. If you draw a 'garter' round each leg with a dampened bar of soap the socks stay neatly in place all day.—Miss I. Tait, 5 Sidney Street, Arbroath.

PEN HOLDER—Use an old flower vase as a pen and pencil holder. Then there's no difficulty for the children to find a pencil. —Mrs J. B. Harrower, 13 Ellangowan Terrace, The Inch, Edinburgh.

BABY PEN—To prevent baby pushing his pen all over the place, scuffing carpets, knocking furniture, etc., place the pen on an old rug or square of sturdy material. Fasten the four corners of the rug to the pen.—Miss A. Whitelaw, 132 Barclay Street, Cowdenbeath.

SAFETY FIRST—There's no crying over spilt ink if you put the ink bottle inside a deep dish or bowl when the children are writing at the table.—V. Stapleton, 6 Thornwood Gardens, Glasgow.

THE SUNDAY POST, AUGUST 4, 1957.

The Sunday Post

Morning Special

PRINTED AND PUBLISHED EVERY SUNDAY MORNING.

No. 2710. | REGISTERED AT THE GENERAL POST OFFICE AS A NEWSPAPER | SUNDAY, AUGUST 4, 1957. | Radio and TV—Page 4. | Price 3d.

COWBOY KISSES HIS BRIDE—

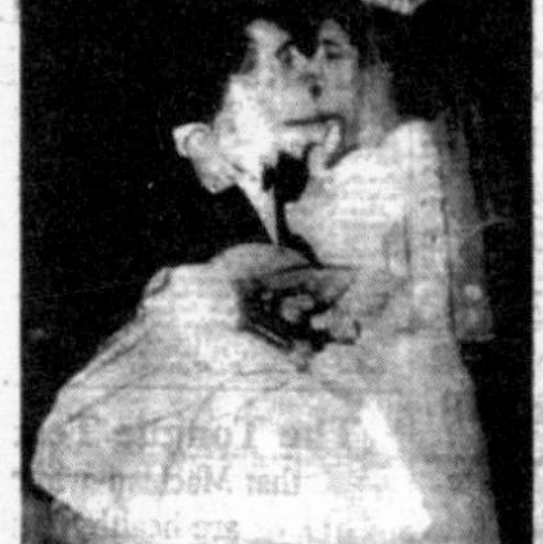

Speed Is Vital In Drive Against Fort

CAMERONIANS—ATTACK WILL BEGIN SOON

THE drive against Oman rebels—in which Cameronians are to take part—will begin as soon as possible.

Speed is vital, it was stated last night.

The Cameronians are among British troops who moved into Muscat territory yesterday.

They will support a planned assault on the big ground fort of Nizwa, H.Q. of the rebel forces in Oman and Muscat.

"We are now ready for the re-entry of the Sultan's forces into Oman, particularly Nizwa," said Air Vice Marshal Laurence Sinclair, commander of British forces in the Arabian Peninsula.

"The key factor in the re-entry of the Sultan's forces is one of speed.

"So far we have been successful at nibbling at the edges, and at the centre we now know there is a fairly hard core of resolute men.

"The rebels have brought in men from outside trained in modern weapons.

"We are therefore going to use adequate forces to do the task.

"The moment we have established the Muscat armed forces in Oman, obviously we will want to get the British forces out as quickly as possible."

Air Vice-Marshal Sinclair said—"Subsidiary operations are going on now," but he did not want to disclose them.

APPEAL FOR HELP

● The Imam of Oman has appealed to all nations represented at the Afro-Asian Bandung conference in 1955 for "immediate help . . . as Oman is completely encircled by the British."

A spokesman of the nine-nation Arab League said they were urgently conveying the appeal to the Bandung nations, numbering about 30.

● Britain is keeping U.S.A. fully informed about the sending of troops to Oman.

U.S. is believed to be in agreement with firm British action in this area.

Princess Margaret To Tour Canada

PRINCESS MARGARET will visit Canada for the first time next year.

This was stated in the "Toronto Telegram" yesterday.

The dispatch said Princess Margaret would go direct to British Columbia to officiate at the opening of that Province's centennial celebrations.

Additional plans are being made for her to visit other parts of Canada, including Toronto.

"Princess Margaret is to visit British Columbia in July, probably going there by air," stated the Telegram.

"On the return journey, however, it is expected that she will cross the major part of Canada by train.

"While the draft schedule has not yet been submitted to the Princess for her approval, it is expected that her itinerary will include major cities such as Edmonton, Regina, Winnipeg, Ottawa, Montreal and Quebec."

TOUCHED 20,000 VOLT WIRE

A PERTH man received severe burning and other injuries after accidentally earthing a 20,000 volt electric wire at Tummel Bridge yesterday.

He is dangerously ill in Bridge of Earn Hospital.

Driver Hurt When Car Somersaults Into Field

Today's Weather

Surprise Attack Would Come Through Arctic

ANY surprise attack by aggressors in a modern war would be launched via the Arctic.

This was stated by Mr Selwyn Lloyd, the Foreign Secretary, yesterday.

He was speaking at Warrington, Lancs.

"We mean business about disarmament," he said.

"There is complete agreement between the Western Governments.

"We have further said that if this is too big a proposition for the Soviets to accept at first, the United States and Canada are prepared to accept a limited zone, and we in Europe are also prepared to discuss such a limited zone in Europe.

"Some people laugh at that, but those who laugh should look at one of the old-fashioned globes and they will see that the Arctic is in fact the realistic frontier area between Russia and North America.

"That is the area from which any surprise attack would be launched."

Nehru's Plan To Make Some Strikes Illegal

MR NEHRU faces one of the stormiest Parliamentary sessions of his Premiership, after a walk-out by all Opposition members yesterday.

Chapter 22
In The Garden

GARDENING has changed, and also not changed in the past 60 years. There were fantastic gardeners cultivating exotic flora then, as now. But (especially in the early '50s) a plot of land was often used to grow vegetables, and some fruit, to augment rations.

Not all tenement-dwellers had access to a plot, although middens had mostly, but not entirely, been replaced by back greens. As ever, Sunday Post readers had good advice.

GARDENERS—I find combining a rake and hoe on one shaft helps considerably in easing work in the garden. The idea is to put the rake on one end of the shaft and the hoe on the other.—John A. Lawrie, 1 Traquair Park East, Edinburgh.

LAWN-MAKING—Before sowing a lawn, allow ground to stand until you've taken off one or two crops of weeds. If weather is settled, sow about mid-August. This gives a healthy, weed-free green.—R. McLean, Glasgow.

FOR THE LAWN—When sowing lawn seed I use an ordinary vegetable sieve. Put the seed in the sieve and walk over the lawn shaking the sieve. It gives an even distribution of seed.—Jas. Gillespie, 19 Robert Smillie Crescent, Larkhall.

CYCLAMEN PLANTS—Never pour water on the corm of the plant, but round the edge of the pot. Keep it away from direct heat of the fire and draughts. As the blooms fade they should be pulled out, not cut off, or the stump causes decay.—George T. Steel, Gaulsbridge, Kirtlebridge, Lockerbie.

GARDENING TIP—I put all my lawn mowings between the drills of my potatoes. This not only acts as a fertiliser but keeps the ground moist during a dry spell.—D. Slater, 6 Commercial Road, Portknockie.

FREE FROM BIRDS—If a net isn't large enough to prevent birds eating my ripening strawberries, I lay a glass jam jar beside each plant and push the clump of strawberries into it.—M. Reid, Homewood, Kemnay, Aberdeen.

MAK SICCAR—Now that spring is round the corner, it is wise to sprinkle the drains and back yard with carbolic. This keeps down pests and insects when the warmer weather comes.—Mrs Appleton, 19 Ellengowan Drive, Dundee.

LAWN CUTTING—Wait until after a shower of rain before cutting the lawn and you'll get an easier and cleaner cut.—S. T. Cobb, Murella, Milton of Campsie, by Glasgow.

HANDY GAUGE—When planting seed, etc, it's important to put them at the right depth in the soil. A handy gauge is made by painting or notching rings on your trowel handle at, say, one inch intervals.—Mrs C. F. Forrester, 1 Mitchell Place, Markinch.

FOR GARDENERS—When planting seeds, remember the old saying: One for the mouse, one for the crow, one to rot, and one to grow.—Dougall Smith, 208 New City Road, Glasgow.

★ TOP TIP ★

KEEPS GARDEN TOOLS FROM RUSTING—To keep tools free from rust during the busy season, get a box one foot deep and fill three-quarters full with clean sand lightly mixed with a good household oil. Run the metal parts of tools (but not keen-edged tools) through the sand before putting them away.—Miss J. Dow, Brae Street, Dunkeld, wins a pair of towels.

USEFUL IN THE GARDEN—I save my broken clothes pegs and use them for marking garden seedbeds.—Mrs M. Kelsey, 23 Gartons Road, Barmulloch, Glasgow.

FRESH FLOWERS—To make picked violets last longer, plunge them head-down in cold water for a few minutes.—Helen Symington, 11 Windyedge Crescent, Glasgow.

WEED REMOVER—For clearing the lawn of dandelions, plantains, and other weeds, use a potato peeler, the apple corer type. One scoop and they come out, root and all.—S. Kincaid, 23 Ossian Crescent, Methil.

EVEN SOWING—Keep an old pepper box for sowing very small seeds and an old flour dredger for the larger variety. This ensures an even distribution and prevents bare patches.—G. Hadden, 3 Neville Terrace, Priestgate, Peterborough.

CARE OF BULBS—Make a small hole in the centre of bowl, place a pie funnel in hole and water through the funnel. In this way only the roots are watered and the bulbs remain dry.—Mrs L. Frazer, 10 Ridgewood Gardens, South Gosforth, Newcastle.

FOR GARDENERS—Keep a discarded whitewash or distemper brush for cleaning the lawnmower after cutting damp grass. It makes the tedious cleaning job easy.—Mrs R. Alderson, 29 Hylton Street, North Shields.

SNOW CLEARING—Before clearing paths of snow, rub both sides of the shovel with an oily rag. The snow slides off the shovel and makes the job much easier.—Mrs E. Muers, 19 Cecil Street, Sunderland.

WINDOW BOXES—To prevent rain spattering dirt from them on to the windows, scatter a layer of gravel over the earth.—Mrs W. M. Brisbin, Brockway, Oregon, USA.

HANDY SCRAPER—If you've an old spade not in use, bury it, shaft downwards, at the bottom of the garden path, leaving about three to four inches bare. This makes an ideal boot scraper.—David Forrester, Craigmaud, Newmills, Fife.

GARDEN GATES—Put a ball castor on the bottom outside edge of your garden gate. This takes the strain off the hinges and the gate lasts for years without becoming loose.—P. McEvoy, 11 Montfode Drive, Ardrossan, wins a pair of towels.

CUT FLOWERS—Lupins usually fall to bits after a couple of days in the house. To make them last for a week or longer, fill each hollow stem with water, put finger over open end, then place in vase of water.—Nurseryman, Dundee.

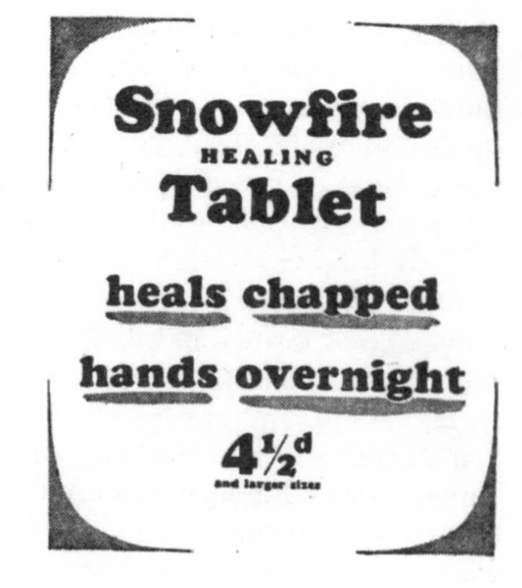

RUST—Stubborn rust is removed by rubbing with a piece of emery paper soaked in paraffin. Very obstinate patches should be wrapped in paraffin-soaked rags and left for a day or two.—Mrs Blacklaws, 42 Cameron Street, Stonehaven.

MAKES CUT FLOWERS LAST—When changing water add a teaspoonful of sugar. Chrysanths last four weeks this way and still look fresh.—Mrs B. Livingston, 20 Nithsdale Road, Glasgow.

GARDEN TIP—If a rubber ring from the stopper of a screw-top bottle is pushed on to your garden dibber, it can be adjusted to different depths. It's a great help in planting seedlings at a uniform depth.—Tom Macaulay, 33 The Wynd, Cumbernauld, Glasgow.

SAVE THE FRUIT—When gathering berries from bushes, spread clean sacking or brown paper under each bush. This keeps clean any berries which fall. It's surprising the amount of fruit that can be salvaged in this way.—Tom Macaulay sen., 33 The Wynd, Cumbernauld, Glasgow.

GARDEN GATE—To make a wooden garden gate self-closing, without the use of a spring, remove the hinges. When refitting them, slope them slightly downwards towards the bottom of the gate. The gate then rises when opened and its own weight pulls it down and shut after you have entered.—D. McLaren, 155 Thomson Street, Glasgow.

SEEDS—To bring on seeds such as sweet peas, when one has no greenhouse or frame, utilise a sunny window sill. Put the seeds in small pots and cover with plastic bags.—Mrs B. Bain, 23 Townhead, Auchterarder.

BULBS—To keep outdoor bulbs warm during frost, I spread fallen leaves thickly over them and then ashes on top. To keep indoor bulbs free from draughts, wrap newspapers round and well up the bowls and stand them on a pile of papers in the dark.—Mrs I. McEwen, 23 Bruce Street, Macduff, wins a pair of towels.

FOR THE GARDEN—Don't throw away any odd ends of covered flex of the electric type. They are useful in the garden for tying up rose bushes and shrubs, and they don't damage the plants. —R. Bruce MacLaren, Redstone, Darnaway, Forres.

PLANTS—When plants are placed in ornamental bowls or vases, surplus drainage water must not be allowed to remain in the bottom of the receptacle. Plants dislike sitting with their roots in water.—Mrs B. Warwick, The Gardens, Auchincruive.

CHRYSANTHS—To give chrysanthemums a longer life, each time you change the water, rush the cold water tap over the slimy stalks.—Mrs E. Murphy, 92 Gaitside Drive, Aberdeen, wins a pair of towels.

INDOOR PLANTS—Never water plants growing indoors (eg geraniums) with cold water. Use warm water and you'll have stronger plants.—W. Legge, 3 Council House, Silverhillock, by Banff.

WORTH KNOWING—If you break the stem of a flower, "bandage" the break with adhesive tape, and it will last as long as the others.—Mrs H. Smith, 14 John Street, Ruabon, Wrexham.

INDOOR FLOWERS—Did you know lily of the valley can now be grown indoors just as easily as other bulbs? This newly-developed type flowers a few weeks after planting. Cost, 3s. 6d. a dozen.—Mrs V. Hart, Glasgow.

THE SUNDAY POST, DECEMBER 1, 1957.

The Sunday Post

Morning Special

PRINTED AND PUBLISHED EVERY SUNDAY MORNING.

No 2727. [REGISTERED AT THE GENERAL POST OFFICE AS A NEWSPAPER.] SUNDAY, DECEMBER 1, 1957. Radio and TV—Page 4. Price 4d.

Scots In Drama Of The Polar Seas

SHACKLETON RESCUE!

The Skipper Of The "Shack"

Captain Norman Roy Brown, Wembley Park, Middlesex, master of the Shackleton.

TERSE MESSAGES FROM ANTARCTIC

A DRAMATIC eight-word message was flashed from the Antarctic last night.

"A RESCUE IS BEING EFFECTED. NO IMMEDIATE DANGER."

This was the first news since a series of terse messages telling that the research ship Shackleton had struck on ice-floe.

Water was reported to be up to her between-decks and boats had been slung out ready for use.

The first rescue message was followed by news that she was returning to South Georgia to make repairs.

The information was contained in a message to the Admiralty despatched from the Shackleton at 12.30 p.m.

It said that her No. 2 hold was filled with water, some cargo had been jettisoned and the remainder was under water.

Two whalers from the whale factory ship Southern Harvester were expected to reach the Shackleton about midnight and were to stand by her.

The Southern Harvester has Dundee men on board.

The drama is taking place in the icy wastes of the South Atlantic, on the edge of Antarctica.

It is a story of a stout ship, with 56 aboard, forcing her way through the ice to the remote and desolate bases where British scientists are living and working.

Ships were soon racing to the rescue after the S O S.

Dundee Men

The whale factory ship Southern Harvester was reported yesterday morning to be about 210 miles away, and H.M.S. Protector, a converted net layer, was about 300 miles away.

Chief engineer of the Southern Harvester is Mr Charles K. Crockett, O.B.E., 9 Ancrum Gardens, Dundee.

Among several other Dundonians aboard are Messrs Frank Stewart, 14 Park Place, Ancrum Road, and George Sinclair, 73 Dens Road.

Hole In Hold

The Colonial Office stated last night—

"Additional information received from the Acting Governor of the Falkland Islands indicates that the Shackleton has sustained damage from ice in the form of a hole in the aft hold, which has filled with water. Some cargo has been jettisoned.

"Temporary repairs are being attempted, as a result of which the master of the vessel hopes to be able to reach South Georgia."

Earlier last week the Shackleton was reported to be beset by ice, 20 miles from the South Orkneys.

A scene in the Antarctic.

Scots Parents Wait For News

LAST night relatives were anxiously waiting at their homes for news of their loved ones aboard the stricken ship.

Two Scots families waited all day for news.

Eighteen-year-old Terry Teal, Murrayfield Gardens, Stranraer, is galley boy aboard the Shackleton.

This is his second trip to the Antarctic.

He went to sea at 15 and joined the John Biscoe as cabin boy two years later.

He was then chosen for the Shackleton.

Last night his parents told "The Sunday Post" they were very relieved to know their boy was all right.

The ship's doctor is Dr John Graham, 17 Beaumont Gate, Hillhead, Glasgow.

He joined the Shackleton in October last year as part of his National Service.

His mother tried to contact Lloyd's in London yesterday, but she couldn't get through.

"All we know is what we read in the papers," she said.

"There seems to be nothing we can do but wait."

Injured Motorist Stops Bus—Then Collapses

TWO men were admitted to Dundee Royal Infirmary last night with multiple injuries after a car had plunged over a bank at Spittalburn Corner, on the Forfar-Dundee road.

They were John A. Divers (42), coal merchant, 2 Stewart Street, Lochee, and Denis McGurk (46), caretaker of St Joseph's School, the Schoolhouse, Wilkie's Lane, Dundee.

A Dundee-bound Alexander bus was approaching the corner, when a man with a blood-stained head limped from the roadside verge waving a handkerchief.

As the bus stopped he collapsed at the roadside.

Driver, conductress and passengers went to his assistance.

It was Mr Divers, and he pointed to Mr McGurk who lay beside a damaged Riley car at the foot of a grassy bank.

The bus driver ran to Invergowrie police office a short distance down the road, and called police and ambulance, while conductress and passengers looked after the injured men.

The car, which was returning from Aberdeen, had skidded on the wet road, crashed through a fence, plunged down the bank and collided with a tree. It remained upright.

Mr McGurk appeared to have been thrown out.

Mr Divers, the driver, despite leg and head injuries, had struggled up the bank to get help.

Both men are well known in the city.

Mr Divers is a coal merchant in the Lochee district, and Mr McGurk is a junior footballer and football legislator.

He ran Dunkeld Amateurs, who won the Scottish Under-16 Cup, and St Mary's Youth Club FC, who supplied several players to the senior ranks.

IKE MAKES PROGRESS

PRESIDENT EISENHOWER is continuing to make excellent progress from his cerebral attack.

The White House spokesman said this last night.

Mr James Hagerty, the spokesman, said, "Dr Snyder (the President's personal physician) told me that the President had another good night's sleep."

Today's Weather

CLOUDY, perhaps occasional drizzle, mild. Midday temperatures 48-50 degrees.

Members of the scientific party, who were aboard the Shackleton when she sailed from Southampton on October 1.

Chapter 23
Good Shoes

THEY used to say a man could be judged by the shine on his shoes. Many had learned this in wartime and National Service experiences that had rubbed the habit of highly-polished boots into their very souls.

Shoes were to be cleaned, then, and were also expensive items which couldn't be cast aside merely because they chafed the heel a little. A remedy had to be found that didn't involve buying new ones.

TIGHT SHOES—Leave a peeled raw potato overnight in a tight-fitting pair of shoes. You'll be surprised at the comfortable fitting afterwards.—Mrs M. Martin, 43 Auldhill Bridgend, Linlithgow.

SHOE CARE—If polish is put on shoes at night it saves a lot of time and trouble in the morning. It is also good for leather when polish is allowed to soak in.—Mrs Nan Mackinnon, 4 Observatory Lane, Hillhead, Glasgow.

SUMMER SHOES—If you have two or three different colours of summer shoes, add a few drops of colouring to white shoe cleaner and you have a different colour to match each pair.—Mrs C. J. Kennedy, 68 Crookings Lane, Penwortham, Preston.

DANCE SHOES—An inexpensive way to brighten satin dance shoes is to dab spots of colourless nail varnish on the heels and toes and sprinkle hair glitter on the spots while wet. A variety of glitter can be bought to ring the changes.—Mrs Margaret Price, 17 Phythian Street, Kensington, Liverpool.

★ TOP TIP ★

IF YOUR CREPE SOLES SKITE ON THE WET PAVEMENTS—I had a pair of crepe-soled shoes which had worn smooth and were dangerous in the street in wet weather. With a rough file I cut V-shaped grooves in the soles, and find they now grip better.—Mrs A. W. Paterson, 57 Taylor's Lane, Dundee, wins a pair of towels.

DRY SHOES—Hang wet shoes under a chair by hooking the heels on to the bar. The circulation of air on both sides of the shoes dries them quickly.—Miss M. Williams, 19 Wrenbury Street, Holt Road, Edge Hill, Lancs.

PREVENTS SLIPPING.—Summer sandals with slingbacks don't keep slipping off the heel if a piece of sticking plaster, cut in a thin strip, is placed inside the strap. This grips the heel.—Miss Agnes Wilson, 109 Ashdown Road, Farringdon, Sunderland.

THE VERY THING FOR WINTER BOOTS—I've restored my winter boots by briskly rubbing the lambswool linings with powdered magnesia. Rub well in, then brush out.—Mrs A. Penman, 62 Onslow Road, Clydebank, wins a pair of towels.

COMFY SHOES—When children's shoes are too large, stuff toes with a piece of rubber sponge cut into shape. The rubber remains soft, whereas cotton wool goes hard and tends to hurt the toes.—Miss F. H Powell, White House of Milliken, Brookfield.

WINTER HEELS—To get rid of scarlet and purple "winter heels", massage them gently with castor oil every night before going to bed. In summer you'll be able to wear sandals without being heel-conscious.—Mrs L. Waugh, 18 Wardlaw Street, Edinburgh.

PATENT LEATHER—To preserve patent leather, massage a little petroleum jelly into it from time to time. Wipe off excess jelly with clean, soft cloth. This keeps the leather pliable. It's also less apt to crack.—M. Wollaston, 8 Tame Street, Palfrey, Walsall.

PROTECTS HEELS—To prevent sore and blistered heels caused by bare feet rubbing against shoes in summer, glue a piece of foam rubber into the inside of the heels of shoes.—Miss B. M. Stevens, 12 Hillpark Avenue, Edinburgh.

SHOE PATCH—When children scuff the toes of their shoes, put on a cycle patch. It's neat and wears well.—Mrs E. Redpath, 130 Clarendon Road, Morecambe.

LOOSE SHOES—To prevent shoes from sliding up and down, rub gently inside the heels with a wire suede brush to give a rough surface.—Mrs Maria Black, 24 Mayfield Road, Saltcoats.

SANDALS—To keep children's sandals fresh and clean, moisten a piece of cotton wool with water and clean out all sand. Then, with another piece of cotton wool smeared with skin cream or lotion, rub inside the sandals. This helps to protect the skin and makes the sandals more comfortable.—Mrs E. K. Wilmott, 10 Thomas Street, Carnoustie.

COSY—Wear a pair of fleecy-lined insoles with your last year's boots if the lining is wearing a bit thin.—G. Ritchie, 22 Tayside Street, Carnoustie.

NEW SHOES FROM OLD—When dance shoes become shabby, paint them with a vivid chinese lacquer and you have a smart pair of sandals.—Mrs M. Fisher, 178 Bartiebeith Road, Easterhouse, Glasgow.

NEW LOOK—To make a pair of court shoes look more exciting, firmly attach a pair of clip-on earrings either to the centre or the side of the shoe.—Mrs Gibson, 45 Springfield Road, Glasgow.

SHOE BUTTONS—Sew the buttons on toddlers' shoes with shirring elastic. They stay on much longer than when sewn with thread.—Mrs E. Rodger, 64 Craighill Drive, Clarkston, Glasgow.

GOOD CLEANER—If you have a pair of suede boots or shoes that are dusty or soiled, switch on your vacuum cleaner and run the nozzle over them. The suction brings up the pile and makes the boots look as good as new.—Miss L. D. Ruditz, 64 Westwood Road, Glasgow.

HANDY SCRAPER—Nail a lemonade bottle top to the back of a shoe brush, and you have a useful gadget for scraping mud off boots and shoes.—Mrs P. Scott, c/o 73 Almond Street, Grangemouth.

BROWN SHOES—To remove stains from brown shoes, rub them with a soft cloth dipped in methylated spirits. Put on brown shoe cream and leave for a day without polishing. Finally, brush the shoes with a soft brush.—J. McG., Glasgow.

FOR WINTER BOOTS—If the lambswool lining in the heels of your boots has worn out, try placing a powder puff, cut to size, over the hole. A little adhesive keeps it in place. It saves the heels of your stockings.—Mrs R. Smith, 90 Seedhill Road, Paisley.

SLIPPERS—A pair of stiff heel grips sewn into the backs of soft slippers prevent that down-trodden look.—Mrs Birchall, 6 Primrose Terrace, Mill Hill, Blackburn.

A TIP-TOP IDEA FOR THE KIDDIES' SHOES—Buckles on children's sandals won't come off if sewn on with 5-amp fuse wire. Use holes made by previous stitching.—Mrs L. E. Saxton, 31 Bolton Lane, Bradford, wins a pair of towels.

NEW SHOES—Before wearing new leather shoes, especially brown or coloured shoes, give them a good thorough polish. This keeps them from spotting if caught in the rain.—Kit Jarrod, 160 Bromley Heath Road, Downend, near Bristol.

STILETTO HEELS—The leather covering on stiletto heels sometimes tears. Cover with one of the new self-adhesive plastics which can be bought in all colours.—Mrs Murdoch, 67 New Dykes Road, Prestwick.

MARKING INK—Use ordinary bleach as ink when marking children's names on dark gym shoes. Write on the dark part of the tongue with a firm nib.—Mrs Murdoch, 7 Ogilvie Terrace, Edinburgh.

NO SLIPPING NOW—New boot and shoe laces often work loose at first. When tying, moisten knot at crossover with finger-tip and they'll stay put.—Miss B. Forrest, 16 Primrose Street, Glasgow.

HAPPY FEET—Cut inner soles in good, white blotting paper. Place in children's shoes and sandals in hot weather. These prove comfortable when they go out without socks, for the paper absorbs perspiration.—Mrs M. Gellatly, 58 Church Street, Dundee.

STITCH IN TIME—Children's shoe laces sometimes don't last long. Do a few rows of machine stitching up and down the laces and they last much longer.—Mrs R. Horsham, 289 Maryhill Road, Glasgow.

SCUFFED SHOES—A little white of egg rubbed on the toes of children's shoes conceals scratches in the leather. Leave to dry and polish well.—Mrs Murdoch, 7 Ogilvie Terrace, Edinburgh.

DRYING WELLINGTON BOOTS—This drying job can be difficult. But the solution is to attach the vacuum tube to the blowing end and slip it into the boot. Loop it over a chair, and it can be raised or lowered according to where you want it to dry the boot.—V. Allan, 4 Tillydrone Terrace, Aberdeen, wins a pair of towels.

THE SUNDAY POST, JANUARY 5, 1958.

The Sunday Post

Morning Special

PRINTED AND PUBLISHED EVERY SUNDAY MORNING.

No. 2732. [REGISTERED AT THE GENERAL POST OFFICE AS A NEWSPAPER.] SUNDAY, JANUARY 5, 1958. Radio and TV—Page 4. Price 4d.

"Sunday Post" Man Sees Maureen Found In Restaurant

MISSING SCHOOLGIRL'S AMAZING STORY

Maureen, with her brothers, photographed at her home last night.

A "SUNDAY POST" man was present when the missing 13-year-old Dundee schoolgirl—Maureen Kidd—was found in a restaurant yesterday.

The restaurant and store—D. M. Brown's—were packed when Maureen was spotted, heating herself at a radiator, by the cashier and a waitress.

She was asked if she was the missing girl, and admitted she was.

The police were informed and Maureen left the store in a police car.

She returned to her home at 114 Findowrie Street, Fintry, with a woman police officer yesterday afternoon.

Maureen, who is the second oldest of six children of Mrs Christina Steele, told "The Sunday Post" of her experiences.

She sat with swollen eyes at the side of a roaring fire with the youngest member of the family, seven-month-old Andrew, crawling round her feet, and described how she had slept during freezing nights in her recesses.

The temperatures on those nights were down to nine degrees below freezing—the coldest nights of the year.

Maureen said she left home at 10.30 a.m. on Hogmanay for a message for her mother.

Slept In Shed

She wandered about until Tuesday night, when she went to City Square and watched the programme until the New Year was seen in.

"I walked up to Fintry," said Maureen. "I hung about the shops till about two in the morning, then went along Fintry Drive."

She saw a partly-built shed at the rear of one of the houses and decided to sleep there.

"I was very cold, and I kept my coat over my face. I used the shopping bag as a pillow.

Slept On Doormat

"On Wednesday morning I just wandered about watching folk passing with wee hats and singing.

"At night I went into Mid Craigie and found a place to sleep—a bin place with a door on it.

"There was only one bin in the recess and I took a door mat from a door and used it to sleep on. I had had nothing to eat all day.

"I Was Freezing"

"I was freezing and I was not feeling very well. I slept for a little while," she added.

She heard the milkman in the morning and after replacing the door mat wandered about for a time.

She boarded a bus and got off at D. M. Brown's.

She went to the restaurant there and had tea, a pie, a cake and a biscuit.

"About four o'clock I went back to the restaurant and got something else—three cakes, a cup of tea and lemonade."

At night she returned to her bin retreat, but didn't have a very restful night.

On Friday morning she got on a bus for town.

(CONTINUED ON PAGE TWO.)

Climber's Body Found On Ben Nevis Range

SEARCHERS yesterday recovered the body of Peter Brassington (24), a Royal Naval instructor-lieutenant, of New Road, South Chingford, Essex, who fell over a precipice on Sgurr Chaimbeach Mor, a 3600-foot mountain in the Ben Nevis range, on Friday.

Lieut. Brassington was with a party of 14 climbers, but they were unable to find him, and a rescue party of six police and eight mountaineers set out from Fort William at six o'clock yesterday morning.

From Fort William to the scene of the accident is about 48 miles.

The rescue party covered the first 24 miles by car to Kinlochleven, a further 11 miles over rough mountain track by jeep and then footslogged the remaining five miles over moorland and mountain.

Brassington was with a party who set out from the mountaineers' hut at Steall, Glen Nevis, on Friday to climb the snow-covered mountain.

They were near the top and descending when Brassington slipped and vanished over the precipice.

He was with a small group detached from the main party at the time.

They made a search in the neighbourhood, but were unable to find him, and some of them went to Fort William to inform the police.

Climbers who had been with Brassington when they set out from the Glen Nevis hut took part in the search.

Brassington's body was carried by stretcher down the mountain and then by jeep and car to Fort William.

Lieut. Brassington was spending the second half of his Christmas leave at Fort William.

In April he was to have married Miss Susan Collinson, of Dulwich.

ISABELLE – POLICE SEARCH FOR MAN

LANARKSHIRE police searching for Isabelle Cooke, the 17-year-old schoolgirl who disappeared last Saturday night, announced last night that they wished to interview a man.

Superintendent Myles Duncan, in charge of investigations, said that the man is about 30, dark-haired and wearing dark clothing and about 5 ft. 6 in. tall. He was seen leaving the Shettleston-Bothwell branch railway line four hours after Isabelle disappeared.

Police believe she may have been chased along the branch line from a point near her bungalow home in Carrick Drive, North Mount Vernon.

Her purse was found on the line near her home and some of her clothes on the banks of the River Calder under a railway viaduct.

Superintendent Duncan said the man was seen near the disused railway halt at Calderpark Zoo at about 11.30 p.m. last Saturday.

He went on to the Baillieston Road, then down some steps to Hamilton Road and turned west towards Uddingston.

"That is all we know about him. We don't know where he comes from, and we would like him to come forward."

The Superintendent said police were also trying to trace a small green van which was seen in Mount Vernon Avenue, about 20 or 30 yards from Hamilton Road, at about 7.25 p.m. last Saturday.

He appealed to the driver and anyone else who was in the van to report to the police.

A search of the River Calder from the viaduct on the Shettleston-Bothwell line to its junction with the River Clyde had been completed, and had proved fruitless.

Pumping operations at water holes in the area had also been completed, at least for the time being.

When the search is resumed, police will be assisted by some civilian volunteers.

100 Waggons Searched

● Police in five counties were yesterday checking railway waggons.

It was thought that, if a body had been dropped from a bridge where the Shettleston-Bothwell railway line crosses a line to Hamilton, it might have landed in a waggon of a mineral train.

The waggons are now distributed through the industrial belt of Scotland, in places as far apart as Fife, Renfrewshire, Stirlingshire and the Lothians.

British Railways said they had been co-operating, and that more than 100 waggons had been searched in various parts of the country without success.

Today's Weather

SHOWERS with bright intervals, with snow on hills. Near average temperatures.

The Man Who Gave His Name To The Anderson Shelter

VISCOUNT WAVERLEY, who, as Sir John Anderson, gave his name to the famous back-garden air-raid shelter, died yesterday aged 75.

Lord Waverley was a former Home Secretary, Lord President of the Council and Chancellor of the Exchequer.

He died from bronchial pneumonia.

Like his former chief, Sir Winston Churchill, Lord Waverley believed in plenty of work to keep himself youthful.

As well as being chairman of the Port of London Authority, he was a director of four companies and the head of a Government committee on the recruitment of doctors for the armed forces.

He also carried out a considerable amount of public work, particularly in the scientific field.

Chapter 24
Nylons

IN an era in which a female in trousers was a rare sight, every woman wore nylon stockings. What are now referred to as "tights" weren't even invented until 1959.

The first task was to make your stockings last, of course. Those terrible wartime days, when there was a stockings shortage, had left a deep scar on the collective female psyche. Stockings were to be protected at all costs.

But the life of a stocking, in those waste-not, want-not days, wasn't over even when, after a long life, it was too shabby or torn to wear.

Nylon is a synthetic polymer and a highly durable material. Indeed, industry has found many uses for it since it was first produced in the 1930s. But '50s housewives found more, a lot more, ways to employ it than mere textile scientists.

The stocking, in the hands of an ingenious woman, was made to work very hard, for a long time, and in surprising ways.

STOCKING SAVER—Put a few coloured stitches at the centre front of new stocking tops. This makes for easy suspendering and keeps seams straight. It also helps to pair them after washing.—Mrs A. W. Henderson, 34 White Street, Glasgow, wins a pair of towels.

SHOES TREES—Fill a pair of old stockings with sawdust. Sew up the tops, they make good shoe trees. The sawdust absorbs perspiration.—Mrs F. W. Bell, 18 Westlands, Sunderland.

UMBRELLAS—To protect the silk of your umbrella, slip and old nylon stocking over it when not in use.—Mrs A. Anderson, 9 Arlington Street, Glasgow.

NEW-LOOK CLOTHES HORSE—Rub the clothes horse lightly with medium-rough sandpaper and then cover with self-adhesive plastic material. A yard goes a long way. The material is kind to nylon and other delicate materials where a pulled thread means disaster.—Mrs J. Brown, 64 Grange Estate, Church Crookham, near Aldershot, wins a pair of towels.

LONGER LASTING—When darning holes in socks, place a double thickness of old nylon stocking over the hole, then darn as usual. The nylon makes the socks last longer.—Mrs H. Allan, 9 Commerce Street, Aberdeen, wins a pair of towels.

NON-SLIP—To prevent heels of nylon stockings slipping under instep when wearing lined boots, wear an old pair of nylons over the good ones, rolling them at the ankle.—Mrs K. E. Mackenzie, 8 Dal-na-Beich, North Connel, Argyll.

A STITCH IN TIME—When the seams of my fully-fashioned stockings give way, I use buttonhole stitch to mend them, as I find it stretches to take the strain.—Miss M. Clifford, Strathloanhead, Avonbridge, wins a pair of towels.

DRESS SHIELDS—Instead of sewing dress shields into woollen jumpers or cardigans, a piece of fine nylon stocking sewn into the armholes prevents perspiration from discolouring the garment. It is invisible if neatly done.—L. K., 19 Houghton Avenue, Cullercoats.

SLIPPER SAVERS—When doing housework, slip a pair of old nylons over your slippers and tuck them in at the ankles. They save the slippers from becoming soiled, especially at the toes.—Elizabeth McLeish, 25 Birkwood Street, Glasgow.

★ TOP TIP ★

NO DARNING NOW—My husband has been wearing my old nylons on top of his socks with his working boots. Since starting this he hasn't had a hole in his socks. Before that I was forever darning. —Mrs E. Somerville, 14 Buchanan Street, Edinburgh, wins a pair of towels.

NO EYESTRAIN NOW WHEN YOU'RE MENDING NYLONS—When repairing nylons, wear a black glove on the hand you slip into the stocking. You'll see the ladder more clearly.—Miss A. Drysdale, 64 Westquarter Avenue, Westquarter, by Falkirk, wins a pair of towels.

NYLONS—When darning nylons, the ordinary mending silk is too thick, so pull a thread from an old silk or rayon stocking and repair with this. The result is an invisible mend which is very durable.—Miss Violet McCallum, Campbeltown, Argyll.

FOR PLANTS—When tying a plant to a stake, cut a strip from an old nylon stocking and use instead of garden twine. The nylon, being soft, doesn't bruise the stem and also stretches as the stem grows thicker.—Miss E. M. Herbert, 1 Stoney Brae, Potterhill, Paisley.

BRUSHING TIP—Place a piece of old nylon stocking over your dog's wire or hair brush. When finished brushing dog, lift off the nylon complete with all cast-off hair.—Mrs H. Lang, 132 University Avenue, Glasgow.

WARDROBE FRESHNESS—Place a cake of scented soap inside an old stocking, sew on a tab at the top and hang among the clothes in the wardrobe. This keeps a refreshing smell in clothes and wardrobe.—Mrs G. Wood, 31 Loaning Road, Edinburgh.

NYLON TIP—When washing nylons, put them into a small, clean, cotton flour bag. Squeeze in soapy water, rinse, and hang out to dry inside the bag. There's no fear of harming them with a finger nail, or a rough line, and they can be kept in the bag.—Miss W. Purves, 5 Lamberton, Berwick-upon-Tweed.

MAKES THEM SHINE—To take streaky marks off windows and give a good polish, put your duster into an old nylon stocking and rub well.—Mrs J. Allan, 9 Commerce Street, Aberdeen.

SHOULDER PADS—Nylon hose make good filling for shoulder pads. After washing, the pads dry as quickly as the rest of the garment.—Miss L. Sinclair, 35 Lorne Street, Edinburgh.

THE SUNDAY POST, FEBRUARY 9, 1958

The Sunday Post

PRINTED AND PUBLISHED EVERY SUNDAY MORNING.

No. 2737. [REGISTERED AT THE GENERAL POST OFFICE AS A NEWSPAPER.] SUNDAY, FEBRUARY 9, 1958. Radio and TV—Page 5. Price 4d.

Worst Blizzard For 40 Years In Some Areas

IT'S ABSOLUTE CHAOS!

Hundreds Of Buses And Cars Stranded

THE Big Blizzard brought chaos all over the country yesterday.

Towns were cut off.

Trains were held up. Some were cancelled.

Drifts were up to 10 feet high.

VERY MANY ROADS IN SCOTLAND WERE BLOCKED, AN A.A. SPOKESMAN SAID AT 5 P.M.

An R.A.C. spokesman said last night that road conditions in some parts of Scotland were the worst for 40 years.

All over the country roadmen with snowploughs battled to open the roads.

Every First and Second Division football match in Scotland was cancelled.

Last night Aberdeen was all but completely isolated.

Out of the city practically every main road was blocked deep with snow.

Communications—road, rail and air—were either completely at a standstill or else seriously disrupted.

It was a state of affairs that couldn't be matched by anything within living memory.

A comparison with the last major blizzard—that of 1947—showed that conditions this time were very much worse.

All over the North-East, hundreds of vehicles were stranded.

They included buses, lorries and private cars.

Many of them were ditched.

Blocked signals and points handicapped services to Carnoustie.

Hundreds Abandon Cars

Hundreds of buses, cars, lorries and vans were abandoned on roads throughout the area. Late last night drivers were still struggling by foot to Montrose, Brechin and other towns and villages.

(CONTINUED ON PAGE TWO).

STORM PRISONERS

Miss Beryl Dow going to church.

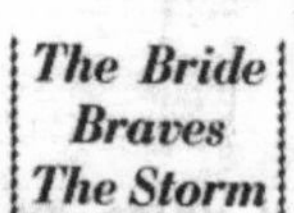

The Bride Braves The Storm

YESTERDAY will hold mixed memories for many brides and bridegrooms.

One couple affected by the blizzard were Miss Beryl A. E. Dow and Mr David V. Bates.

Mr Bates, whose home is in London, spent the morning anxiously inquiring about the arrival time of the Aberdonian, which should have reached Dundee at 7.20.

His parents, Mr and Mrs Philip Bates, were travelling on the train together with the best man, Mr Ivor Bayliss, second officer on the P. & O. ship Bendigo.

But by 2 p.m., the time of the ceremony, there was no word of the train.

It seemed to have been enveloped in snow somewhere between the Border and Edinburgh. The bride and bridegroom had to be married without the bridegroom's parents, the best man and some of his relatives.

They were also without the page, Master Donald L. Mackintosh, who had travelled with his parents from Carlisle and had reached Dundee, but had been stranded in the Hilltown, where they were staying.

Miss Dow was held up for 35 minutes with taxi trouble owing to the shocking road conditions.

She is the only daughter of Mr and Mrs James E. Dow, 282 Strathmartine Road, Dundee.

B.E.A. CHIEF SAYS HOUSE MADE MUNICH MISHAP A MAJOR DISASTER

SPORTSMEN at home and abroad remembered in silence yesterday the men of Manchester United.

In England on this black Saturday for football, crowds stood with heads bowed in quiet tribute before the kick-off of soccer and rugger games. (See picture on Page 27.)

As flags flew at half-mast and players, wearing black armbands, lined up, the nation's football lovers thought of the seven stars killed in the crash and of those still lying injured in hospital at Munich.

"Abide With Me"

At some grounds bands played and crowds sang "Abide With Me."

He said at London Airport that sabotage had never been considered a cause of the crash.

Should The House Be There?

MATT BUSBY A LITTLE BETTER —SEE PAGE TWO.

World Cup Draw

THE draw for the World Cup football finals, which take place in Sweden in June, was made in Stockholm last night.

Scotland are in the same group as France, Yugoslavia and Paraguay.

Full details are on page 27.

Today's Weather

SLEET or snow. Slightly higher temperatures in some places.

Chapter 25
Painting And Decorating

IN the early part of the decade, the types of wallpaper available were so difficult to work with that tradesmen had to serve lengthy apprenticeships. And pre-war wallpaper that had been varnished over was fiendishly difficult to prise off the plaster-and-horsehair wall underneath.

All ceilings had to be whitewashed or distempered. Any paint you bought had to be vigorously stirred.

But by the mid-1950s materials started being produced that could be worked by a handy husband. Easy-hang paper and non-drip paint were even available.

It became a revolution. Soon, the expectation was that if your house was to be "done up" you did the job yourself. Barry Bucknell's Do It Yourself became a must-watch TV show and every young wife set her heart on G-plan furniture.

Shops and stores rushed to feed this home-making rage. By the time the '60s drew near there were daring new wallpaper patterns and all shades of bright, bonny paint available to transform your wee hoose into a wee palace.

And the work was done by Britain's have-a-go home heroes. This new breed of DIY experts found marvellous methods of pasting paper and slick tricks for slapping on paint.

They used the Pass It On column to share their wisdom.

PAINTING HINT—If you are using a roller for painting, line the pan with aluminium foil before filling with paint. When finished, discard the foil. Then you have a clean pan, with no scouring and no flakes of old paint to mar your next job.—Miss A. Cooper, 63 Cambuslang Road, Rutherglen, Glasgow, wins a pair of towels.

HOUSEHOLD LOG—Make a handy record of such information as room measurements, quantity of paint and paper required, curtain sizes, etc.—W. R. Bowie, High Street, Brora.

NO MESS NOW WHEN YOU'RE PAINTING—When painting windows, skirting boards, etc., have one clean paint brush dipped ready in turpentine. Use it to instantly clean off any paint that accidently falls on surrounding woodwork, lino etc., it makes a tidy job.—Mrs W. Stewart, 56 Dudhope Street, Dundee, wins a pair of towels.

MATCHING COLOUR—When patching walls with plaster of paris, add a little powdered chalk of the same colour as the wall. This saves subsequent distempering to match existing colour. —Mrs J. Wilson, 10 Pundeavon Avenue, Kilbirnie.

THE SECRET IS ALL IN THE DRYING—I've just painted my bath and found the secret of the successful job is in the drying. Before painting, sandpaper it, wash with soda water, rinse and dry thoroughly. Apply good, hard undercoat and leave for at least two days before sandpapering again. Then use a reliable bath enamel. Leave to dry for three days or more. Fill bath with cold water and wait another day before using hot water.—R. Thomson, Edinburgh, wins a pair of towels.

PAINTING HARDBOARD—If you have to paint both sides of hardboard, mix plaster of paris into a smooth paste. Add a drop of linseed oil. Spread this all over the rough side of the board and allow to dry. Then glass paper all over, to give a smooth surface.—Mr J. Pearce, 61 Ferry Street, Montrose.

PAINT BRUSHES—When painting, I find my brushes keep quite soft from one day to another by just standing them in a jar or tin which has in it a strong mixture of soap powder and water to cover the bristles.—Roy Steward, 46 Sidney Road, Beeston, Notts.

★ TOP TIP ★

IT HELPS TO GET WALLPAPER OFF—When stripping wallpaper from a room, add two dessert spoonfuls of ammonia to a quart of water and soak the wall. Before trying this my paper was coming off in small scraps. Afterwards, long sheets came off without effort.—Mrs Bradley, 4 Wraes Avenue, Barrhead, wins a pair of towels.

STAIR CARPET CLIPS—Put a matchstick or a nail in the screw hole when taking stair clips off to paint stairs. This avoids the holes being painted over, and makes it easier to re-screw on clips.—Miss S. Bovill, 34 Batson Street, Govanhill, Glasgow.

PAPERING—When you have stripped off old wallpaper, go over the walls with a wire pot-cleaner. This removes little bits and pieces which are often left and makes the wall smooth for redecorating.—Mrs J. Philip, 16 Huddersfield Street, Galashiels.

PAINTING—When doing home painting, place the tin of paint in a child's seaside pail, which is easily held by the handle. This saves strain on the hand caused by holding the tin. —M. Murray, 59 Keptie Road, Arbroath.

PAINT REMOVER—To remove paint from frosted glass, rub with a dry nylon pot scourer.—Mrs McLellan, 53 Craigend Drive, Kirkwood, Coatbridge.

NO SPLASHES NOW—While whitewashing a ceiling the other week the splashes from the brush annoyed me. I decided to try an experiment. I added a small quantity of cellulose adhesive powder to the whiting. Splashes were eliminated as the whiting tended to cling to the brush. Also, the whiting does not easily rub off the ceiling.—William S. Jack, 9 Windsor Gardens, Alloa, wins a pair of towels.

DUST DODGE—Freshly varnished or painted surfaces of tables and chairs dry dust-free if hung upside-down from a pulley.—Mrs Andrew, 69 Battlefield Avenue, Glasgow.

TILES—When choosing wall or floor tiles, a single tile may look attractive, but laid out in a mass may be overpowering or rather disappointing. Take time to choose your colour schemes. —Mrs M. Kerr, 3 Coronation Buildings, Gilroy Road, Wirral.

PAPERING—A darning mushroom is ideal for removing "blisters" or air pockets which may form when papering a room. Place the smooth top of the mushroom at side of the blister and, with a rotary motion, press gently but firmly over it, keeping it moving in the direction of the edge of the paper. The air bubble is expelled without damage to the paper.—J. B. Lavery, 32 Huntly Gardens, Glasgow.

CEILINGS—Before whitewashing the ceiling, add 1 oz. of alum to a pail of water, and brush on to the ceiling. This prevents whitewash from peeling off.—Mrs R. Cunningham, 21 Pembridge Square, London.

A LOT OF PEOPLE SPOIL THEIR CEILINGS THIS WAY—Before putting water paint on a ceiling previously distempered or whitewashed, thoroughly clean it back to bare plaster (and on no account use size). Otherwise paint will flake off. A lot of people ruin their work this way.—Mrs Ritchie, Carlisle, wins a pair of towels.

PAINTING—Instead of using black paint as a dividing line between two shades of paint on a kitchenette wall, procure a roll of narrow black insulating tape. Mix 2oz. of size with ¼ pint of water and beat till gluey. Smear the tape and paste to the wall. This ensures a neat finish.—Miss Nancy Tod, 'Aroa', Edzell, Angus.

PAPERING—When papering a room, start from each side of the window and work towards the door. This prevents a shadow showing the overlap of paper.—Mrs D. McInnes, Avonlea, Luss, by Alexandria.

CAREFUL—Varnish made for outside paintwork such as front doors, should not be used inside the house. It will stay sticky over a long period, because it cannot dry properly indoors.—Mrs T. Duncan, Derby.

PRECAUTION—Before redecorating a room, rub chromium fittings with Vaseline. Afterwards, any paint on them can be easily cleaned off.—Miss D. Richardson, 8 Bevan Avenue, Ryhope, Sunderland.

WALLS—When washing down scullery walls, add two tablespoonfuls glue size to a bucket of soapy water. This removes grease and leaves paintwork bright. But before repainting, walls must be thoroughly cleaned.—Mrs S. Cunningham, 23 Willoughby Road, North Shields.

WATCH OUT WHEN YOU'RE PAINTING NEW WOOD—As new wood for doors, etc., is often not fully seasoned, it should get a first coat of aluminium paint. This seals the wood and prevents resin coming through (it can come through five coats of ordinary paint). Then put on flat paint, and finish off with glossy.—Painter, Edinburgh, wins a pair of towels.

REPAINTING—Never attempt to repaint a surface (such as a stairway) until you've removed any traces of polish. This delays the drying process and causes a dull finish.—Miss L. D. Ruditz, 64 Westwood Road, Glasgow.

WHEN YOU'RE PAPERING A ROOM—Before re-papering walls, check to see if there are any grease spots on the old surface. If so, cover each spot with a thin coat of shellac, and the grease doesn't seep through to the new paper.—Andrew C. Lonie, William Street, Tayport, wins a pair of towels.

PAINTING—Before starting a painting job, people wearing glasses should slightly smear the lenses with soap. The fine pinpoint paint spots can then be easily removed from the lenses on completion of the job.—W. Malcolm, Cora House, Portknockie, wins a pair of towels.

CLEAN JOB—When painting kitchen or bathroom, tie plastic bags over the taps. They will be kept nice and clean.—Mrs C. L. Beattie, 8 Kilberry Street, Dundee.

PAPERING—When doing a papering job, try using a paint roller to apply the paste. It spreads the paste evenly, is quicker, and less messy than the brush.—Mrs C. Hooper, 180F Centre Street, Glasgow.

PAPER PROTECTION—Place the back of your against-the-wall vase on a piece of blotting paper and draw the outline. Cut around and attach lightly to the vase with Sellotape. This prevents any surplus moisture or marks from spoiling the wallpaper or freshly-painted wall.—Mrs A. Kelly, 353 Warwick Road, Carlisle.

GREASE MARKS—I removed grease marks from my wallpaper by soaking a piece of soft rag in turps substitute and gently patting the marks, making sure the edges of the marks were well treated.—Mrs I. Cummings, 3 Brackenwood Grove, Tunstall, Sunderland.

STRIPPING WALLPAPER—Use a foam sponge self-wringing mop for soaking wallpaper prior to stripping. It's less messy than a brush and the long handle enables you to reach the top of the wall easily—Mrs S. B. Guy, Hirst Road, Harthill.

KEEP IT IN MIND WHEN PAPERING THE ROOM—If you haven't an odd table on which to paste wallpaper, buy a piece of plastic large enough to cover your dining table, and paste on this. It gives enough protection. The plastic can be washed and used over and over again.—Mrs M. B. Johnston, 27 Kelso Gardens, Newcastle-upon-Tyne, wins a pair of towels.

COLOUR GUIDE—If you want to make sure of the colour before painting walls, brush a little on to blotting paper. It works best with flat paint.—Mrs J. Ferrol, Netherwood Bank Cottage, Clencaple Road, Dumfries.

SIMPLE DECORATION—Use autumn leaves to decorate a plain parchment lampshade. Press the prettiest leaves from your garden then stick on to the shade. When lamp is lit, the colours in the leaves show up in all their glory.—Mrs H. Bell, Hylcroft, 33 Whiteclosegate, Carlisle.

LESS WORK—When you want to screen the windows of a room you are decorating, use window-cleaning fluid instead of whiting (which is messy and needs to be carefully washed off after). When finished, just give the windows a final polish and they're clean.—Mrs L. Wreghitt, 10 Railway Terrace, Holgate, York.

COLOURFUL POTS—I had several tins of paint with just a little in each. So I made myself a pretty harlequin set of flower pots by painting each a different colour.—Mrs M. Hughes, 5 Green Lane, Llangollen.

HOLE FILLING—To fill holes after painting and there's no paint left, use children's Plasticine, which can be bought in almost any colour.—Mrs M. Smith, 60 North Hill Street, Liverpool.

DISTEMPERING—Screw a cup hook into the handle of the distemper brush. Slip the hook over the edge of the bucket to keep the brush from slipping into the distemper.—Miss M. Chalmers, 30 Constitution Street, Inverurie.

BATH PAINTING—Before painting a bath, get a length of old cycle tubing and push one end over the hot water tap and the other end over the cold. This will catch all the drips and allow the painting and drying to proceed without a mark of any sort. The tubing can be slipped off and the water poured into the wash basin. —J. C. J. Albin, 39 Stewartville Street, Partick, Glasgow, wins a pair of towels.

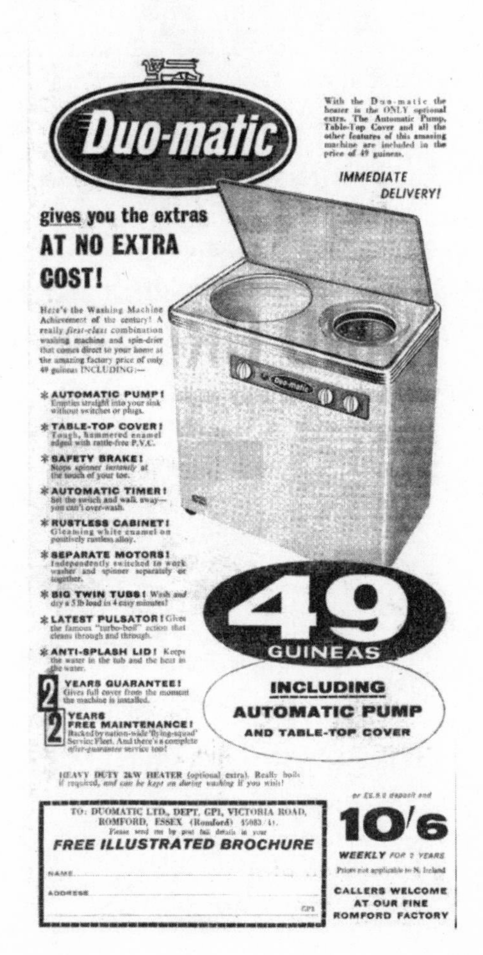

The Sunday Post

Morning Special

PRINTED AND PUBLISHED EVERY SUNDAY MORNING.

No. 2744 — SUNDAY, MARCH 30, 1958. — Radio and TV—Page 26 — Price 4d.

First Death Penalty On Woman Under New Act

WIDOW OF WINDY NOOK SENTENCED TO BE HANGED

MRS MARY ELIZABETH WILSON.

THE drama of the trial of the Widow of Windy Nook, 66-year-old Mrs Mary Elizabeth Wilson, ended at Leeds Assises when Mr Justice Hinchcliffe — black cap on his head — sentenced her to death for the murder by poison of her second and third husbands.

She is the first woman to be sentenced to death under the Homicide Act of 1957, and the first person to be sentenced under the Act for more than one murder.

The Act preserved the death penalty where a person is convicted for two murders tried together, but done on different occasions.

Mrs Wilson stood in the dock, a nurse on one side of her and a woman prison officer on the other, and heard the foreman of the jury announce that they had found her guilty on both charges.

IMPASSIVE

LAST WOMAN EXECUTED

BEETLE POISON

(SEE ALSO PAGE 2)

"Very Sad," Says Princess

PRINCESS MARGARET told British troops at a parade at Munster yesterday she was "very sad" because she was addressing them for the last time as their Colonel-in-Chief.

Snow Ploughs Are Out Again!

POLICEMAN SHOT

Today's Weather

Chapter 26
The Elixir That Was Vinegar

VINEGAR is composed of acetic acid, diluted in water. It's an ancient substance, traces have been found in Egyptian urns from 3000BC.

Some vinegars have as much as 20% acid and it is that chemical element which is useful beyond its normal job of adding flavour. Acetic acid will break down wax, resin and mould, and kills bacteria.

Households of the 1950s put it to a great many good uses. And no doubt at some point it was also used, along with salt, on fish and chips.

PREVENTS MOULD—Before sealing jars of jam or jelly for storing, brush over with a very little vinegar. It prevents mould and preserves keep a long time. I have done this for years with good results.—Mrs E. Keir, Rosewood, Lade Braes, St Andrews, wins a pair of towels.

MEAT IN HOT WEATHER—Pour a little vinegar into a large dish and place two pieces of stick across the dish. Stand the meat on the sticks. The vinegar wards off flies and also helps to keep the meat sweet.—Mrs Ellis, 121 Sinclair Drive, Glasgow.

TARNISHED BRASS—To remove tarnish from brass, put some salt on a saucer and soak with vinegar. Apply with a soft rag. Allow to dry, brush off, and polish in the usual way.—Mrs J. Devlin, 29 Coltmuir Street, Glasgow.

FOR THE PANTRY—Wipe your pantry shelves with a cloth that has been dipped in vinegar. This helps to keep them fresh and free from flies during hot weather.—M. Duncan, The Firs, Crudie, by Turriff.

HERRINGS—Dip fresh herring and mackerel in vinegar before coating with seasoned oatmeal. This makes them nice and crisp and takes away any excessive greasiness.—Mrs J. Scott, Benholm, Montrose.

STRONG GLUE—If you want a firm fix with glue, add a teaspoonful of vinegar to a small amount of glue. This makes it extra strong.—Mrs L. R. Hill, 48 Constitution Street, Dundee.

GLUE—A little vinegar put into a bottle of glue which has dried up will moisten and make it liquid again.—Mrs M. Robson, 32 Whitehall Place, Aberdeen.

PREVENTS LEATHER CRACKS—To keep leather furniture soft and free from cracking, mix one part vinegar to two parts boiled linseed oil. Put the mixture into a bottle and shake till creamy. Apply with soft rag and polish with soft duster.—Miss M. Currie, 20 Stirling Road, Camelon.

FOR GREENS—When washing greens, put a teaspoonful of vinegar in the water instead of salt. Leave to stand for a little. —Mrs Hawthorne, 97 Riversdale Road, Romford.

★ TOP TIP ★

YOUR FLOORS WILL LOOK TWICE AS GOOD—Before varnishing a wooden floor, wipe the wood with a soft rag wrung out of vinegar. This removes grease from the surface and helps the varnish to dry quickly with a good surface.—Mrs Cathie Brown, 480 Tollcross Road, Glasgow, wins this week's guinea.

PICKLES—When making pickles, rinse out the jars with cold vinegar before bottling to prevent fermentation.—M. Thompson, 12 Davidson Street, Lancaster.

FRESH AIR—When you have friends in or are giving a party, place an open bowl of vinegar in the room. It keeps the air fresh and sweet.—Mrs Selbie, 194 Seatown, Cullen.

FLIES—Saturate a piece of silk-knit material with vinegar, rub over inside of window panes. Flies hate vinegar. It also brightens the glass.—Mrs J. Thomson, 9A Biggar Road, Cleland.

PLASTER—When treating ceiling or wall cracks, mix plaster of paris with vinegar instead of water. It then takes longer to set and gives more time to smooth it down.—Mrs H. Webster, 8 Thistle Terrace, Leven.

CHAIRS—Leather-covered chairs should be cleaned with a cloth slightly moistened with linseed oil and a very little vinegar. Carefully remove all dust first.—Mrs F. Alexander, 40 Mill Lane, Whitburn, Sunderland.

VINEGAR FOR BRASS—If brass curtain rings and hooks get corroded, soak them in vinegar for three hours, wash in water, and dry with a soft cloth.—Mrs F. Cobb, 21 Portland Street, London.

BREAD BIN—To prevent a bread bin from becoming mildewed after washing, wipe it over with a cloth dipped in a little vinegar. —Mrs M. Sinclair, 10 Great Western Terrace, Glasgow.

SUNDAY POST, DECEMBER 27, 1959

The Sunday Post

Morning Special

PRINTED AND PUBLISHED EVERY SUNDAY MORNING.

No. 2835 | [REGISTERED AT THE GENERAL POST OFFICE AS A NEWSPAPER.] | SUNDAY, DECEMBER 27, 1959. | Radio and TV—Page 5 | Price 4d

2 Killed, 4 Injured, In Scots Collision

SO MANY XMAS CRASHES—HOSPITAL SENDS FOR EXTRA STAFF

THERE were so many road crashes over the Christmas and Boxing Day period that:—

A hospital had to call out extra staff.

A mayor—making his usual Christmas week-end visit to hospitals—said: "It was pitiful to see how many patients had just been admitted after road crashes."

At least 16 people were killed, and scores injured, all over the country.

● In Scotland, two men were killed and four badly injured in a head-on crash between Barrhead and Lugton late last night.

Both cars were wrecked.

Motorists and ambulance men had difficulty in extricating the casualties from the wreckage.

The four injured were taken to Paisley Infirmary.

ONE A MINUTE

● On Teesside, in England, the Christmas road toll was the worst in living memory—three deaths, 30 people seriously injured, and an unknown total less seriously injured.

Police, ambulance and hospital workers had rarely known a night like it.

Casualties were arriving at the accident centre at Middlesbrough General Hospital at the rate of one a minute.

Extra staff had to be called in.

MOTHER KILLED

Shocked

Xmas Hold-Up

IN Los Angeles, a gunman stole 315 dollars (about £112) from a cocktail bar, and shouted from the doorway—" If anybody follows me I'll kill him—Merry Christmas to you all."

Edinburgh And Dundee Factories May Get £20 Million Contract

Chain Reaction!

Caroline Finds Her Mummy At Last

CAROLINE DALZELL-PAYNE and B.E.A. receptionist Mrs Marianne Gabriel together at London Airport waiting for news of Caroline's mother.

Today's Weather

THE WOMAN WITH THE 50-GUINEA SHOES

ONE young lady in the Borders received the Christmas present of a lifetime—a pair of shoes.

But no ordinary shoes, these.

They cost 50 guineas.

For some time, these shoes have been the centre of a window display in Mr John Rennie's shoe shop at 10 Bourtree Place, Hawick.

They were evening shoes made of cream satin, slip-on courts with a painted toe and a three-inch heel.

Embedded all over the shoes were £45 worth of semi-precious stones—among them garnets which gave a dazzling orange, green and red effect.

People from all over the Borders travelled to Hawick to see the sumptuous shoes.

Women gazed for minutes at them—and the price.

Then a man came into the shop and bought them.

By now someone has slipped the size three and a half shoes on—and will be feeling like Cinderella!

Chapter 27
Christmas Was Better

CHRISTMAS was different in the 1950s. A lot of the festive tips were about saving money, or not spending any in the first place. This was a time when putting up the paper decorations, stored from last year, was exciting, never mind the prospect of an apple, orange and florin in your stocking.

And, as anyone who lived through it will confirm, Christmas then was a lot better than it is today.

HOLLY—Holly stays fresh and green if, before arranging it round the house, the ends of the stems are split and soaked for a day or two in a deep, narrow vase containing one part glycerine to three parts water.—Mrs M. Connon, 8 Market Street, Turriff, wins a pair of towels.

OLD HULA-HOOP—A hula-hoop, no longer played with, is attractive covered with Christmas decorations, holly and cards and hung in the hall.—Mrs Janet Crouch, 12 Seton Street, Ardrossan.

STUFFED TOYS—If making stuffed toys for Christmas gifting, stuff with pieces of plastic foam. The toys are wonderfully light to handle, and can be washed more often, as the plastic foam dries quickly. They can be put through the wringer, they spring back into shape.—Mrs A. Ganrow, 4 Brimmond Place, Torry, Aberdeen.

TIMELY GIFT—A selection of Christmas cards, with envelopes already stamped makes an acceptable pre-Christmas gift for an invalid.—M. T. Paterson, Cairndhu, 44 Oak Street, Windermere.

LONG LASTING—Place your decorative candles in the refrigerator for 24 hours prior to using. This increases their burning time.—R. Harris, 8 Denholm Drive, Giffnock.

BALLOONS—Balloons for parties can be inflated with safety and ease by putting a cigarette holder in the mouthpiece.—Mrs E. Morley, c/o 27 Salisbury Road, Hexthrope, Near Doncaster.

TIDY-BOX—Put castors on a wooden box, paint it brightly, and give it to the children at Christmas. They can wheel it about to pick up their scattered toys.—Mrs L. Hook c/o 2 Oakwood Villas, Lisburn Street, Alnwick.

CARDS—To enhance the beauty of ordinary Christmas cards, I use my daughter's glitter set. I paste the tops of trees, church spires, candles, windows, etc., then sprinkle on glitter in different colours. Result: some very expensive-looking Christmas cards.—Mrs Morrison, 67 Kenilworth Road, Kirkintilloch.

PLUM PUDDING—If you are adding rum, sherry, or brandy to your plum pudding let the fruit soak in it for 24 hours before adding the dry ingredients. In this way the spirit is evenly distributed, with the full flavour through the whole mixture.—Mrs R. W. Henry, Dunairn, 16 Mill Street, Kirriemuir.

INEXPENSIVE GIFT—Embroider the days of the week in bright colours on seven white handkerchiefs. Inexpensive and sure to please.—Mrs Dishington, Muirfield Farm, Gullane.

HAVING A PARTY—Prepare your plates of savouries, sandwiches, cakes etc., early in the day. Place them in polythene bags folded in at the end. Everything is perfectly fresh for serving, and you are spared that last-minute rush. —Mrs G. M. Pratt, 95 Beach Crescent, Broughty Ferry.

AFTER THE PARTY—If your living-room is heavy with smoke after a party, put a basin of cold water in the room and leave overnight. The air is quite fresh in the morning.—Mrs A. Galt, Avils Hill, Kilbirnie.

CHRISTMAS EXTRAS—Now is the time to start a Christmas shelf by buying an extra tin of fruit, meat, etc., every week.—Mrs J. L. Young, 23 Swanston Grove, Fairmilehead, Edinburgh.

BOOKS—When sending books at Christmas, protect the corners from damage by cutting the corners from strong, heavy envelopes, and place one on each corner of the book.—Mrs M. Craig, 37 Kilburn Street, Donegall Road, Belfast.

ICING FOR CAKE—When covering the top of my Christmas cake with almond icing, I roll out the icing, place the tin the cake was baked in on the icing, and cut round it. The icing then fits the cake perfectly.—Mrs E. Dainty, 48 Honor Avenue, Goldthorn Park, Wolverhampton.

CHRISTMAS GIFTS—If you are covering coat hangers for Christmas gifts, try this. After padding, wind with tissue paper, then cover with material. This little extra effort gives a crisp and professional finish.—Margaret C. Kinnear, Lochside Cottage, Tayport.

★ TOP TIP ★

LESS CHANCE OF FIRE WITH THE CHRISTMAS TREE—To minimise the risk of fire, put a thick layer of salt round the Christmas tree in tub instead of cotton wool. It looks just like snow.—Mrs E. Archer, 27 Salisbury Road, Hexthorpe, near Doncaster, wins a pair of towels.

KEEP IT MOIST—After boiling a clootie dumpling, remove cloth and immediately sprinkle sugar over the dumpling. This keeps it from forming a hard, leathery skin.—Miss N. Gall, 1 Chapel Court, Justice Street, Aberdeen.

LABOUR SAVER—When boiling a pudding, line the cloth with greased paper, and all the flavour will be kept in. In addition, the cloth will not be soiled.—Mrs M. Robson, 22 Whitehall Place, Aberdeen.

CHRISTMAS CANDLES—Cut a large potato in half. Lay the flat side down, make a hole on the top, and insert a candle. Put sprigs of holly all round, and you have a very decorative pair of Christmas candles.—Morag Murray (aged 13), 26 McAllister Avenue, Airdrie.

ROASTING—When roasting meat or a Christmas fowl, I find it best to cover it with several thicknesses of cheesecloth and baste over it. Done this way, it comes from the oven juicy and tender. —Mrs A. Southwell, Hythe, Alberta, Canada.

SAFETY TIP—When using drawing pins, push them into a large cork. It can be carried round in your pocket when pulling up Christmas decorations, and there is no pricking of fingers.—Mrs John Logan, 320 Castle Street, Glasgow.

DECORATIONS—When hanging up Christmas decorations thread a piece of fine string through centre of paper chains. This prevents them tearing apart or falling against fires or electric heaters.—Mrs E. Shaw, 5C Menzies Drive, Stirling.

DOUBLE MINCEMEAT—Chop two sweet apples with handful each of currants and sultanas, grate a lemon or orange skin, and add two dessertspoons moist sugar. Turn into a large basin a 1lb. jar of mincemeat. Mix well with above ingredients and fill two jars.—Mrs R. Paton, 42 Clarence Road, Southport.

bt. 74n

They're good-very good!

1/8 FOR 10 · 3/4 FOR 20

TWELFTH NIGHT—If paper streamers, bells, etc., are folded in their natural creases, put between two sheets of greaseproof paper, then through the mangle, they retain their freshness for next time.—Mrs E. Durrant, 17 Lilburn Street, Chirton, North Shields.

CHRISTMAS TREES—If your tree has a root that hasn't been severely pruned, it can be successfully planted back out in the garden. Sprinkle all over with tepid water, dig a fairly deep hole in the garden, and into this pour a kettle of hot water. Plunge the root in and press firmly down. I have done this for years, always with success. —Miss R. Simpson, 9 Erskine House, Oxley Drive, South Oxley, near Watford.

LEFT-OVERS—Mince pies are as good as new if popped into deep, hot fat for a few seconds and sprinkled with caster sugar. Covered with a pouring custard, they make a delicious sweet. —Miss L. Murdoch, 45 Wheatlands Avenue, Bonnybridge.

YULETIDE LOG—Make some suet crust, roll out thinly, and spread with layer of mincemeat, leaving ½-inch paste all round. Moisten edges with water, roll up, and put in a straight 2lb. jam jar, well greased. Cover with greaseproof paper and steam for two hours. Serve with custard sauce.—Mrs Slater, 17 Geddes Avenue. Portknockie.

FOR A PARTY—Stand a swiss roll on end and cover with glace icing, allowing it to run down the sides to look like wax. Then tint a piece of marzipan red to represent a flame and stick on.—Mrs Sievewright, 6 Castle Street, Turriff.

NUTS—Remove Brazil nuts whole by putting them in water and bringing to the boil. Then crack in the normal way.—Mrs H. Dale, 70 Manuel Street, Goole.

ARTIFICIAL BERRIES—If your holly has no red berries, make them of red modelling wax. Pierce them with a pin and fix to the stems.—Mrs A. Cowan, 103 North High Street, Musselburgh.

TINSEL—If your last year's tinsel for Christmas decorations has become tarnished, dip it in silver cleaning liquid and rinse in clean water. It comes up sparkling.—Mrs A. B. Allen, Stafford House, Dunbar.

FOR SPARKLE—When using holly for decorations, paint over a few of the leaves with clear nail varnish and then sprinkle on some glitter frost. Do this quickly before varnish dries.—Mrs A. Wheeler, 13 Palmerston Street, Montrose.

EXACT SIZE—After rolling out the almond paste for my Christmas cake, I use the tin in which the cake was baked as a cutter. I then get the exact size without the bother of cutting and trimming.—Miss N. Richmond, Ballytaggart, Ballymoney, Co. Antrim.

FOR SAFETY—When the glass balls come down from the Christmas tree, it is sometimes difficult to pack them away safely for a whole year. Try using a cardboard egg container. They fit snugly, just like eggs.—Mrs M. Glen, 21 Amisfield Place, Longniddry.

CHRISTMAS PARCELS—I work at a Post Office counter. Here are my tips for wrapping Christmas parcels. Don't tie them with string of different thicknesses knotted together. Don't use paper that's been through the post a few times already. Try to have parcels well balanced (I've seen many with a heavy item bursting through). If possible, put parcel in a cardboard box before final wrapping.—Postmistress.

TIT-BIT—Pink apple froth makes a lovely surround for a festive jelly. Peel, core and sweeten apples, cook gently and when cool add the white of an egg and a drop of cochineal. Beat till fluffy.—Mrs L. Waugh, 18 Wardlaw Street, Edinburgh.

To End, A Look Forward

THIS article was printed on January 3, 1960. The first Sunday Post of the 1960s. It details changes readers could expect in the next decade. It's a rosy picture, if not an entirely accurate one. It is of its time. If only more of these predictions had come true…

A NEW decade has begun We've left the Fifties behind. And it's now for the sizzling Sixties! Without a single doubt, amazing changes will take place in all our lives. Science—advancing at breakneck speed—will see to that.

In the next ten years Britain will have at least twenty nuclear power stations, producing fifty per cent. of the country's electricity. Our first atomic-powered tanker will be on the seas in a few years. At least two huge nuclear liners will be sailing the Atlantic flying the British flag. Waste products from the nuclear furnaces will be harnessed to domestic use. Radiation from this residue will toughen plastics to such an extent that houses will be built with it. Yes, plastic houses. Milk that won't go sour. Potatoes and onions that won't sprout in storing. Cattle food made from sawdust. All from the radiation of waste products that were sunk to the depths of the sea in the Fifties.

What about the motorist? A network of motorways will be completed. All arterial roads turned into dual carriageways. Road bridges will span the Forth, the Tay and the Severn. Special trucks with a speed of seventy miles per hour. These trucks, equipped with superchargers and disc brakes, will cut costs by up to 30 per cent. Dangerous bends and hills will be free of ice and snow during winter. They'll be kept above freezing by an electric current. This will pass through surfacing material mixed with graphite powder. It will do away with the elaborate network of wires below the surface in 1959.

Next, our standard of living. It'll rocket like a sputnik. In the period 1951-59 the standard of living increased by 15 per cent. In 1960 to 1970 it will increase by another 25 per cent. at least. It will be the era of two-car families. One for the husband to go to work. A smaller one for the wife to go shopping, and taking the children to school.

Next—health. The assault on cancer and leukaemia will stride on. Some hope that at last both will be tamed, and the average expectation of life will take men to 75 and women to 80.

Space? Russia predicts the first man on the moon in 1965. In 1970 both America and Russia will be planning to send up whole expeditions to set up observatories.

Clothes—Suits that will outlive the wearer. The fibre will be treated with radiation from waste fission products to make them almost everlasting.

Now, a peep into the kitchen of the Sixties. The cooker will be split, so that the oven is built into the walls, and the hotplate is in another part of the kitchen. Washing machines will be entirely automatic. Clothes fed in one end will be washed, rinsed, and dried without the help of the housewife. Transistor fridges. Cooling units in miniature will be placed in food cupboards to give a "cold" larder. Miniature fridges will be taken by families on motoring tours and picnics. Even the small food shops will take on the appearance of supermarkets. The food will be practically all of the frozen variety—even frozen bread and cakes.

Other features of the Sizzling Sixties in brief—

- **Huge supplies of oil will come from the Arctic in submarine tankers.**
- **Colour television. Twenty-one-inch screens will be replaced by thirty-inch screens. Trans-Atlantic TV will be possible by relay stations attached to satellites circling the earth.**
- **In industry the 30-hour week will come in sight.**
- **The Atlantic will be crossed in a few hours by jets with a maximum speed of 2000 miles per hour.**
- **In athletics seconds will be gradually knocked off the mile record until it will be run in three-and-a-half minutes.**
- **On the football pools, it's possible the prize for the treble chance could reach the staggering total of one million pounds for a 2d stake.**
- **Heated grandstands at football grounds. Pitches free from frost and snow by electrical soil heating.**
- **By 1963. Scotland's new strip mill at Ravenscraig will be producing up to 500,000 tons of steel.**
- **Scotland will have at least one car factory.**
- **A heliport in Glasgow by the mid-Sixties. Inter-city helicopter services throughout Britain.**

Yes, it's to be the Sizzling Sixties all right.